Rachel Vorona Cote writes for publications like the *New Republic, Longreads, Pitchfork, Catapult, Hazlitt, Rolling Stone, the Poetry Foundation, Buzzfeed,* and *Literary Hub.* She was also a contributor at *Jezebel.*

She has a BA from the College of William and Mary and an MA in Literature from the George Washington University. She is ABD at the University of Maryland, College Park, where she studied Victorian literature. She lives in Takoma Park, Maryland.

TOO MUCH

How Victorian Constraints
Still Bind Women Today

RACHEL VORONA COTE

SPHERE

First published in the United States in 2020 by Grand Central Publishing,
a division of Hachette Book Group, Inc
First published in Great Britain in 2020 by Sphere

13 5 7 9 10 8 6 4 2

The stories in this book are true.
A few names have been changed to protect the privacy of people involved.

A previous version of 'Nerve' appeared in *Literary Hub*, October 27, 2016.
Previous versions of 'Close' appeared in *Jezebel*, April 21, 2015, and September 23,
2015. 'Close' also includes excerpts from 'Painted Ladies', an essay first published
online by The Poetry Foundation. A previous version of 'Cut' appeared in
Broadly (now *Vice*), March 15, 2017. A previous version of 'Old'
appeared in *Literary Hub*, January 5, 2017.

A CIP catalogue record for this book is available from the British Library.

ISBN 978-0-7515-8052-5

Printed and bound in Great Britain by Clays Ltd, Elcograf S.p.A.

Papers used by Sphere are from well-managed forests
and other responsible sources.

MIX
Paper from
responsible sources
FSC® C104740

Sphere
An imprint of
Little, Brown Book Group
Carmelite House
50 Victoria Embankment
London EC4Y 0DZ

An Hachette UK Company
www.hachette.co.uk

www.littlebrown.co.uk

For my mother, Katherine Florio Vorona, whose compassionate heart and boundless empathy taught me that no amount of love is too much. If she had not raised me, and embraced everything I am — with all my excess, unruliness, and contradictions — I could not have written this book.

AUTHOR'S NOTE

Before venturing any further, it's important that I address a few matters related to diversity in source material. Victorian literature is a useful tool for exploring the phenomenon of too muchness, but like so many mechanisms for critical thought, it is limited, racially and otherwise. Throughout the book, I will reference and draw principally from Victorian narratives and conduct manuals. However, I will also place them alongside others in order to, I hope, provide a broader purview beyond that of the cisgender white woman. That said, I will, for the sake of (relative) brevity, primarily focus on woman identifying persons over the course of the book, although there remains much work to be done in considering the emotional circumscription of transgender persons, gender nonconforming persons, and men, queer and straight. This is a long and intricate conversation: I submit the following book as one rivulet leading to vaster waters.

Finally, I want to turn this narrative of too muchness on its head without letting empathy out of sight—this isn't an excuse to do and say whatever we want, context and consideration be damned. It is, however, a call for others to witness a broad, more complex range of emotional presentation and utterance, and a demand for the space we cohabit to be treated as capacious ground for any expression that is neither malicious nor harmful to folk, flora, and fauna. I believe that this is possible. In writing this book, I am declaring my belief that it will exist, that we are, gradually, making it so.

Chapter One

WONDERLAND: AN INTRODUCTION

A weeping woman is a monster. So too is a fat woman, a horny woman, a woman shrieking with laughter. Women who are one or more of these things have heard, or perhaps simply intuited, that we are repugnantly excessive, that we have taken illicit liberties to feel or fuck or eat with abandon. After bellowing like a barn animal in orgasm, hoovering a plate of mashed potatoes, or spraying out spit in the heat of expostulation, we've flinched in self-scorn—*ugh, that was so gross. I am so gross.* On rare occasions, we might revel in our excess—belting out anthems with our friends over karaoke, perhaps—but in the company of less sympathetic souls, our uncertainty always returns. A woman who meets the world with intensity is a woman who endures lashes of shame and disapproval, from within as well as without.

In Victorian England, the medical establishment would have labeled us hysterical, pathologically immoderate in emotional and physiological expression. Here's how a German-born doctor practicing in London, one Julius Althaus, defined the condition in 1866: "All the symptoms of hysteria have their prototype in those vital actions by which grief, terror, disappointment, and other painful emotions and affections, are manifested under ordinary circumstances, and which become signs of hysteria as soon as they attain a certain degree of intensity."[1] Of course, "a certain degree of intensity" invites a vast range of interpretation, and when it came to emotional eruptions, the Victorians were none too generous. Hysteria was a convenient means of pathologizing—and thus regulating— feminine feeling and its expression. Today, as many among us grieve our political optimism and hammer out our anger on social media, we find our husbands, our boyfriends, our parents, our politicians diagnosing us with similar maladies: we're wallowing in it, why are we so freaked out, we must be bleeding out of our wherever. Take a Xanax, girl, and *calm down*.

We are the women who can hardly contain our screams, and, oftentimes, we don't. Our muchness oozes from our pores like acidic sweat: ranker, more caustic, less concealable than ever. But however brutally the stigma may sizzle in this political moment, this sense that we are somehow Too Much is hardly new to us—nor will it dissipate whenever Donald Trump's vise finally unclenches from our skulls. I conceived the idea for this book—a critical cry of bullshit against this concept, Too Much—some years ago, during a comparatively happier presidency. This term, Too Much, pernicious in its ambiguity,

attacks with the force of history. It's the overdetermined ex-
ponent of ideologies, centuries old, structured by misogyny,
racism, and homophobia. American society fetishizes white
heteronormative propriety: it wants its girls pliable and
demure—girls who safeguard both tears and sex for the privacy
of the bedroom, who keep their voices measured during meet-
ings, and who brush their hair and blot their lipstick. It worships the woman who, if she should experience distress, will
wear her sadness like Lana Del Rey or *Middlemarch*'s Dorothea
Brooke: with genteel sensuality and relative quiet. Anything
more—well, that would be excessive.

Accordingly, "You're just too much!" is the threat of patriarchy disguised as playful admonition. It is a warning, even a
diagnosis. It is saying, "This space is not yours to colonize. This
power is not yours to claim." Systemic oppression relies on the
careful partitioning of social space. Specifically, it requires that
marginalized peoples—of which women are one broad example, and women of color and queer persons are more pointedly
targeted ones—dwell within corners, that we shrink inside walls
that loom and compress.

The public devises unspoken rules of deportment born from
anxieties over what we can bear to see expressed—and accordingly, whom we are willing to allow the privilege of expression. Reluctant to countenance emotional and physical extremes
in any case, women, long regarded as the lodestars of excess,
are eyed like shape-shifters with the power to transform into
Medusa. But I've since realized that there is power in what others
call monstrosity. Our refusal to abide, to prioritize the comfort of the West's hegemonic governance, lays bare the rickety
scaffolding of culture's so-called behavioral norms. The roots of

rules are never so deep that they cannot be wrenched from the soil; man-made boundaries remain at the mercy of the creatures who erected them. For when we are Too Much—and when we refuse to apologize for that—we burst against those walls and marvel as they give way like sand.

"LOST MY MUCHNESS, HAVE I?"

I remember little about the circumstances of seeing Tim Burton's adaptation of *Alice in Wonderland*. It must have been 2010, because that was the year it was released, and I saw it in a movie theater. My impressions were, and still are, few. Mia Wasikowska is a sweet-faced, impertinent Alice. It disappoints me that she and Anne Hathaway's White Queen do not embark on a love affair, though I'm certain they develop a queer affection (they're *absolutely* making eyes at each other, and you will not convince me otherwise). Tossing the Jabberwocky into the mix seemed a lazy narrative decision. But above all in my recollection, there is the question of "muchness," and whether nineteen-year-old Alice has retained it after her protracted absence from Wonderland and all the ravages and impositions of early adulthood.

Muchness: what a word! It was new to my lexicon, and yet it seemed as if I had always known it, my kinship with it sensed, if not fully comprehended, as if its letters were threaded into my veins. But as I left the theater, I contemplated how, for Alice, the Mad Hatter, and the rest of her bizarro entourage, "muchness" although vague in definition, evokes an unambiguously positive quality—something that surprised me, even if I hadn't yet parsed the reason. Alice's muchness is her passion, her verve, and her courage. "Lost my muchness, have I?" Alice mutters to herself as she gingerly traverses the Red Queen's moat, littered with the petrified heads of her victims. When it returns—or had it ever really gone?—she transforms into a mighty warrior, fit to slay a monster fifty times her size. When she returns to her conventional English milieu, this muchness also supplies her with the confidence to reject a marriage proposal in front of an expectant crowd and dash off in pursuit of a more auspicious future. From there the film veers into regrettably imperialist territory, but in any case, Alice's muchness spares her a life tethered to a sniveling boob and instead sends her on adventures, like a mercantile Mary Kingsley (fittingly enough, Kingsley is her last name in this adaptation).[2]

Had I, without context, been asked to describe muchness, I would have offered a definition shot through with censure and cruel self-assessment. Muchness, I might have told you then, was a characteristic—an affliction—possessed by those who were in every way *too much*: too emotional, first of all, but also too exuberant, too loud, too talkative, too volatile, too brimful of desire. It also connoted mental illness: a genetic cocktail of anxiety and depression primed to seize the brain at any moment. The way I saw it, a woman plagued by muchness is likely to call her friend in a panic at three a.m., gripped by terror over seemingly trivial circumstances. She has more than once cowered in humiliation after someone has told her to lower her voice. Perhaps she is inclined to obsess or to engage in acts of compulsion—maybe she's even depressed, masochistic. Probably she spends each day stuffing herself into an invisible carton more palatable to general company, like a jack-in-the-box where the head lolls outside the top, a smile slapdashed over a scramble of ugly, brambly feelings. And, if my experience was any indication, she lives in perpetual fear of the time when those she loves will tire of her—when her muchness becomes cause for expulsion, and renders her irrevocably alone.

A few years later I was working on a doctorate in Victorian literature, and, inevitably, my eye always wandered to passages where female characters erupted with feeling, whether of love or defiance or fury. They were the women I preferred, and with whom I felt an affinity—the ones who wept and feverishly declared their love and rarely apologized. After a tormented resistance, Tess Durbeyfield nakedly expresses her desire for Angel Clare (who, alas, is the unworthiest of feckless assholes). Catherine Earnshaw of *Wuthering Heights* is cruel to the bone, but I am endlessly in awe of her uncompromising and voracious demand for adoration. Most tellingly, Maggie Tulliver of George Eliot's *The Mill on the Floss*—impulsive, sometimes baffled by her own excesses—became my Victorian avatar, textual evidence that the vigorous pulsing of my veins was, perhaps, not wholly incompatible with life (though, if you know Maggie's tragic story, I realize this might seem an ironic comment to make).

I detected "too muchness" in each of these characters, and in so many more—Victorian literature breeds Too Much women—though I never wrote about it directly, or even mentioned it, for that matter. Graduate school seemed inhospitable to too muchness, privileging those who endured austere conditions of intellectual labor as if training for a bookish Spartan army. What a bizarre badge of pride: the first time a professor skewered my work, I thought, "At least I didn't cry in his office." It would be unseemly—presumptuous—and a mark of excessive sensitivity in a context where one was expected to take her lumps with stoic submission. There was no space for Maggie Tulliver or Catherine Earnshaw in graduate school, and by that logic I often wondered whether there was room for me: someone who attempted to be who she wasn't—measured, demure, cool—and who failed gloriously most of the time.

But gradually, I spooned meager portions of hope into a theory: that my maximalist personality, my muchness, was no reason for shame but, dare I say it, pride. I had never forgotten about muchness, the word and the notion of it, and as I began to regard its assignations with timid dignity, I considered the possibility of a reinterpretation, one that summoned greater self-regard. Perhaps what others had condemned in me, what I had condemned in myself—this muchness, or because I thought of it in terms of fundamental excess, too muchness— held promise I was only beginning to discern.

A THEORY OF TOO MUCHNESS

Although "muchness" is the term that galvanized my idea for this book, "too much" and "too muchness"—the latter a clunky noun form of my own devising—are the phrases I will return to throughout these pages. My reasoning, beyond being loath to steal another's verbiage, is this: The insidiously destructive accusation of being "too much" has traveled American discourse for decades. Thoroughly vague, it can refer to nearly anything, and often does. We call individual people "too much" the same way

we might describe an aggravating workday or an overwhelming
to-do list or a night of babysitting three squalling toddlers and
an incontinent puppy. In so doing, Too Much persons are maligned as inconvenient bothers, people to avoid because their
dispositions, embodiments, sexualities, disabilities, and so forth
are disconcerting or uncomfortable to behold.

This wide-ranging scorn for too muchness is no coincidence
or matter of social caprice. Our culture, for all its staggering
toward progress, possesses a meager threshold for discomfort
when faced with examples of nonnormative difference. We
should not be surprised that those most often stigmatized as disagreeably or even dangerously excessive are those who contest
white masculine heteronormative and capitalist ideologies. For
centuries, white cisgender straight men have defined excess according to the terms that most benefit them, cementing, brick
by brick, a culture that caters to their proclivities, comforts, and
benefits.

After all, not all forms of excess are condemned as too muchness. A soldier's valor in battle, achieved through intense feats of
physical duress, violence, and the willingness to sacrifice oneself, has always been hailed as morally upstanding and the most
preeminent index of patriotism. Machismo, for all its hazards,
commands unflagging cultural respect and racks up sexual cur-
rency. Indeed, metrics of excess are rarely, if ever, calibrated according to their masculine appeal, but—still—books and films
are every day dismissed for being "too girly." Although we've
garnered powerful heroines like Buffy the Vampire Slayer and
Jessica Jones and films like *Captain Marvel* and *Mad Max: Fury
Road*, the action film has, to a severe extent, been interpreted as
a showcase for outsize feats of masculine strength and stamina.

The Rambo franchise, initiated with the 1982 film *First Blood*, showcases the swarthy and sweat-sheened warrior, John Rambo, who grimaces and cocks his machine gun like an accessorized appendage. Portrayed by Sylvester Stallone, Rambo is a Vietnam War veteran who, over the course of five films, transforms into a herculean, renegade killing machine. His character is not empty of nuance—like so many soldiers, he suffers from post-traumatic stress disorder—but Rambo's intensity, his too muchness, has cultivated near-idolatry not because he thwarts expectations of masculine normativity, but because of the ways he becomes a cartoonish embodiment of them. He is heroic, yes, but his heroism is a feral sort: ferocious and filthy and violent.

We've long understood that masculine experience is posited as universal, or at least as more compelling (women are not necessarily invited to relate to John Rambo, but then, the Rambo franchise, like so many cultural entities, was not created with us in mind). It is also the case that, from childhood, we are all of us instructed to revere stories of boys becoming men—in the most conventional sense—while the feats of others, particularly women, are understood as so exceptional as to nearly be taken as fiction. Moreover, bravery that wears a feminine face is rarely applauded without the lurking question of whether it should exist in the first place—Disney's *Mulan* (1998) is one such example. Though we cheer for her, it is always our understanding that her adventures, should she survive them, will end. Eventually, she will return home, to her parents, and reassume the mantle of dutiful daughter. And what luck: dressing in drag, joining the Chinese army, and nearly being slaughtered—both for breaking the law and by the Hun army—results in her snagging sexy soldier Shang (whose over-the-top masculinity and verve is presented as both inspirational and, for a children's film, weirdly titillating).

Then of course there are the scattered shards of popular culture that reify privileged male excess in more granular and mundane ways. After all, one need not—and probably should not—go full Rambo to enact hypermasculinity. When I was an undergraduate in Virginia, and AIM profiles operated as intertextual self-endorsements, the chorus of the Dave Matthews Band's 1996 hit "Too Much" made the rounds as a cyber-epigraph. Its inclusion seemed a choreographed shrug in the face of debauchery, a barely coy means of expressing, through performed pseudo self-deprecation, that one was living the good life of Pabst Blue Ribbon, Wawa hoagies, and boozy, wet kisses.

Ultimately—and this is the logic upon which the song turns—we expect men to be hungry and horny and to wet their whistles with a beer or five; we overlook and even giggle at their vices. Gleefully, ravenously, Matthews sings, "I eat too much / I drink too much / I want too much / Too much." What strikes me most about this debauched anthem is how it deploys the rhetoric of self-critique in order to revel in a prism of desires: food, booze, sex, merrymaking. Matthews acknowledges—celebrates—his gluttonous passion; his insatiability is championed by a melody both vigorous and urgent. He is the fraternity brother's composite of the Heat and Snow Misers from *The Year Without a Santa Claus*, announcing with cheery gusto, "I'm TOO MUCH!"

And while it's reductive to designate experiences as either "masculine" or "feminine," Dave Matthews's iconic status among twenty-something men is by no means coincidence. Nor am I surprised that the lyrics to "Too Much" tended to populate the profiles of the male college students with whom I was acquainted, rather than those of their female counterparts—though, admittedly, I think I may have posted them at some point. (I had a brief, strange love affair with the Dave Matthews Band that I entirely blame on my Virginian upbringing; the band assembled in 1991 at the University of Virginia in Charlottesville.) For the Dave Matthewses of the world, "too much" is associated with power and virility. But for women—for whom excess is constantly tethered to some perceived lack of emotional or physical control—the concept of "too much" carries the unwieldy baggage of cultural stigma. As Jess Zimmerman writes in her 2016 essay "Hunger Makes Me," "A man's appetite can be hearty, but a woman with an appetite is always voracious: her hunger always overreaches, because it is not supposed to exist. If she wants food, she is a glutton. If she wants sex, she is a slut. If she wants emotional care-taking, she is a high-maintenance bitch or, worse, an 'attention whore': an amalgam of sex-hunger and care-hunger, greedy to not only be fucked and paid but, most unforgivably of all, to be noticed."[3]

Accordingly, when we tell a woman she is "too much," it is not with the grin and playful tap that the Dave Matthewses of the world smugly expect, but with a wagging finger and the intonations of a warning. Remember that you, and your de-sires, must be small—diminishing—preferably nonexistent. Ask only for that which you are invited to receive, which is to say, basically nothing.

And yet, Americans are bathed in economic excess, our lives marshalled by it. Capitalism is defined by overabundance, set to a score of "more and more and more," a yen gurgling in its belly to create and destroy with the sloppiest strokes of greed. The fashion industry, despite some recent fragmental efforts by brands to embrace "sustainability," has long urged avid, bottomless consumption through the proliferation of fast fashion, garments meant to be both bought and tossed on a whim, within months. But for these companies, the prevailing ethos has been one that turns on extravagant production and wallets coaxed open by savvy marketing—that we owe it to ourselves to gorge on knitwear and stilettos, that greed is self-care. We owe it to ourselves, although the fashion industry, if it continues apace, is likely to gobble a quarter of the planet's carbon supply by the year 2050.[4] Female hunger, when driven by consumerist fantasies that fill the coffers of the wealthy, is— sometimes—more palatable.

Our excesses are stridently policed in this way: when in the service of a capitalist hegemony, they may be overlooked or excused—even when, in certain cases, they ought not be— and sometimes they may even be encouraged. But to be "too much," as I define it, connotes a state of excess that either directly or indirectly derives from an emotional and mental intemperance: exuberance, chattiness, a tendency to burst into tears or toward what is typically labeled mental instability. In the last several years, the colloquialism "extra" seems to have become something of a near neighbor, although without quite the same bite and with more of an emphasis on absurd or flamboyant behavior than on one's vulnerabilities or deviations from normative behavior. Often too muchness carries a significant emotional component, because excess, whatever form it takes, is conceived of as a basic function of unbridled feeling. Women who are taken to task for inhabiting unruly bodies, particularly those marked as fat, face stereotypes of immoderacy: on the one hand, they are castigated for not simply choosing and committing to weight loss; on the other, they are lampooned as people constitutionally unable to regulate their appetites. In the eyes of patriarchal medicine, women are endlessly diagnosable, and yet the verdict is always the same: we are fat or horny or skinny or depressed precisely because we are women, and women—that broad, rangy, insufficient category—are predisposed to all manner of prodigality.

Demolishing capitalism and patriarchy are, alas, beyond the reach of this book. We can, however, take stock of the social corset that encircles those of us seeking to live in ways that are deemed inconvenient or messy—or, in the most extreme cases, altogether unacceptable. We have acquiesced to a climate that is hospitable to a statistical minimum, while the margins heave with the rest of us, the Too Much people: humans straining for breath in a milieu that has constricted our air supply, who may be uncomfortable to countenance or even contemplate—that is, if we are to live in the world the way that is truest for us. Now, we inhale and exhale with big, ravenous gulps, urgent and socially verboten. We must take them anyway, these caches of oxygen and sweeps of space: breathing in, shrieking our exhales.

WHY THE VICTORIANS?

This book draws significantly from nineteenth-century literature and culture, grounding its discussion in a historical period when women's too muchness underwent vigorous medical scrunity, routinely receiving a specific, vexed verdict—one that had already dogged women for centuries and that would continue to haunt those of us who live with mental illness or who so much as manifest acute emotional intensity: hysteria. The Too Much diagnosis par excellence, hysteria became an especially ubiquitous catchall for women in the nineteenth century when doctors like French neuropsychiatrist Pierre Janet and American physician Frederick Hollick took grandiose measures to explore the so-called disease's symptoms and treatments. (Others, like British doctors Robert Brudenell Carter and F. C. Skey, doubted the existence of hysteria, not because they were sympathetic to women, but precisely the opposite: they believed those who complained of symptoms to be both duplicitous and solipsistic.)[5] Janet's work in particular—he posited hypnosis as a preeminently effective means of both study and therapy—manifests itself as an antecedent to Sigmund Freud's mode of psychoanalysis, which catalyzed the psychological theory of hysteria.[6] Hysteria, however, has endured in the medical and larger cultural imagination long after Freud's hypotheses surrounding penis envy and psychosexual complexes: it was listed in the *Diagnostic and Statistical Manual of Mental Disorders* until the third edition was printed in 1980. And even now, its influence is everywhere present, not only distorting prevailing conceptions of femininity but maintaining its antiquated status as a pre-existing medical condition—at once a symptom and a diagnosis.

To be sure, hysteria was not born with the Victorians, although, as historian Carroll Smith-Rosenberg has written, it is construed as "one of the classic diseases of the nineteenth century."[7] Evidence from Ancient Egypt suggests that it was the first mental illness conceived of as uniquely and fundamentally female. The Greek physician Hippocrates was first to use the term "hysteria," the etymological origins of which point to a very telling definition: uterus. For centuries, wild theories about female anatomy have simmered. In the seventeenth century a theory took root that the uterus—long believed to be the root of every female malady—bounced around the body like a rubber ball, wreaking havoc wherever it settled. Victorian women carried smelling salts to revive them when they swooned: apparently the uterus disliked the pungent odor and would be enticed to meander back to its appropriate place within the loins. Men were diagnosed with hysteria too, albeit comparatively rarely; moreover, physicians, entrenched in essentialist medical ideology, debated whether one could be a hysteric if one's biology did not include a uterus, the affliction's perceived locus.[8]

In 1847, Hollick published *The Diseases of Woman, Their Causes and Cure Familiarly Explained; with Practical Hints for their Prevention and for the Preservation of Female Health*, a book meant to become a household staple, a compendium for reference when domestic angels were, for obscure reasons, freaking out. Unsurprisingly, he devotes a lengthy entry to hysteria, with the underlying thesis that women are essentially fragile and prone to malady, particularly—but not always!—when their dispositions are emotionally sensitive, and practically everything can be read as a symptom. Predictably, he pins the site of the malady within the tricky and changeable womb:

In regard to the starting point or original seat of Hysteria, there seems to be no doubt of its being the Uterus, which becomes subject to a peculiar excitement, or disturbance, that exerts a wonderful sympathetic influence on the whole system. The Uterus, it must be remembered, is the *controlling* organ in the female body, being the most excitable of all, and so intimately connected, by the ramifications of its numerous nerves, with every other part.[9]

But although the uterus was charged as the hub of all feminine maladies and distress, Hollick cautions that there is no feasible way to comprehensively document hysteria's every symptom. "The symptoms of this disease comprise, if we were to enumerate them all, those of nearly every other disease under the sun," he writes. "In fact, they are so numerous, so various, and so changeable, that describing them all is out of the question."[10] And yet, he makes a valiant effort, in a passage that is the stuff of dark comedy—for all its absurdity, texts like this one, in which a socially manufactured disease is interpreted as medical fact, have warped women's lives and clipped their liberties:

> The causes of hysteria are as abscure [*sic*] as the symptoms are diversified. Probably some of the most frequent predisposing causes are, weak constitution, scrofula, indolence, a city life, bad physical and moral education, *nervous or sanguine temperaments, the over excitement of certain feelings,* and religious or other enthusiasm... Some of the immediate causes are, the first period, suppressed menstruation, late marriage, chronic inflammation of the womb, vicious habits, and long continued constipation. *Vivid mental emotions, and excited feelings, may also be specially mentioned,*

such as anger, fright, disappointment, particularly in love, read-
ing sentimental and exciting romances, and disagreeable, painful,
or sorrowful sights. Some authors also suppose there is a
hereditary disposition to hysteria, and others that there
is a peculiar temperament which disposes to it. It is certain that immitation [*sic*] has much to do with it, or, in
common parlance, it is catching, for very often when one
female is taken in an assembly, many others will also be
attacked from seeing her.[11] (emphasis mine)

Although Hollick's laundry list indicates, before anything
else, that the illness described is illusory—a fantasy of basic
feminine subordinacy—he returns to references of heightened
affective states, implying both that it is dangerous for a woman
to harbor these feelings and that women who are inclined to
"vivid mental emotions" are social hazards. A hysterical woman
is, above all, an inappropriate one. "She becomes dejected, or
melancholy, and will sigh, or burst into tears, and then as suddenly laugh in the most immoderate manner, and without any
reason for it,"[12] Hollick explains. As he lectures his readers,
his tone waxes with urgent castigation: any woman might be a
hysteric, but those most likely to become so, he determines, are
those whose characters are cracked with moral turpitude:

Women disposed to hysteria are *generally capricious in their*
character, and often whimsical in their conduct. *Some are*
exceedingly excitable and impatient, others obstinate or frivolous;
the slightest thing may make them laugh, or cry, and
exhibit traits which ordinarily they are not supposed to
possess. Like children, the merest trifles may make them

transcendently happy, or cast them into the most gloomy despair. Very frequently they are made much worse by seeing that those around them have no real commiseration for their sufferings, and perhaps even think they are not real. A delicate attention, and properly exhibited sympathy, will soothe and calm the excited feelings more than almost anything else.[13] (emphasis mine)

Hollick's account of hysteria never achieves greater specificity, only an increasingly taut strain of stigmatizing rhetoric, connecting states of exuberance and depression with a disposition predisposed to caprice and frivolity—and of course it's not clear what the doctor considers examples of the latter, besides "reading sentimental and exciting romances." Indeed, his most precise directions for combating the menace of hysteria corroborates contemporary perspectives on suitable pastimes for the gender:

All kinds of sentimental and romantic reading must be avoided, but amusing books, or travels, and descriptions of scenery may be allowed. Music or poetry, when indulged in to excess, and with those of an excitable temperament, is often highly injurious. *More domestic occupation, and less fanciful idling, would prevent numerous disorders in many young females.*

These archaic—and legitimately bonkers—theories have been debunked, but the anxiety underpinning them has lingered, rendering female bodies the landscape of a brutal ideological battlefield. The protracted, but ever vicious, reproductive rights debate asks whether a woman is sovereign of her body: Is she free—is she *reasonable enough*—to treat it as she sees fit, and should that freedom be circumscribed depending on circumstance? And for that matter, how should the body feel to the woman living in it?

It's through literature that we gain access to Victorian female perspectives, through writers like the Brontë sisters and George Eliot and Elizabeth Gaskell and Christina Rossetti, all of whom, in various modes and means, contemplate the circumstances of women in an age when emotion was so viciously policed and pathologized. It's stories like Charlotte Perkins Gilman's "The Yellow Wallpaper" that articulate, with blistering focus, the individual ramifications of widespread hysteria diagnoses, and sensation novelists like Mary Elizabeth Braddon who bear out in their narratives the terror with which Victorian men regarded women, whose bodies and temperaments seemed, to them, irrevocably illegible. In order to account for the fearsome conundrum of women, men resorted to obsessive, stigmatizing taxonomies, legitimized through the medical establishment. Even novelist Thomas Hardy conveys remarkable empathy in the famously tragic *Tess of the d'Urbervilles* (1891) in which the titular woman is doggedly shamed and tortured for her desires—and for the potency of her sexual attractiveness, regarded as something of a character flaw whenever it was convenient for men to do so. As we will see, other male writers, Lewis Carroll, for instance, did not share Hardy's insight into the structural misogyny that could render a woman's reality a waking nightmare: instead *Alice in Wonderland* illuminates the anxieties surrounding female bodies that ignited the hysteria craze and conveys the abiding fear that women were, by virtue of biology, excessive in ways that could be dangerous to men if they were not soundly bridled.

Victorian literature reveals and, often, responds to an enduring principle that has since lurked in cultural understandings of femininity: women's bodies, historical sites of male anxiety and consternation, are not trusted to register maladies in ways legible to the institution of medicine—and we, the custodians, cannot be trusted to accurately represent our interiorities. Perhaps we are Freudian hysterics or hypochondriacs or, to draw on recent conversations surrounding the #MeToo movement, perhaps our real diagnosis is anger, even bloodlust—for one man, or for cisgender men at large. Moreover, through the lenses of fear and prejudice, biological processes like menstruation and childbirth distort and appear dubiously associated with black magic—what sorts of creatures bleed for days without dying? Perhaps we are monsters after all.

Chapter Two

CHATTERBOX

"Do you know where the wicked go after death?"

"They go to hell," was my ready and orthodox answer.

"And what is hell? Can you tell me that?"

"A pit full of fire."

"And should you like to fall into that pit, and to be burning there for ever?"

"No, sir."

"What must you do to avoid it?"

I deliberated a moment: my answer, when it did come, was objectionable: "I must keep in good health, and not die."[1]

If you know Charlotte Brontë's *Jane Eyre* (1847), then it's likely you recall this moment, in which a little girl—our orphaned titular protagonist—guilelessly, and to the horror of her adult audience, suggests her certain damnation. It's a delightful scene, all the more so because it functions as a pressure valve for readers who have fumed through the novel's opening chapters. After all, Jane's plight is maddening: she's brutalized by a boorish older cousin, and then punished for his sins by her aunt, the spiteful Mrs. Reed. The household treats her as a pariah, and when she is introduced to Mr. Brocklehurst, the oppressive and hypocritical head of Lowood School, Mrs. Reed willfully misrepresents Jane as a veritable hellion. What relief when Jane responds to Mr. Brocklehurst's interrogation with—albeit unintentional—comedy. And after Brocklehurst's departure, we enjoy even sweeter satisfaction as Jane, who can no longer countenance her aunt's injustice, summons her mettle and delivers a withering indictment of Mrs. Reed's character. It is equal parts delicious and heartbreaking: "You think I have no feelings, and that I can do without one bit of love or kindness; but I cannot live so: and you have no pity."

For Jane to assert a fundamental claim to parental tenderness—to declare that her feelings are inherently important—is a meaningful moment in the context of the novel, but, as you might suppose, it would not have been supported by Victorian guides to children's discipline or the morally didactic literature for young Britons that, since the middle of the previous century, had become commonplace.[2] We love Jane Eyre because, from childhood, she understands the sanctity of one's emotional life and, despite poverty, low social position, and a dearth of physical charms, she demands to be respected—for her sensibility to be respected—on her own terms. This is not the first time that she will draw attention to her passionate inner life: years later, she will confront Mr. Rochester, both her secret beloved and her employer, in a similar manner. For many of us, Jane's moxie renders her all the more dear and all the more heroic. It also illuminates her singularity in a period that balked at female excess of any kind, and at any age. To broadcast the intensity of one's emotions shattered every rule of decorum guiding feminine behavior in the nineteenth century. And while we're no longer quite so constricted, a girl like Jane—ardent, uncouth, and uncompromisingly candid—would make others squeamish. Don't be so *aggressive*, some would tell her. Calm down. Shush.

Charlotte Brontë might have bristled at these directives; after all, she and her siblings were reared with leniency relative to contemporary Victorian children. Their reading material extended far beyond the typical stock of childish morality tales, which was both fortunate and a necessity: the Brontës were a voraciously intellectual set with roving and precocious interests. Too often, however, this shared creative luminescence became a mode of contemplating their sorrows; for the Brontë siblings, youth was wracked with tragic loss. The family matriarch, Maria Brontë, née Branwell, died of cancer in 1821, when the children were still too young to vividly remember her. She was followed in relatively short order by her two eldest, Maria and Elizabeth, who caught tuberculosis while away at school. Ages eleven and ten, respectively, the girls returned to Haworth only to die at the family hearth: Maria on May 6, 1825, and Elizabeth just over a month later, on June 15. Cowan Bridge School, which Charlotte and Emily also attended—they were withdrawn after their sisters fell ill—appears, scarcely disguised, in *Jane Eyre*, the clear model for Lowood School. Charlotte depicts the brutish treatment the four sisters experienced there and the outbreak of illness that felled Maria and

Elizabeth. The character of Helen Burns, Jane's first and most cherished friend, is, according to Charlotte, a portrait of her eldest sister, Maria, "a little mother among the rest"[3] of the Brontë children, brimful of benevolent sagacity.

The Brontës often seem like a literary flash in the pan, a brilliant crackle out on the English heath: glimmering in sudden, triumphant glory, and then, just as quickly, extinguished. Charlotte, who died on March 31, 1855, at age thirty-eight, likely from complications in pregnancy, outlived her other sisters and brother considerably. In fact, she lost Emily, Anne, and Branwell—her three remaining siblings, playmates, and literary co-conspirators, in the spindly timeframe of eight months. Emily, famous for her ferocious, desolately passionate novel *Wuthering Heights* (1847), was thirty years old when she died on December 19, 1848; Anne, author of the predominantly autobiographical *Agnes Grey* (1847) and *The Tenant of Wildfell Hall* (1848), died on May 28 of the next year, at twenty-nine years old. Branwell died in September 1848 at age thirty-one, his poor health agitated by alcoholism. After their deaths, Charlotte published two novels, *Shirley* (1849) and her last, the cagey, meditative, achingly lonely *Villette* (1853). Her first novel, *The Professor*, originally rejected by editors, was published posthumously by her husband in 1857.[4]

The old chestnut in which one claims that a young, deceased person burned too brightly for the world is hopelessly cheesy; frankly, our world would be a better one with more Brontë novels. Yet the Brontës, a coterie of idiosyncratic brilliance, relatively isolated from the churn of the British literary marketplace, have always seemed to me a family that dwelled in a haunted, gossamer space indiscernible to the

rest of us. Charlotte and her siblings were, I believe, rife
with too muchness, and whatever else that may have meant,
they were virtuosos. They also enjoyed a certain mental and
physical freedom that facilitated their collective imaginings.
Rather than be circumscribed to specific, domesticated spaces,
they were encouraged to wander the moors that engulfed
their Yorkshire home, and which Emily rendered in *Wuthering
Heights* with ghostly reverie. Moreover, their father, Patrick
Brontë, taught his daughters a range of subjects that others
would have deemed unsuitable, or at least unnecessary, for
young women: mathematics and classics, for example. The
Brontë girls were not raised to diminish their talents or to suppress either their appetite for knowledge or the fruits of their
studies.

But, of course, an unconventional childhood does not
necessarily shield a little girl from cultural insinuations, particularly where feminine propriety is involved. Accordingly,
Charlotte was not immune to the stigma attached to expressing, or even harboring, abundant feeling. While both studying
and teaching in Brussels under Monsieur Constantin Héger—
for whom she developed a deep, but unrequited, romantic
affection—Brontë devised a fictional character to give voice
to the frustrations she suffered as a young woman of ardent
temperament:

> There was always excess in what I did; I was either too
> excited or too despondent; without wanting to I allowed
> everything that passed through my heart to be seen and
> sometimes there were storms passing through it; in vain
> I tried to imitate the sweet gaity, the serene and equable

spirits which I saw in the faces of my companions and which I found so worthy of admirations; all my efforts were useless; I could not restrain the ebb and flow of blood in my arteries and that ebb and flow always showed itself in my face and in my hard and unattractive features. I wept in secret.[5]

Héger, it seems, recognized these traits as belonging to his pupil, and although he didn't reciprocate her love—he was married and taught alongside his wife—the professor encouraged her to regard herself as exceptional, as a genius, in fact. But then it has often been the case that we make allowances for those whom society designates as uncommonly skilled or clever. (When, later in life, Charlotte made the rare visit to London literary society, she did not slip easily into the fold, although contemporaries like author William Makepeace Thackeray were bemused by her brash honesty.) Yet the account she provides of herself indicates a queasy recognition that her emotional tumult, the pulsing passion of her inner life, could not be reconciled with any context, whether at home at Haworth or among strange company.

In 1835, several years before her tenure in Brussels, Charlotte took a teaching position at Roe Head School, which she had once attended as a star pupil and where she cultivated intimate friendships, most famously with her longtime pen pal Ellen Nussey. Her return, however, delivered her into the misery that was the drudging life available to a single woman without independent wealth. She resented her less intelligent pupils—and privately referred to them as "fat-headed oafs"[6]—ached for her family, and, in general, viciously preferred the fantastic worlds to which she escaped through writing, even when it was ill-advised: for instance, when she was supposed to be teaching class. Meanwhile, she sent bushels of letters to Ellen chronicling her guilt: she was, she feared, not capable of the mild goodness she attributed to her friend. She even frets, as Brontë biographer Claire Harman writes, that she was "*too much* for Ellen, and was censoring her own post when it became too sentimental."[7] Attuned to the violence of her attachment, which she more or less suggests through elimination, Charlotte writes, "I will not tell you all I think, and feel about you Ellen. I will preserve unbroken that reserve which alone enables me to maintain a decent character for judgment."[8] A tension throbs between Charlotte's stubborn passion, her yearning to indulge her fantasies and more or less do as she pleased, and her chagrin over her emotional intensity, particularly when what she felt was not especially charitable. A similar vacillation emerges in the character of Jane Eyre: while she never quite capitulates to Victorian expectations of gentle femininity, she is duly chastened for her brash, childish defiance and learns, with time, a quieter form of resistance.

The strictures of twenty-first-century little girlhood might, at a glance, seem inconsequential when set alongside the demands laid before Victorian children—including the Brontës—and yet, present-day expectations are enduringly rigid. It is true that the last few years have yielded a modest offering of feminine fictional icons modeling less constrained behavior—both *Brave*'s Merida and *Moana*'s titular heroine are standout examples. The latter's release was nothing short of sensational: here, finally, is a nonwhite female character who is reduced to neither racial nor gender stereotype. Accordingly, she's positioned neither as a damsel in distress nor as an object of desire— Moana's romantic life receives no narrative attention, and her chutzpah saves her island, however much it unsettles her father, the film's benevolent patriarch. But our excitement over these young heroines belies their enduring paucity. And if we're delighted over the representation of sassy, brave girls—if we're still registering them as novelties and dazzling exceptions—it emphasizes the extent to which American popular culture continues to proffer an idealized version of young femininity as white, docile, and amiably stifled (Moana, after all, is one of the only nonwhite heroines Disney offers its viewers).

Despite nearly two centuries of shifting perceptions, our ideologies of gender and emotion, and the art so finely shaped by them, derive from an enduringly Victorian perspective of little girlhood. Perhaps we are more secular—the Disney Channel does not necessarily threaten its young viewers with a "pit full of fire"—and we're certainly invested in the window dressings of female empowerment, but claims of progress ring hollow in the wake of cultural ephemera stubbornly insisting that the best little girls are the quiet ones, the ones who smile benignly and who behave.

Child rearing has a long and knotted history, but along that timeline we can pinpoint certain significant personages who wrote on the subject, namely, late eighteenth/early nineteenth-century British writer Maria Edgeworth, a figure who looms large as an influence in gendered discipline. Edgeworth wrote careful narratives meant to instruct both boys and girls in the appropriate decorum specific to their respective genders. In these moralistic tales, a child would disobey, be punished accordingly, and ultimately learn a lesson about docility in the face of authority. Specifically, early nineteenth-century conceptions of proper, Anglo girlhood were informed by the domestic duties they would perform later in life. If donning a corset— a functionally restrictive undergarment—signaled the transition to womanhood, then the lessons learned by little girls corseted them in figurative ways. There was no room for too muchness when a child was bent over needlework or, in the cases of the less affluent, learning duties in the kitchen. These were tasks that necessitated slight, measured movements and taut physical rigidity. Moreover, they certainly did not require chatter.

In *The Parent's Assistant; Or, Stories for Children* (1796), Edgeworth penned brief, chaste tales intended to instruct young boys and girls in the proper decorum for English youth. Although boys receive greater attention throughout the collection, expectations for young girls are made eminently—not to mention exasperatingly—clear. In "Simple Susan" the titular character provides a template; she is, the narrator extols, a "sweet tempered, modest, sprightly, industrious lass." But lest we underestimate her virtues, Edgeworth's narrator elaborates in a fastidious benediction:

> Susan's affectionate, dexterous, sensible activity was never more wanted, or more effectual. She understood so readily, she obeyed so exactly; and when she was left to her own discretion, judged so prudently, that her mother had little trouble and no anxiety in directing her. She said that Susan never did too little, or too much.[9]

To my mind, Simple Susan is simply fucking insufferable. But how could she be anything else? She's not so much a feasible representation of humanity, let alone a role model; rather, she is an archetype—an assemblage of character traits that Edgeworth deems critical for any little girl's repertoire. And, of course, our attention is specifically drawn to Susan's ability to eschew any sort of disagreeable excess. She neither does "too little or too much," a vague assessment of character if ever there was one, but Edgeworth makes her point. With the utmost diligence, Susan calibrates herself according to contemporary dictates of femininity. She possesses the verve and initiative to be both unwaveringly honest and sedulous, yet her modesty and dedication to serving her parents—like so many fictional mothers of the time period, hers is in poor health—ensures that she will never interrogate the boundaries circumscribing her world. She is exactly what is expected of her.

I'm not questioning Susan's specific and, we must admit, bountiful virtues. Goodness has no precise calculus: if Susan's parents treat her with kindness and care, then she has every reason to respect their wishes. Were modesty not an evident cultural mandate for every person identifying as something other than white, heterosexual, and male, then perhaps its inclusion in Susan's grab bag of righteousness would not prickle me in the way it does. But Edgeworth's narrative is prescriptive; she indicates in no uncertain terms that there is a particular, paradoxically impossible way for a young girl to be. Young readers, I imagine, were tasked with striving along that asymptote of good behavior in an effort to mimic Simple Susan's perfection. They must have sensed the futility, that their moral trajectory would trudge onward toward infinity, never—no matter their efforts—reaching that endpoint exalted by the era's disciplinarians: where little girls were more akin to little angels who never did or never were too much.

It follows, then, that Edgeworth's bad girls were hyperbolic animated ids, little monsters reared through piss-poor parenting. Barbara, Susan's counterpart, the daughter of wealthy Mr. Case, sits slothfully at home unless she has the opportunity to torment one of the village's ruddy-cheeked children. She reads lascivious novels—which, even in the era of Fanny Burney, Jane Austen's eighteenth-century literary predecessor, continued to suffer from prevailing masculine assumptions about their intellectual vacuity—indulges in gluttony, and watches idly as Susan, her nemesis, perkily accomplishes her daily chores. Of course Barbara resents Susan for being universally beloved and assuages her envy by seeking to torment her by any means available. For wicked Seven Deadly Sin practitioners like Barbara, the future—at least in Edgeworth's universe—is dim. She will be humiliated, humbled, and, if she's lucky, rehabilitated. Barbara's antics lead her to be stung by a nasty horde of bees and then, horror of horrors, to endure the unsightly welts that blossom on her face, rendering her physically unbecoming, at least temporarily. In fact, the story ends here for rotten Barbara: too swollen and grotesque to attend a ball upon which she had set her sticky sights, we assume that she remains wretched, unreformed, and, thus, no longer of any concern to us. For Barbara, like Susan, is an archetype of vice more than she is a feasible depiction of little girlhood. She's so vile, in fact, that it's difficult to imagine any child without an acute psychotic disorder mimicking her villainy. But ultimately, we're not to concern

ourselves with the complexities of why Barbara is bad but
rather to understand, through her impossibly naughty behavior,
why Susan is so good.

Edgeworth and authors who wrote in a similar vein influenced other Victorian and Edwardian authors who, in turn,
provided more body to the milieu's conceptions of girlhood.
In 1880, editor Charles Peters began publishing *The Girl's Own
Paper*—a periodical that became extremely popular—in an effort "to foster and develop that which was highest and noblest
in the girlhood and womanhood in England."[10] At the same
time, *The Boy's Own Paper* was also in wide circulation, and
while it too encouraged Christian morals and decorum, its focus on adventure and rigorous activity differed markedly from
the female-oriented periodical lauding quiet, domestic pastimes
and occupations.

Author Lewis Carroll—given name Charles Dodgson—
betrays even deeper cultural anxiety about exuberant or overly
demonstrative feminine behavior in his children's stories,
specifically in the canonical yet chimerical *Alice's Adventures
in Wonderland* (1865). Likely enough you know the premise,
whether because you've read the book, seen Disney's 1951
animated feature, or even seen Tim Burton's aforementioned
fanciful, off-kilter—and therefore utterly Burton-esque—
adaptation from 2010. A young girl is listlessly dozing outside,
too soporific to listen to her older sister read, when she suddenly catches sight of a white rabbit—one who happens to
be clothed and sporting posh accessories. He dashes across
her line of vision and, her curiosity piqued, she follows him,
subsequently tumbling down a rabbit hole and into Wonderland. There she encounters a bevy of phantasmagoric creatures,

including a fragmentally disappearing cat with a deranged grin, a flimsy-willed, sentient deck of cards, and a caterpillar who, given his hookah habit, seems like he should be rather more patient and amiable than he is.

As soon as Alice enters this psychedelic fantasy world, her human form summons curiosity, and sometimes disquiet, from the inhabitants who themselves manifest in all manner of bizarre embodiments. But while these creatures engage in spectacles mesmerizing to young readers, Carroll's narrator fastens his sights on the little girl stumbling through this dizzyingly monochromatic world: it is her unruly body that concerns him and that, consequently, propels the narrative. As author, Carroll asserts his authority predominantly by regulating his muse's size fluctuations; however, the rapidity of said fluctuations betrays apprehension, stemming from Carroll's conception of female maturity as uncontainable and chaotic—that is to say, fundamentally *too much*. If a little girl's body could not be made to behave—that is to say, to submit to perennial youth—what else might she do? What churned beneath that learned veneer of docility, behind those eyes, reverently downcast? Perhaps even the most pliable little girls would prefer to be otherwise.

Setting aside garden-variety Victorian agitation, it's not especially surprising that Dodgson would concoct a narrative so manically concerned with a little girl's behaviors and bodily changes. He cultivated friendships with children—"child-friends," he called them—and even took up the hobby of photographing them in the nude, which, while never documented as foul play during his lifetime, certainly registers squeamishly now. Dodgson's child-friend Alice Liddell, probably his favorite of the bunch, inspired the character that would come to define his career. She was twelve years old when she received as a gift *Alice's Adventures Under Ground*, bound and lettered by Dodgson himself and, most significantly, containing a photograph[11] of seven-year-old Alice at the end. Critic U. C. Knoepflmacher remarks that the picture is "mirror-like," a laden, if embedded, message to its recipient, for "this mirror reflects a face that cannot age." It's difficult to locate many pictures of Liddell during the early years of pubescence when she received this gift from Dodgson—and when, to his consternation, her body would have experienced the first quakes of maturation. The photograph tucked inside Liddell's book is the gift of her former self, memorialized by Dodgson as an impossible fantasy: the female body, unfettered, fledgling, in perpetuity.

Yet Dodgson is not merely privileging a prepubescent moment that he regards as less chaotic; he also yearns for Liddell to join him in this nostalgia, even as she inevitably propels toward adulthood. For, when Liddell receives her copy of *Alice's Adventures Under Ground*, she embodies the reality resisted by Carroll in his narratives. The photograph is a plea: "Mourn with me, Alice," it beseeches. "Tell me that your new, mature body, which is too much for me to bear, is too much for you, too."

When *Alice's Adventures in Wonderland* was published in 1865, Dodgson and Liddell no longer shared the intimacy that had accompanied the latter's childhood.[12] Dodgson's diary indicates that the two were still in contact with each other; however, Liddell's appearance—she would now be about thirteen years old—had begun to repel him. He writes on May 11, 1865, "Alice seems changed a good deal, and hardly for the better—

probably going through the usual awkward age of transition."[13] Nowadays this "usual awkward age of transition" is designated as its own era, adolescence—those blistering years that roil with infamous physical and emotional tribulations. But the Victorians possessed no such category, at least not until the turn of the century,[14] and thus the space between girl and woman presented as vexingly ill-defined. Dodgson refers to the transition as "usual," but certainly in *Alice's Adventures in Wonderland* bodily change is presented as poignantly *unusual* and, thus, confined to a parallel world that parodies our own in the most haywire ways. The pleasure of the story turns on the fish-out-of-water narrative: one young, human girl collides with a legion of kooky persons, like the exasperatingly helter-skelter Mad Hatter, condemned to temporal imprisonment—after offending the Queen of Hearts, he must endure a perpetual tea party or else lose his head—and, of course, the variously neurotic, anthropomorphic creatures she encounters across her haphazard adventures. Alice is befuddled, sometimes even incensed, by Wonderland's nonsense, and yet, Carroll insinuates that a growing girl is better suited to a mercurial parallel universe of amoral absurdity—that her own, maturing body designates her as such—rather than to the Victorian world, where puberty is abject.

Charles Dodgson, like any other person, ultimately had no choice but to accept the fact of Liddell's developing body regardless of the displeasure it provoked. But the authorial persona of Lewis Carroll—fictitious and, thus, free—enabled the meek clergyman to imagine himself master of a magical domain and, more to the point, master of his heroine: he could "write" Alice's body in the manner of his choice and subject it to his whims—even punish it, in some cases. As he watched Liddell

grow, with what he seemingly perceived as wretched inevitability, Dodgson imagined a female body that is always precariously
close to changing, but whose changes were impermanent and
always fell within his jurisdiction.

But for all his aversion to bodily transformation, *Alice's Adventures in Wonderland* is a very fleshy novel, with narrative
elements belying Dodgson's sensitivity to feminine rhythms. It
wears its anxiety on its sleeve: little girls grow and harbor voracious appetites and sob buckets of tears, and as their size and
confidence burgeon they become more difficult to control. In
fact, in Carroll's psychedelic dream, bodies are always in peril—
particularly Alice's body as she encounters the decapitation-
inclined Queen of Hearts. But beyond demonstrating their
terrible mortality through a monarch's incessant murderous
threats, Carroll reminds us, insistently, of what a body can do—
particularly ones with gestational capability. The rabbit hole
that transports Alice to Wonderland might as well be a birth
canal concealed within the vast corpus of the earth. Alice's
bodily changes produce a cyclical trajectory characteristic of
women's biological experiences. And while no actual blood-
shed mars the desexualized text, it is nonetheless awash in
Alice's fluids. At Wonderland's threshold, suddenly turned nine
feet high after consuming some unattended snacks, Alice—
disoriented and frightened—begins to weep. The vestibule fills
with her prodigious tears, signaling Alice as a sort of "leaky vessel,"[15] a term that, in Renaissance England, implicated women
as unable to control their bodies precisely because of emissions
like tears, menstrual blood, and amniotic fluid. Alice's hearty
sobs are treated similarly—unseemly in their excessiveness, a
sign that she is an unpredictable, troublesome organism. And

once she is shrunk, she realizes that her transgression will be duly punished:

> Her first idea was that she had somehow fallen into the sea...However, she soon made out that she was in the pool of tears which she had wept when she was nine feet high..."I wish I hadn't cried so much!" said Alice..."I shall be punished for it now, I suppose, by being drowned in my own tears!"[16]

The text treats it as a matter of course, despite the fact that death by drowning in one's own tears is uniquely sadistic. It is a penalty precisely designed to fit the crime: too much noisy, wet sobbing. Perhaps the narration's equanimity is a form of tonal reassurance: Alice will, ultimately, survive this predicament. But first, she must do penance for her body's too muchness—too many emotions, tears, *secretions*. In Wonderland, the stakes are high for a female body in flux; but then, that has always been the case, everywhere.

———

The twentieth century gave rise to children's films and books that celebrated imagination and subversion—kids suddenly were invited to explore the pleasures and excitement of rule breaking. And yet, this was a privilege reserved for boys; girls were, for the most part, excluded from the narrative—and frolicking beyond the spokes of decorum remained a punishable offense. Dr. Seuss's books, the most famous of which were written in the 1950s, are chock-full of little boys dreaming up

wild schemes and adventures. But in contrast, the little sister
in *The Cat in the Hat* sits passively by in the midst of the pan-
demonium. We find a female protagonist in *Gertrude McFuzz*,
but in a well-traveled context: she serves as an explicit warning
against excess. This "girl-bird," Gertrude, is distraught that she
only possesses a stump of a tail feather, unlike one of her companions, who boasts two luxuriously long plumes. As directed,
she eats "pill-berries" in order to grow an extra feather or two.
But, delighted by the effect of two pill-berries, she gorges until
her plumage multiplies to exorbitant lengths, incapacitating her
in the process. At last, her uncle remedies the predicament, and
Gertrude learns to squelch both vanity and jealousy and thus
the desire for more vibrant feathers.

While Dr. Seuss penned these frolicking rhymes, Disney released films like *Cinderella* (1950) and *Snow White* (1937) where
desire is punished by near-death, and disobedience—attending
a glamorous ball without permission—becomes a last resort in
pursuit of heteronormative romance. As it happens, Disney also
released their adaptation of *Alice in Wonderland* (1951), which
demonstrates fidelity to the story and, accordingly, condemns
Alice to the usual gamut of size-shifting and bodily peril. On
Looney Tunes, Bugs Bunny donned drag and wreaked havoc
across his animated universe—which, like Seuss's domain, was
overwhelmingly male, and included within its ranks Pepé Le
Pew, a skunk for whom rules of romantic consent were at best
negligible guidelines.

Plucky heroines abound across Anglo and American children's literature, yet their own struggles with gendered strictures
and the trajectories of their comings-of-age often present con-
flicting narratives. Perhaps one of the most uncompromising—

and uncompromised—children's heroines from the twentieth century is Pippi Longstocking, literary creation of Swedish writer Astrid Lindgren. Disgusted by the ways in which adults "browbeat"[17] and "trampled on" their children, she dreamed up Pippi, "the strongest girl in the world," in the winter of 1941. Her daughter, Karin, seven years old at the time, was confined to her bed with pneumonia, and yearning for entertainment. By 1945, the first book, named for the titular character, was published to great acclaim, although one reviewer, aghast, referred to Pippi as "psychotic."[18]

Certainly Lindgren's character would have been unconventional in any case, but she is all the more extraordinary for her femaleness. Like Anne Shirley of L. M. Montgomery's *Anne of Green Gables*, her plaited hair blazes a combustible red—though, unlike Anne, she is perfectly content with her appearance. She wears her freckles proudly and is offended by beauty products vowing to eliminate them. And she wields wild, magical strength—she can easily lift a horse—although she adheres to a code of pacifism. The child of a mother who died when she was a baby and a ship captain father who is lost at sea, Pippi lives alone with a pet monkey, and she resists with vivacity adults' attempts to corral her into conventional childhood activities. For instance, she refuses to attend school, eludes those who would toss her into foster care, and she goes to bed whenever she pleases (she also drinks coffee). It's a staggeringly solitary life for a nine-year-old, but Pippi isn't frightened: "Don't you worry about me," she assures everyone who indicates solicitude. "I'll always come out on top." Although Lindgren never referred to herself as a feminist[19] per se, Pippi's staunch independence, and her gusto for life, one lived entirely

according to her own calibrations, reveals a progressive interpretation of gender that remains relatively conspicuous even
today. Pippi's disinclination toward conformity and her disinterest in yielding to the crush of adult authority posits a little girl's
entitlement to disrupt—not because she harbors some precocious agenda, but because she demands the right to be fully
herself, fully too much.

In 1955, Ramona Quimby, a near American cousin of Pippi
Longstocking, tumbled into the picture, all scraped knees and
exuberant doodles. She and her creator, author Beverly Cleary,
united with Pippi and Lindgren in literary confederation,
bright beacons for little girls who have been variously told
they are too much: too loud or pesky or hyperactive. Upon
a cursory read, it might be tempting to describe Ramona as
mischievous, but Cleary herself has protested against this accusation,[20] and with good reason. Ramona loves the world
with ferocity; she does not so much want to disturb it as she
yearns to discover, to turn it over, examine every piece and
crook and marvel at why each creature, commodity, and substance exists the way it does. "She was a girl who could not
wait. Life was so interesting she had to find out what happened
next," explains Cleary in *Ramona the Pest*. But when put in
practice, Ramona's philosophy stirs controversy, and all too frequently the intrepid heroine contends with indictments of her
disposition. Her demure, long-suffering older sister, Beatrice—
dubbed "Beezus" by Ramona when she is learning to speak—
lobs them at her regularly. "Beezus felt that the biggest trouble
with four-year-old Ramona was that she was just plain exasperating," writes Cleary at the start of the series' first book,
Beezus and Ramona. "If Ramona drank lemonade through a

straw, she blew into the straw as hard as she could to see what would happen. If she played with her finger paints in the front yard, she wiped her hands on the neighbors' cat."[21] But as we quickly understand, Beezus is not the enemy. Focalizing *Beezus and Ramona* through Beezus's perspective—when Ramona is still in preschool—prompts us to empathize with the aggrieved older sister, the girl who is steadied by rules and orderliness and placid afternoons stitching potholders. Beezus struggles to comprehend how Ramona, whom she dearly loves, could be so defiantly opposed to convention.

And yet, Ramona, whose family lives in the working-class Pacific Northwest, does not eschew gender and behavioral norms out of calculated defiance, but rather out of disbelief that metrics of femininity and propriety could matter in the grand scheme of things. It would be vastly oversimplifying to refer to Ramona as a tomboy; she nurtures crushes on classmates and wants a pair of gleaming red galoshes that match the ones worn by other girls in her kindergarten class. But most crucially, Ramona is dissatisfied by the template for any childhood that doesn't accommodate her brash exuberance, or that would compel her to assimilate into the status quo. Two of Ramona's most prickling fears are impossibly intertwined: first, that her affection for all those most important to her goes unrequited, and second, that she cannot be loved for precisely who she is—impetuous, temperamental, profoundly sensitive, and, yes, a little bit of a show-off. Her fondness, once coaxed, thumps ardently from her staunch and earnest heart. However irksome her family might be, she is both fiercely proud and protective of them. She intuits threads of kindness stitched inside the grimy cheeks of playground boys—the infamous "yard apes."

She idolizes her kindergarten and third grade teachers, Miss
Binney and Miss Whaley, respectively, and registers their mentorship as maternity—the schema she knows best. But teachers, ·
Ramona learns, cannot love with the exclusivity of a parent.
Miss Binney in particular breaks Ramona's heart again and again
when she lavishes praise on other students, especially those
whose personalities contrast sharply with Ramona's own rough-
and-tumble demeanor—the prim, smug Susan, for instance,
who lacks the bona fide sweetness of her similarly aggravating
forebear, Simple Susan, but who also knows the benefits to
performing docility. Even if Ramona were capable of such a
masquerade, she would reject it on principle. And she is discon-
solate when beloved Miss Binney resorts to harsher methods of
discipline in an effort to teach Ramona the necessity of boundaries (is it really her fault if Simple Susan 2.0 has "boing boing
curls" that are every moment pleading to be pulled?).

It's in the atmosphere, our disdain for too muchness, and Ramona absorbs it, recognizing in her quivering little bones that
this quality propels her and that sometimes it leads her astray.
But if Ramona senses that her impulses are not always compatible with suburban niceties, she refuses to diminish herself. Her
character is not a problem to be solved. She demands that those
who comprise her universe bear witness to her tangled, wild
yearnings—and, what's more, that they embrace her for them.

She cried harder than she ever had cried in her life. She
cried until she was limp and exhausted.

Then Ramona felt her mother's hand on her back.
"Ramona," she said gently, "what are we going to do
with you?"

With red eyes, a swollen face, and a streaming nose, Ramona sat up and glared at her mother. "Love me!" Her voice was fierce with hurt. Shocked at her own words, she buried her face in the pillow. She had no tears left.[22]

Ramona is devastated by her first grade progress report, in which her well-meaning but aseptic teacher notates her lack of self-control, and her mother's subsequent remark that she "must try to grow up." She interprets these criticisms as a larger condemnation of her person. And we can easily understand her position. Although readers are meant to empathize with those who are baffled by Ramona—like her teacher, the pedestrian Mrs. Griggs—and although Ramona, like most children, neglects to consider the impact of her every action, Cleary never leaves us in doubt of Ramona's singularly queasy fit within a society that can oftentimes feel tight and chafing. With the same instinct that directs her antics, Ramona understands that the world does not anticipate her full-throttle vivacity and that, as such, it does not always appreciate her.

Nonetheless, she does not ask to be loved; like Jane Eyre she demands it, and she doesn't question her due as a person stumbling through a bewildering world. Her tear-filled imperative—love me—is fraught with the barbs of growing pains, but it is assertive. It is, moreover, analogous to what she asks of herself.

For the first time Ramona looked into her very own mirror in her very own room. She saw a stranger, a girl with red eyes and a puffy, tearstained face, who did not look at all the way Ramona pictured herself. Ramona thought of

herself as the kind of girl everyone should like, but this
girl...

Ramona scowled, and the girl scowled back. Ramona
managed a small smile. So did the girl. Ramona felt
better. She wanted the girl in the mirror to like her.[23]

This moment of self-recognition follows on the heels of a
furious outburst at school, where Ramona, upon realizing the
horrid Susan has copied her artwork, destroys it and her own
as well. Ramona's young sense of self turns on the conviction
that she is inimitable: consequently, Susan's offense—the illegitimate invocation of sameness—stirs in Ramona an aversion so
extreme as to be indecipherable, especially to adults like Mrs.
Griggs. But Ramona does not always attempt to explain, to
usher along those who cannot easily empathize with her decisions. After all, for the duration of Ramona the Brave, she is only
six years old, and she assumes, in confident hastiness, that even
if she is misunderstood, she need not account for herself.

Because exuberant little girls are so often compelled to de-
mystify their emotions and the behaviors motivated by them,
Ramona's tendency to act and then delay the debriefing satisfies
our ache of recognition. Yet, as Ramona peers at her reflection,
damp and flush, it's clear that she is rarely served well by this
approach. Too Much little girls like Ramona, the fortunate
ones, anyway, learn a flinty lesson—that their self-preservation
demands near-saintly patience with a world disinclined to accommodate them. Cleary's heroine must learn how to negotiate with the Griggses of the world, who would prefer it if
she returned to her seat, folded her hands, and emulated the
youthful femininity of her sister, Beezus, and even the dreaded

Susan. Ramona's first duty is to the little girl in the mirror, and Cleary suggests that she will, as she grows older, devise ways to live in the brash, loud way she relishes—in the way that feels truest—without always being so handily diminished. But she will struggle in this endeavor. There is never a guarantee that Ramona the Brave—the Ramona who demands every day to exist according to her own metrics, whose dedication to self-honesty will not permit her to behave as anything other than her instinctual self—will ever be regarded as anything but a pest.

To this day, a little girl's too muchness is not a right, but a privileged exception typically reserved for white, able-bodied heroines. Ramona Quimby remains an exemplar of young, girlish empowerment not only because of Cleary's literary perceptiveness, but also because the ranks of Too Much girls have hardly thickened, even if the atmosphere has softened. We no longer languish beneath the oppressive virtue of a thousand Simple Susans, thank goodness. We've slogged to the lip of Wonderland's inhospitable terrain, in which Lewis Carroll's Alice—adventuresome, inquisitive, but ultimately marked by authorial neuroses—ambles through a punishing world devised to clip at her fluctuating body. Nor do our heroines suffer like young Jane Eyre when they screw their courage to the sticking place and speak truth to power. From her first years at Hogwarts, J. K. Rowling's famous heroine, Hermione Granger—intellectually nimble, earnest without apology, and rarely intimidated—demands attention from even her most bullying professors. She raises her hand in class whenever she knows the answer (she always knows the answer), and the series' titular hero, Harry Potter, would be royally fucked a dozen times over without Hermione's steady guidance, which, of course, Harry and Ron bemoan as bossiness.

Charlotte Brontë's heroines, sometimes churlish, but stridently devoted to a trusted few, are granted—perhaps unexpectedly—an emotional afterlife in Katniss Everdeen of Suzanne Collins's Hunger Games trilogy. An arrow-slinging misanthrope, she, like Jane Eyre and Hermione, would sooner sacrifice herself than submit those she loves to suffering. After all, Katniss loves so few people. She is flinty and withholding, Lucy Snowe—the tricksy, taciturn heroine of Brontë's *Villette*— as a dystopian action hero, and Collins doesn't shield her young readers from the scorch of trauma that sears brain and body like a torch blazing in her abdomen. Of the contemporary young heroines we know best, Katniss supplies evidence that little girls in pain can still be warriors—that, indeed, they may be the ones to save us.

These are formidable characters, but they nonetheless comprise paltry offerings. Disney, the same animation behemoth that offered us Cinderella, Snow White, and even Alice in Wonderland, together with Pixar, brought us the aforementioned Merida, who, unlike her fellow champion Mulan, doesn't pursue conventionally masculine pursuits as an extreme means to an end. On the contrary, she heaves against the strictures imposed upon a Scottish princess and prefers wild adventures with her bow and arrow—the weapon of choice, it seems, for the atypical female character who is still intended to attract readers and audiences with her grace and beauty. Merida's too muchness is signified in the film by her ebullient and meandering red curls, but even Anne Shirley would have resigned herself to life as a redhead if she had such a wealth of sinuous locks.

By far, *Moana* is the studio's greatest achievement, and the most trenchant marker of its evolution, with a courageous, keen, and splendidly silly titular character who flourishes throughout her coming-of-age hero's journey. In fact, before Moana embarks on her sea voyage, she is trained carefully by her parents to inherit rule of the Polynesian island without the explicit support of a companion. There is no dispute over Moana's gender presentation: the film's central interpersonal conflict resides in her desire for a more expansive life than the one she's offered: she is yet another precocious, bighearted girl who wants too much and cannot resist the tidal pull of exploration.

And as for characters like Arya Stark, from George R. R. Martin's *Game of Thrones*, or Eleven from Netflix's *Stranger Things*, they are little girls who are not precisely written for children—of course, neither was Jane Eyre. Maisie Williams's interpretation of Arya, angry but maniacally focused, is revelatory, but HBO's adaptation of Martin's novel would be difficult to digest for young girls (it would have been—and still is—for me, anyway). But these characters have been brought into the fold; they are there, waiting, when today's little girls search beyond Hermione and Ramona and Moana. They await together with Jane, plain-faced and stouthearted, seething in the gnarled face of injustice. And when they encounter Eleven, whose bounteous power surges from her wellspring of emotion—in marked contrast with Alice, who suffers in a deluge born from her tear ducts—perhaps they will not say, as we did, "Thank goodness." As Wonderland recedes into the distance—its punishing and confounding landscape melting at the horizon—the view brightens, and what we are owed becomes ever clearer. Perhaps instead they will nod and remark, "Of course."

Chapter Three

NERVE

My mother might have told you that my too muchness blossomed inside her womb, within the thump-thump-thump of my fledgling heart. While she was in labor with me, toiling to bring me into the world, *I* was preoccupied with staying out of it, thank you very much. In fact, my determination was such that the doctor resorted to using forceps, at last dragging me into the hospital room's antiseptic cool and away from the safe, wet warmth of maternity. I would never be as close to Mom again; thankfully, my instinct to withdraw from waking life dissipated with exposure.

So it came to pass: I was, after much protest, born.

I like this story because it so precisely adheres to the cliché of the difficult and neurotic child whose disposition manifests from the absolute start—when she revolts against vacating the cozy womb: the one who knows in some ineffable, visceral way that nothing could possibly improve by exiting a temperature-controlled chamber in which all of her basic needs were met, and where she was bathed in an embrace, utterly surrounded by the body that loved her best.

But I also consider it a fitting metaphor for what has long felt to me like a physiological incompatibility with the world. Maybe I sensed it: my tiny limbs buzzing with alarm, head crackling in confusion. From the very start, I was a problem, an agitated little body requiring extraction by hardware. This world wouldn't know what to do with me, nor I with it. Regardless, this whole enterprise of being born was sure to be a catastrophe.

And at first, it was. I screamed and wailed relentlessly, as if tormented by some obscure demon, distraught by the mere fact of being in the world. According to my parents, they finally resorted to a practice of driving me throughout the night, meandering in a weary circuit through the streets of Durham, North Carolina, silence and motion the only things that could subdue me. If either Mom or Dad uttered so much as a word, I began to cry again.

By adolescence, I had acclimated somewhat to my existence, but in the meantime had accumulated a bundle of neuroses and obsessive-compulsive habits. Mom often likened me to Anne Shirley of the Edwardian series *Anne of Green Gables*—a compliment, mostly, because she wanted to encourage the pleasure I took in writing and in fanciful games. I suppose the comparison was apt enough, if Anne also balked at the thought of leaving her room without ensuring, five separate times, that her Walkman remained precisely where she had deposited it. There was, everywhere, so much possibility for error—accident—

disaster! It was imperative that I attend to the minutest details of the everyday, lest my wobbly, fear-filled life collapse. I checked the inside of my locker multiple times to ensure my books were there—and then passed the night fretting that, somehow, they weren't. If a teacher awarded our class the coveted gift of "no homework," I would confirm the news with them multiple times before departing the classroom. (Anne would have done this, I bet.) I harbored an obsession for patterns of all sorts. It was not just desirable, but cosmically imperative, that my report card never bear the shame of a scarlet "B" (I was forced to become more lax in high school, when my brain explained, with weeping exhaustion, that it could accommodate neither calculus nor chemistry). I still cried habitually, but, at the very least, I had some idea why.

This much seems like honest inheritance. Everyone in my immediate family is stridently Type-A, and we all nurture our respective eccentricities like rose gardens. My mother, a kindred spirit in galactic feeling and perfectionism, was convinced that our bannister was crooked by three sixteenths of an inch. When, years ago, she fretted that new wallpaper had been applied unevenly to the dining room walls, she stationed herself across from the offending portion and stared it down like a tiger, chasing truth with her canny eyes (merely taking measurements was insufficient; she required optical verification too). Her sensitivity, like mine, was steep: she was the sort of person who felt the world in her bones, whose empathy at times seemed unsafe—though, as I am learning, that's the point of empathy in the first place. She cried during maudlin commercials, throughout *Bambi*, and when, in the 1985 film series, Matthew Cuthbert dies in Anne's arms, out in the fields of

Green Gables. She wept bitterly for the baby bird she discovered in our backyard, pecked brutally to death by a blue jay,
and for Ginger in Anna Sewell's *Black Beauty* (1877), which we
both read and then watched—habitually—when the 1994 film
adaptation was released on VHS. When, in 1994, newspapers
broke the story of Susan Smith drowning her two young sons,
she was inconsolable for days. If my younger sisters or I angered
her—and we were quite adept at this—Mom's volcanic yelling
gave way to thick, red-faced sobs.

I was rarely privy to Mom's marital frustrations—to my
knowledge they were infrequent—but I knew that her approach
to solving them involved a degree of self-policing. Our household was calibrated according to our father's preferences for engagement. If we were upset over some domestic or interpersonal
matter, it only made matters worse to approach him in tears.
Recognizing Dad's disinclination to meet with unbridled distress,
Mom—who absorbed her daughters' schoolday strifes and waded
into the quagmires of homeownership—trained herself to wait
until her upset dissipated and, instead, approached him in the
calm aftermath. She admonished me to follow suit, and we both
did our best. If I misbehaved and was punished, I learned not to
attempt an emotional plea in the moment. Instead, I took to leaving letters on Dad's pillow when I wanted to apologize for some
trespass—and to negotiate my punishment—but was too intimidated to ask him directly. Dad always mitigated my sentence.
He helmed a conventionally patriarchal household, but was kindhearted in the face of my pleas for reduced sentences ("no television for a week" became "no television until the weekend").
As for Mom, I couldn't imagine anyone meeting her tenderness
with flinty chill, least of all the person who was so in love with

her. When she spoke, he listened with careful appreciation. They were, I believe, as happy as two people could be.

My father never asked us to comport ourselves with his own characteristic placidity, nor did he explicitly demand stoicism; we only saw how highly he revered it and adjusted our behavior accordingly. This protocol was largely the result of unspoken deduction. It most often fell to me—or so I thought—to wrangle my too muchness before approaching Dad, whether I was in shambles over my algebra homework or because he had denied my request to see a PG-13-rated film. Had Mom not imparted it to me, I still would have divined this familial covenant. After all, she was my template. In all the years she lived, I observed her careful self-monitoring: withdrawing to an unoccupied room to sob through some affliction, shushing an impassioned conversation into the ether as soon as the door to Dad's parking spot in the garage grumbled its ascent.

Our too muchness, as I understood it, was an obstruction to familial harmony, rather than a disposition entitled to empathy, and it was our responsibility to tame the beasts that made us wild. As a family, we were imbued by the larger cultural organizing principle that instructs men to both model and reward shows of emotional reserve and admonishes against too muchness. Throughout her life, Mom must have been taught this—that her lavishness of feeling was shameful, and that she ought to be grateful when it was tolerated. I bore witness as she crammed herself into more seemly boxes, and tried to emulate her efforts. I ached for the both of us.

Eventually, I arrived at a striking realization: for someone like my mother, the world brimmed with emotional hazards. Years later, when I read George Eliot's *Middlemarch*, I wondered to what extent she had been afforded the sort of emotional protection presumed fundamental to a happy life:

If we had a keen vision and feeling of all ordinary human life, it would be like hearing the grass grow and the squirrel's heart beat, and we should die of that roar which lies on the other side of silence. As it is, the quickest of us walk about well wadded with stupidity.[1]

She died before I thought to ask: *Did* the world seem to roar inside you, Mom? I'm merely left with my own experience of empathy, which I smugly consider one of my better qualities until I remember her compassion: it flowed from a wellspring deeper and more bountiful than my own. She was happy, often cheery, but the world's sorrows and joys and fears filtered through her like rainwater frizzled with electricity. Somehow, she maintained her balance with a heart that—whether she willed it to or not—always extended and exerted itself, accommodating a new woe that was relevant to her precisely because she was aware of it. Thus, it mattered.

When it came to her three daughters, the boundaries between our sorrows and hers were unsurprisingly labile. "I can't help it," she once sobbed, devastated upon hearing the news that Sarah, my youngest sister, had been dumped by her jerk boyfriend. Sarah sat at the kitchen table, soused in her own misery, and Mom embraced her, resting her cheek upon my sister's bowed head. "My heart is tied to yours."

Yet her empathy, so often a gateway to rage, could unnerve, even embarrass me. Years before this, when I was in eighth grade, I had become unwittingly embroiled in a debacle regarding student censorship, and Mom was livid on my behalf, champing at the bit to charge into battle with the academic authorities. I attended an elite private school in Winston-Salem, North Carolina, where the liberal arts education was extraordinary and the student body was, to a significant degree, comprised of wealthy, coddled bullies who harbored little interest in me unless I was the convenient butt of a joke.

This dynamic shifted briefly when, for a school assignment in which we were instructed to compose satires, I took as my focus our own social ecosystem, which was as sordid as junior high relations come. I delighted in the project and wrote without considering the potential consequences: these essays were intended to be read not only by our teachers but our classmates. Then, during a draft workshop, one of the more popular girls, Carrie, was assigned my essay to review. I watched her as she read, the corners of her mouth turning gently downward. She said very little when she handed back my draft, but I observed, anxiously, that she seemed upset, or at the very least preoccupied.

Of course you know what follows. Before the next period, Carrie had apprised her friends of my transgression, and they were duly affronted. Within the next few days, their well-monied parents had called the school to complain, and our milquetoast headmaster was prepared to demand that I rewrite the essay. My parents found the controversy to be preposterous and, what's more, unfair. Dad penned a strongly worded letter to the school with the dictionary's definition of "satire" typed in full at the top of the page. I would not, he declared, rewrite an assignment that I had completed exactly as instructed. Mom raged and readied herself for confrontation with school administrators, teachers, basically anyone who might suggest that my rather benign thoughts on the school's social web were based in malice.

I was baffled that everybody cared so much. Rather than dwell in self-righteous anger, I focused on the thought of having to write a new essay when I liked the one I had already composed. Neither Anne Shirley nor Emily Byrd Starr—the proudly obdurate heroine of L. M. Montgomery's Emily trilogy—would have acquiesced where their writing was concerned, although I never considered myself in possession of their courage. For my part, I skirted any possibility of trouble, and had taken care—to the extent that an insecure thirteen-year-old girl could—to critique with humor and insight, rather than to lob ad hominem insults. I genuinely didn't want to be unkind. Mostly, I wanted to be liked.

One day, in the midst of this imbroglio, my English teacher asked me to meet with her and with the other, notoriously intimidating eighth grade English teacher after my last class. Certain that I was bound for punishment, I agonized for the remainder of the day and asked my best friend to wait for Mom at carpool so she could explain why I wasn't there (in my terror it apparently never occurred to me to call home).

Once the meeting began, my fears were assuaged: they supported me wholeheartedly, these teachers assured me, and they were going to ensure that I did not have to rewrite my essay in order to placate my classmates or their parents. My stricken limbs loosened, and I began to breathe with regularity.

Until, as if on cue, Mom appeared at the classroom threshold, windswept and wild-eyed. She was as furious as I had ever seen her, and before I could assure her that all was well, she settled her white-hot glare on this pair of unsuspecting teachers and drew a full-bodied breath. The court of Katherine Florio Vorona was in session.

"My daughter has been treated *like shit* at this school for nearly two years," she snarled. I'm ashamed to say that garden-variety teenage embarrassment nullified what should have been pride. I broke in as quickly as I could, all agitation and squirms—"Mom! Mom! It's okay! They're on my side! I'm not in trouble!" But in retrospect, Mom stormed into that class-room like Athena on a righteous rampage. She was a warrior waving the banner of motherly justice, determined to defend her daughters from the perils of juvenile nastiness.

At the time, I didn't fully appreciate this, didn't appreciate her. Certainly my reaction was born, in part, from snotty ado-lescent panic over my own reputation: Mom was an extension of me, and if her behavior raised eyebrows, or if my classmates overheard this wrath-soaked expostulation, I would be mocked for it. After all, earnest, outsize reactions—a quintessential as-pect of Mom's too muchness and mine—were regarded as absurd and unseemly. Having fully absorbed this ideology, one in which we were premium examples of lesser people, I could not be proud of the mother whose fierce empathy had sum-moned this act of parental heroism. Instead, I was mortified by her too muchness, particularly the aspects of it that seemed to have engendered my own. I saw only what I feared be-coming, what, in my bones, I knew I already was: tremulous and sensitive, constitutionally incapable of feeling anything by half. These were traits that oriented my mother and that begot what was most precious in her. She may have been predisposed to empathy, but she also chose it, cultivated it—even when it burned. It took me years to interpret her fire as something exquisite and rare; finally, I understood that those flames blazing within her—scorching her—had lovingly kept me warm.

———

Mom and I may have fretted over each other's inclinations toward maximalist emotion, but she also orchestrated my literary education in exuberant and temperamental girls—the girls who would become my mentors and, collectively, my solace. My mother came late to classic literature, so I read the Brontë sisters, Jane Austen—oh, the ache of recognition in *Sense and Sensibility*'s Marianne Dashwood—Louisa May Alcott, and L. M. Montgomery not long after she did, and upon her recommendation. Montgomery supplied me with two kindred variations of feminine too muchness: her aforementioned heroines, Anne Shirley of Green Gables and the lesser known but beloved Emily Byrd Starr of New Moon. I gulped these books like Hi-C Ecto Cooler (my beverage of choice) and, as bookish girls do, contemplated their characters with solemnity and devotion equal to the consideration I gave my companions in daily life. But just as my anti–too muchness, wholly internalized by preadolescence, stirred me to look askance at Mom's emotional vulnerabilities, so did I begin evaluating Too Much heroines according to how I thought I ought to navigate, and feel, the world.

Of the two, Anne Shirley, in all her Anne Shirley-ness, has endured more prominently in our cultural zeitgeist. She is the one my mother knew, and prodded me to know as well. Anne, not Emily, was the one bestowed with a now-canonical CBC miniseries, followed by a 2017 reboot; she is the one who has been elevated to archetype. Nowadays, her name functions as the nineties girl's shorthand: to be an "Anne Shirley" is to be bookish and daydreamy and bold, with just a dash of impulsive charm. It's an alluring moniker, one that acknowledges a nerdy, literary soul without professing undesirability—and without the negative connotations of identifying with a Zooey Deschanel character. In this way, her too muchness becomes as palatable as Western culture typically permits. But Anne's widespread appeal also waters down the sense of uniqueness we might feel in identifying with the character; I suspect that most cusp-millennial women have at one point or another fancied ourselves Anne Shirley. With Jonathan Crombie's death in 2015—verily, the death of Gilbert Blythe—our mourning manifested itself as fierce projection. We not only remembered Anne and Gilbert; we remembered *being* her and opining the arrival of our own Gilberts—that is to say, someone who loved and exulted us with steadfast devotion.

It would be satisfying to believe that Mom was motivated by recognition of my blossoming intensities, but I doubt that was the case. I do wonder if she found fragmented reflections of herself in Anne Shirley, thereby inspiring the intermittent comparisons. But when I strongly identified with a character, I was liable to be repulsed, particularly when she reminded me of my own unwieldy feelings, or I recognized in her some of my own, more aggravating traits (like Anne, I was and am a chatterbox). So when I discovered Emily Byrd Starr of the titular Emily trilogy—passionate, poetic, but uncannily self-possessed—she became my object of desire—my aspiration.

My encounters with these characters were significantly staggered. I met Anne Shirley years prior to finding Emily, though whether it was on the page or through the interpretation of

Megan Follows, I can't recall. Either way, I quickly acknowledged our kinship: garrulous and gawky, passionately devoted
to our dearest girlfriends, and eager to love those who loved
us—not to mention some who didn't. Her delicate nose was
the focal point of her wobbling vanity; mine, contrastingly, was
conspicuous in an ungainly, ill-fitting way; it seemed a curse
designed for schoolyard torment. But we both plotted out our
lives according to storybook conventions, and our first attempts
at authorship were similarly schmaltzy.

Anne joined ranks with the coterie of fictional odd girls—
Jane Eyre, Matilda, Jo March—who kept my neurotic, lonely
heart company. L. M. Montgomery, like so many of my favorite
authors, begot a heroine who transcended her narrative. *Anne
of Green Gables* (1908) gave me worthy cause for optimism.
My peers found me peculiar, but perhaps that assessment was
not as damning as I had previously feared. After all, Anne
Shirley befriends kindred spirits scattered throughout Avonlea,
and though she aims to please, she never compromises the sanctity of her selfhood. The Anne novels thus became cherished
evidence: one day, I too would find fellowship.

And yet, I didn't really *love* Anne Shirley.

Instead, love found me when, one weekend—dawdling
through Barnes and Noble—I stumbled upon another Montgomery creation: Emily Byrd Starr, the titular character of the
Emily of New Moon trilogy. Emily enthralled me in a way that
Anne never could: she was haughty and incandescent and altogether intimidating. Her first book was published in 1923, fifteen
years after *Anne of Green Gables*, with *Emily Climbs* and *Emily's
Quest* following in 1925 and 1927, respectively. But in spite of
the distance spanning their publication dates, Emily's story arc

will sound familiar to readers already intimate with Anne. Accustomed to a quiet, companionable life with her widower father, Emily is bereft when he dies of consumption. Now an orphan at age twelve, she must abandon her childhood home to become the ward of her mother's priggish relatives, the Murrays.

But slowly, she comes to love New Moon Farm, where her mother lived as a girl, and which her spinster aunts Elizabeth and Laura, and cousin Jimmy, inhabit and maintain now. The farm and surrounding town of Blair Water are bathed in myths and hauntings—ideal for an aspiring poet. And before long, Emily befriends three similarly maverick souls: the warm-blooded Ilse Burnley—a Too Much girl in her own right—the ambitious Perry Miller, who loves Emily, and the artist Teddy Kent, whom Emily loves (although it is years before she expresses her affections outright). She relies on the un-Murray-like sympathy of her gentle aunt Laura and cousin Jimmy; meanwhile, she and the intractable Aunt Elizabeth assume a power play that, in time, gentles into an affectionate and fiercely loyal kinship. Even more herculean than familial frictions are her efforts to earn a living as a writer, and to suss out the future she desires with Teddy.

Because Montgomery dwells on similar themes in the Emily and Anne books, it's fitting that her heroines share similar preoccupations. Their writerly inclinations and broad imaginations imply a twinned urge to remake the world into something befitting their dreams. And yet, each girl's pious romance with the Prince Edward Island landscape communicates a love for the extant natural world. They revere their pastoral environs as unknowably enchanted, but nevertheless claim fellowship with the copses of trees and twinkling lakes that form the backdrop to their coming-of-age. In this comradely spirit, they christen everything that delights them: the Lake of Shining Waters, the Tomorrow Road, the Disappointed House, Dryad's Bubble. Anne chases "scope for the imagination"; Emily refers to volts of creative energy as "the flash." Their love, when it is bestowed, is lavish and boundless like the sea that compasses their island home.

In my despondent adolescence, when I longed to be someone else—someone who could cool out and care a little less, *be* just a little less—I would confide to Mom, tear-soggy with despair, my fear that nobody could possibly fall in love with me: puberty was, in my experience, a dreadful landscape of pustules, wire-thronged teeth, and graceless extremities. Perhaps my gargantuan emotions—ready tears and piercing outbursts—would have seemed more palatable if I had been beautiful, but I was not, or at least I didn't think so. When Mom, ever the romantic, soothed me with promises that I would encounter my own Gilbert Blythe, I struggled to imagine a person who would not recoil in the face of my too muchness and promptly head for the hills. But Mom seemed confident, perhaps, in part, because she was a Too Much woman happy in love, and so I listed against the comfort of her conviction. And then there was Anne, and Emily, too: weren't they lovable?

So I took consolation in L. M. Montgomery's passionate young heroines; they seemed to me textual evidence that my own coming-of-age would not be a hapless misadventure. Still, my visceral preference for Emily Byrd Starr signaled to me, albeit implicitly, the variety of girlhood. Now, it lays bare the obsessive focus of my anti–too muchness conviction. Convinced that my own outpourings of earnestness and nakedly cellophane skin were detriments to my character, I assumed the same for Anne, cleaving instead to Emily's performative cool. With the exclusion of a few, spare resonances, I shared precious little in common with her, and therein lay the linchpin of my preference. Indeed, I was taken with her precisely because I doubted that she would approve of me or, for that matter, cheery, obliging Anne. Though it would be, as it were, a scenario of the pot calling the kettle black, I wondered if Emily might have found both Anne and me to be too much.

Montgomery writes Emily as basically enigmatic, and in so doing, I could only ever conceive of her in an aspirational context: she feels with a thundersome fullness but, through pride and wellsprings of restraint, conceals the brunt of it. When the CBC announced its plans for the new *Anne of Green Gables* miniseries, the 2017 adaptation, *Anne with an E*, I grumbled, "Always Anne, and never Emily." But, admittedly, I understand. Anne has always wanted us to know her; Emily has never been sure. The latter's book, written as biography, emphasizes our distance from the character—even her diaries, which she intends as posthumous publications, are contextualized as archival materials, temporally removed. She'll never write directly to us.

From the first pages of *Emily of New Moon*, I was primed to favor its heroine. She writes—poems, letters to her deceased father, stories, and diary entries—with an urgency her aunt Elizabeth castigates as pathological. Although she eschews demonstrations of romantic vulnerability, she betrays a curiosity about boys—or at least one boy. And she is sensually porous: the world laps against her skin, seeps underneath, and startles her marrow. Her so-called mysteriousness, of which her family accuses her, is her primary means of self-preservation in a milieu where her quirks and strange delights will always draw suspicion or, at best, confusion. But because she trusts in her façade of stoicism, she need not resort to silence in the face of adversity. On the contrary, she can speak on her own behalf when she chooses, and leave both schoolmates and stony relatives trembling in her wake.

Emily's imperiousness dazzled me. Meek and agitated, I spent my youth far too terrified of judgment to speak with her frankness. Taking issue with others seemed a luxury totally unavailable to me—after all, I was too desperate to be loved. When Gilbert Blythe so crassly calls Anne Shirley "Carrots," she smashes a slate over his head. Under the same duress, Emily's knuckles might have whitened as she gripped her own slate more fixedly, but her revenge would have been delivered as a dart of smooth, rhetorical evisceration. Tormented on the first day of school, Emily returns the gawking of the other schoolchildren with her own tenacious stare. "Why don't you like me?" she asks, eliciting a dumb silence. Finally, her flustered adversary stutters, "Because you ain't a bit like us."[2]

"I wouldn't want to be," said Emily scornfully.

"Oh, my, you are one of the Chosen people," mocked Black-eyes.

"Oh course I am," retorted Emily.[3]

Emily, it seemed to me, had won the too muchness honey pot. It's true: her disposition mixes with those of her peers like oil and water, and perhaps she is a bit eccentric, too. But she's glad of it, regardless of whatever loneliness may result in the schoolroom—even when the duplicity of a supposed friend leads to her exclusion from a much-anticipated birthday party, or when her aunt bars her from chasing fads (bangs, for instance). Whatever tremors of agitation or pain may disturb her proud heart, Emily only endeavors to be precisely who she is.

What's more, her too muchness does not preclude the chilly composure with which she takes the measure of her bullies and, with a few barbed words, summarily levels them. (To be sure, Anne is also quick with a retort. Although more inclined than Emily to make friends, she generally does not find herself in these sorts of showdowns. And if she did, she wouldn't want for support.) Emily, moreover, demands the respect of her elders— even when they refuse it—and she does not shrink from calling injustice by its name. Even in the wake of her father's death, nei- ther grief nor trepidation diminishes her verve. À la *Jane Eyre*, her rigid aunt Elizabeth locks Emily in a darkened spare room as punishment; unlike Jane, Emily escapes through the window and spends the evening cavorting with Ilse.

Still, Emily is not wholly immune to the carping chorus of her relatives and the Blair Water schoolchildren. Adopted by her late mother's half sisters, the Murrays, she recoils from members of the clan whose dispositions chafe against her own. But even as she struggles to adapt, she absorbs the infamous "Murray pride," which fortifies her with self-possession, and a touch of arrogance. "*The time will come when they will not laugh at me*," she avows in a diary entry, with foreboding italics.[4] At the time, it was wonderful to me: here was a young girl who pre- ferred the company of books and her own chimerical thoughts, who could not shrug off the world, even if she pretended, and who was determined not merely to survive, but to thrive like a rose bursting from cracks in slate. Too muchness had always seemed—often still seems—like a condition to be endured, and just barely. I have often felt as if it is organically toxic. When I only knew Anne Shirley, I took comfort in the elegance of her maturation: she does not change in essentials, but she cultivates a discipline that I thought would perhaps, one day, burgeon in-side me, too (the jury is still out on this particular matter). But Emily—she is young when she makes this declaration: she will not suppress her predilections, nor will she police herself for the comfort of others (though, of course, she summons stoicism for a kind of power play). If she is too much for others, then this is an index of her community's failings, not hers, and one day they will stand in awe of her.

I admit, I have never imagined that my too muchness would command the sort of admiration that Emily envisions. Tolerance always seemed to be the most for which I could hope, and so I sought that. Even now, I beat back my sheep-ishness in the face of a culture that barks at us to be thankful for belonging, even when we are difficult pills to swallow. There is no shame is our yen for appreciation, or for com-pliments. Nothing could be more human than hoping others find us pleasant. After all, girls are taught to please with social direction that is both insidious and explicit, and in each case, unceasing. And because I regarded my elders—and, frankly, anyone more popular than me—as authorities, I, too, was vo-racious for approval, particularly in the realm of beauty. To be called "consumptive" or "plain" by my family would have shattered me just as Anne is mortified by references to her homeliness. Emily, however, sustains these blows time and again. Her tenacity discomfits the Murrays; they, accordingly, cast aspersions in a desperate grasp for the upper hand. Emily is less inclined to court approval from those she does not like, but as a matter of principle will not endure the Murray fam-ily's onerous discussion of her appearance while she is seated in the same room:

"She's too pale—if she had a little colour she wouldn't be bad-looking," [said Aunt Addie].

"I don't know who she looks like," said Uncle Oliver, staring at Emily.

"She is not a Murray, that is plain to be seen," said Aunt Elizabeth, decidedly and disapprovingly.

. . .

"She's got her father's forehead," said Aunt Eva, also disapprovingly.

. . .

Emily had reached the limit of her endurance.

"You make me feel as if I was made up of scraps and patches!" she burst out indignantly.[5]

As if the scenario were not sufficiently cruel, Emily's maternal family—these are her late mother's siblings—sees fit to undertake this rhetorical dismemberment just after her father has died, and Emily—orphaned, and soon to be carted away from her family home—is still keening with bitter, distending grief. For the Murrays, their niece's too muchness, exemplified by her precociousness and self-advocacy, is carved into the illegibility of her features: evident genealogy is clarifying and soothing to a family whose identity is firmly buttressed by familial ties. Emily, Montgomery implies, will never be so easily deciphered.

But her heroine prefers it this way. When she bids goodbye to her father, laid out in his casket, she confides to him that she has not allowed his grim set of in-laws to get the better of her: "'Father, I didn't cry before them,' she whispered. 'I'm sure I didn't disgrace the Starrs...oh Father, I don't think any of them like me...And I'm going to cry a little bit now, Father, because I can't keep it back *all* the time.'"[6] Emily's interpretation of honor—withholding the extent of her pain from those she does not trust—was familiar to me. It was a stratagem that I longed to deploy, but found insuperable, like holding my breath indefinitely. Because Emily could—and under the most grievous circumstances at that—I marveled at her, although the restraint is choking and, as her (very understandable) outburst during her audience with the Murrays demonstrates, sometimes wholly impossible to uphold. We congratulate ourselves for self-denial, for holding fast when our nerves cry out, because triumph seems to demand this emotional suffocation. No wonder I felt like an utter loser in middle school when, in the face of childish adversity—someone telling me that I ought to get a nose job or that on a scale of one to ten I was a solid "two"—I cried in the bathroom, in class, or into my pillow for the rest of the night. Still, even Emily feels compelled to warn her dead father that she will "cry a little bit" because she mourns him, fiercely, and because in the midst of her torment, she spends the previous day being ripped limb from limb by a pack of wolfish relatives.

Nineteenth- and early twentieth-century literature reflects a bygone period in which girls and women were told, without ceremony, whether they were attractive or plain or wholly unbecoming. Aesthetic hierarchies were often crystalline. Elizabeth Bennet knows that she is pretty, but is never left in doubt that her older sister, Jane, is the family beauty. When Jo March sells her hair to fund her mother's travel expenses, her family bemoans the loss of her "one beauty."[7] In Frances Hodgson Burnett's *The Secret Garden* (1911), the narrator dwells insistently upon Mary Lennox's limp, homely features, beginning with the very first lines of the book, where she is introduced as "the most disagreeable-looking child ever seen."[8] Soon thereafter, the little orphaned heroine—they abound, do they not?—overhears the uncharitable observations of her uncle's housekeeper, Mrs. Medlock: "My word! She's a plain little piece of goods!...And we'd heard that her mother was a beauty. She hasn't handed much of it down."[9] Today, remarks like these, not to mention the Murrays' calvacade of abuse, would be considered gratuitous and inappropriate, although it remains perfectly commonplace to disparage feminine appearance—anyone who writes for the internet encounters as much, sometimes on a daily basis—or to slavishly insinuate that we ought to adjust ourselves according to the prevailing metrics of beauty. Still, we are horrified when, in *Anne of Green Gables*, the chronically tactless Rachel Lynde eyes a jittery Anne from top to bottom and proclaims, "Well, they didn't pick you for your looks...She's terrible skinny and homely, Marilla."[10] Anne, of course, cannot countenance such nastiness and, like young Jane Eyre before her—and with somewhat less composure than Emily—bursts with pained indignation: "You are a rude, impolite, unfeeling woman!...How would you like to be told that you are fat and clumsy and probably hadn't a spark of imagination in you?"[11] To say the very least, there have been healthier exchanges on the topic of personal appearance, though, admittedly, I have always appreciated Anne's ill-advised, predictably searing outburst—shut up, Rachel Lynde!—and while I often experienced secondhand embarrassment on Anne's behalf, I found her temper to be vicariously cathartic when weaponized in response to physical insults.

Ultimately Anne must, at Marilla's demand, apologize to Rachel, but Montgomery has made her argument: young girls do not attain moral robustness by weathering unwarranted criticism about their bodies. Nor is it frivolous for a young girl or for a woman to fret over her appearance, certainly not when we are culturally mandated to strive for an ever-fluttering set of beauty criteria. Yet Montgomery's narrators are, to an almost bizarre extent, preoccupied with the question of whether or not Anne and Emily grow to be beautiful women (it's pretty clear that they more or less do). The tension buzzes throughout the novels: Montgomery posits the harmfulness of picking apart little girls for being too pale or too skinny or too freckled, but she is nonetheless steeped in a milieu that privileges these assessments of femininity. She cannot fully deliver Emily and Anne from these concerns, or from the conversations that entangle them, but she can vouch for Anne's right to anguish, and thwack against the enduring philosophy that it is better to receive insults quietly, even when they cut us to the quick.

Emily's allure has always been tethered to her inscrutability and her staunch self-sovereignty, both for me and for her fellow characters. Indeed, her very species seems up for debate, yet another case of feminine too muchness sublimated into something witchy or phantasmagoric. Is she, as some men tease, descended from elves or fairies? (Her pointed ears instigate this hypothesis.) In Avonlea—a world rooted firmly in realism— that possibility would be laughingly discarded. But Emily's precocity amasses supernatural gravity: even Aunt Elizabeth begins to doubt her Bible-braced convictions in the face of her niece's otherworldly intuition. Throughout the series, the narrator suggests that Emily possesses "second sight," and we the readers

are supplied with no pragmatic alternative. In a feverish delirium she solves Blair Water's blackest mystery, one that has long
afflicted the relationship between Ilse and her distant father.
Years later, Emily and Teddy share a spontaneous psychic com-
munication that proves life-saving; certain he sees Emily on a
Liverpool dock, Teddy misses the opportunity to book passage on a ship—one doomed to collide with an iceberg in the
middle of the Atlantic Ocean.

These premonitions unsettle Emily—"I don't *want* to have
any such power...I don't feel *human*"—and she endeavors to
forget about them.[12] As a child, I found her reaction rather un-
grateful: who doesn't want superpowers? The magic that Anne
so desperately seeks in the world, that she wills into being,
seems to saturate Emily, so much so that she can hardly know
herself. And while I might have bristled at this lack of enthusiasm for the supernatural, I consider it fitting, now, that Emily
would be unharnessed by these obscure abilities. Suspicious of
vulnerability in any form, Emily perceives her "second sight"
with reticence adjacent to contemporary social codes: it is an
index of her profound sensitivity, its presence a threat to her
hell-bent determination to curate her presentation according to
her own specific predilections. She perhaps intuits the precarity inherent to broad emotional exposure: when society glares
at those who do not self-moderate, it's dangerous in any case,
but particularly so for young women. To be "human," Emily
might say, demands one's groundedness upon the earth, firm-
ness imbuing one's most intimate crevices. Humanity enables us
to choose what we share, and where we are soft. And yet, like
Anne—and like me, at last—she has always known that it is folly
to tether humanness to fundamental self-control, to fullness of

comprehension. Too muchness blossoms in the soil, tickling at our feet: senses, inclinations, and urges at times carry us miles past what we understand ourselves to be. But then, maybe Emily is right. Too muchness *can* trick us into thinking ourselves inhuman; after all, the experience of profound, fiery feeling has always been relegated to the outer lip of cogent experience.

Anne lacks any such powers of premonition; instead, she bewitches her environment through the sheer force of imagination. Under her jurisdiction, the woods neighboring Green Gables become the Haunted Forest; she then contrives ghostly myths so that it lives up to its name. And, aware of her own emotional transparency, she dwells in alternative plotlines that mystify her character as well. As a child she fashions a vast wardrobe of enigmatic identities—"Will you please call me Cordelia?"—and daydreams about the woeful, obscure demise of Tennyson's "Lady of Shalott." Cooking endeavors mutate into disasters because Anne cannot resist plunging into her tragic world of make-believe.

Ultimately, both Anne Shirley and Emily Byrd Starr thrive—in love and friendship, and in intellectual and creative pursuits, where the structural arrangements are organized for men. Both are desired and adored by the person of their choosing (even if, in Anne's case, her feelings for Gilbert Blythe are for some time obfuscated by fantasy). Young Anne aggravated me by exemplifying my own idiosyncrasies and my own susceptibility to the world's most agitating offerings. I was the girl who didn't want to be born, who predicted, in her tiny infant heart, that she couldn't live inside cold, unmoderated chaos. But, evidently, I wasn't an especially perceptive infant—I'll forgive myself for that much—and for years, I read Anne in bad faith.

Yet, even then, I knew that she matured into the sort of woman who embodied my adolescent conception of personal triumph: charming, academically successful, and that bleary red herring, pretty *enough*. In fact, when *I* was not wallowing in the depths of despair, Anne Shirley-ness struck me as not only appealing, but perhaps attainable too. Maybe L. M. Montgomery had inscribed my future for me to seek and uncover in due time. Maybe my mother *had* deciphered these clues first and alerted her flailing daughter. Through this feat of narcissistic projection, Anne's Too Much life becomes a road map for my own. But who has ever loved a map?

Loving Anne necessitated self-acceptance, and I was uninterested in that endeavor. If I stopped aspiring to stoicism, if I checked my effusive earnestness, if I allowed myself to weep in English class after being harassed outside the bathroom, I would be acquiescing. So instead, I worshipped the girl I could never be: cool Emily. In my estimation, magical abilities—no matter the variety—provided a keener means of survival, a too muchness without the social mortification. Alex Mack's telekinesis seemed worth the hassle of hiding from a corrupt chemical plant. When I saw *The Craft*, I bemoaned my own magic-less constitution. And as for Emily Byrd Starr, well, I might have likened her to Matilda or even Willow Rosenberg before placing her within the same domain as Anne Shirley. Something otherworldly had kissed her. No matter what trials befell her on earth—even if she detested her "second sight"—the cosmos had deemed her special.

And yet, aspirations shift and ebb. Anne's avid heart—its bright, broad welcome—we can hear, and if we can't precisely place the melody, we're acquainted with a variation. If we're reticent in our desires or frightened by our yen for belonging, Anne sings in our stead, without fear and without exposing us. If we're just as loud, she'll whoop and laugh and cry in tandem. "My heart is tied to yours," said my mother. It was an Anne Shirley-ish declaration: vehemently and ardently stating something she felt in her bones. As a girl, I balked at that eager warmth—hers, Anne's—because I recognized it, glowing at the bottom of me. Both Anne and my mother fell in love with the world, and on the page, where Avonlea beamed with gentle, bucolic grace, that love seemed marvelous. But I had seen my mother weep. I discerned the worldly hazards that could overwhelm an unguarded soul. Fearing annihilation by too muchness, I lamented my own porous skin, knit like hers.

But my mother was not annihilated. Her prodigious love begot strength, and they reinscribed one another like a double helix. They endure, intertwining and blossoming and holding fast in me, although her body has gone. A shattered heart mends infinitely, although it takes variant shapes. It is stained glass, shifted. It is vibrant, evermore.

I will always love Emily, but I no longer want to be magical, nor am I panting after an aloof façade that I could never approximate, let alone perfect. I want to live wide open, to regard too muchness as my entitlement, and as my dear maternal bequest—not as a burden to bear. I want to embrace what I've inherited from my mother: a heart that hears everything at full volume. And because I want that, because I love what it entails, I must make a confession. I love Anne too.

Chapter Four

CLOSE

I am a composite of the women I have loved. I am built and reconstituted from my memories of them: words and embraces exchanged, the smell of their hair and the soap smoothed into their skin. This sounds romantic, I know, and it is: my most intimate female friendships have always, at least in my perception, been romances of their own, untethered from my erotic life—unless they weren't. I have anguished over strife with women dear to me. And I have fallen in love with a woman without realizing it—until she delivered me a broken heart.

My history of female friendship might be recounted by some as a tale of excessive passion—*too much* passion—as well as conceived, somewhat, as a reckoning with my own bisexuality. Perhaps this is why I've always been preoccupied with "dangerous" female friendships—the intimacies from adolescence to adulthood that exist apart from heteronormative arrangements and that are too intensely passionate to be neatly categorized as platonic: the zealous, fleshy sisterly bond of "Goblin Market"; the chilling case of teenage murderesses Pauline Parker and Juliet Hulme, who kill in the name of their love; Celie's infatuated devotion to Shug Avery in Alice Walker's *The Color Purple*; the gnashing competition that sears the bond between Lena and Lila in Elena Ferrante's Neapolitan novels. My interest, I now realize, has always been in the service of self-absorbed curiosity: why am I so enthralled with women? (Besides the obvious, of course: women are wonderful.) I wondered, too, whether there existed a guiding metric to clarify this excitement kindled by women's companionship. Since high school I would now and again entertain a suspicion loitering at the bottom of my abdomen—that I was attracted to women and to men. Many years later, I determined this to be true. However, my queerness has rarely been a factor in the ardor that charges my friendships. I would argue that many same-sex intimacies trouble the boundary between homoerotic and platonic love, but in my case the only friendships that have made manifest my queer desires are the ones where sexual attraction has transformed from companionate love.

Although it has inspired me to seek resonant narratives, loving women so fervently has never made me anxious or given me especial pause. However, as my search for stories of female homosociality has persisted, I've discerned the crawling hetero-masculine fear that distorts so many of them as cautionary tales against excess and obsession. In the myopic gaze of contemporary culture, some girls simply love each other too much and, as a result, become tangled in what we might refer to as

Too Much friendships—that is, friendships so absorbing that those involved evince interest in little else, particularly hetero-normative rituals of dating and flirting. They are intimacies that ignore the arrangements by which conventional American society replicates itself and which, often, refuse to answer questions of definition—What is this affection you share? Are you lesbians?—because in the beaming incandescence of girl love, we are disinclined to pay attention to formalities.

———

On a placid spring night, I leaned against my best friend, Leigha, on the steps of the Thomas Jefferson Memorial and re-alized that I wanted to kiss her. It wasn't precisely sexual, but it listed against that boundary. Moreover, I knew that no one in the world was as dear to me as she was—and that included my fiancé, Nick. Roughly a month later, Nick and I departed for three weeks of travel and an extended visit with his family. Faced with this parting, Leigha and I were bereft; and I espe-cially was inconsolable. Early in our trip, I rapidly tip-tapped through a flurry of lovelorn emails to Leigha. One day, Nick glanced over as I was signing off with a frenzy of "x's," "o's," and "I love you's." "I'm not comfortable with this," he said. My relationship with Leigha certainly seemed dangerous to Nick, and, to be fair, I had not concealed my attachment from him. But, in fact, it was not so much a hazard as a warning. Engulfed by my love of a best friend, and yearning for a stretch of time where I was unburdened with a man's emotional well-being, it was becoming clear that I did not want to marry the person to whom I was engaged.

At the time, I defended myself in the way most legible
to me: with literary scholarship and Victorian novels. In
nineteenth-century England, society didn't bat an eye at romantic female friendships, and in her book *Between Women:
Friendship, Desire, and Marriage in Victorian England*, critic
Sharon Marcus goes so far as to argue that this "world...made
relationships between women central to femininity, marriage,
and family life."[1] She moreover posits that "relationships between women were a constitutive element of Victorian gender
and sexuality" and that these intimacies existed peaceably
alongside heterosexual partnerings.[2] Often, Marcus emphasizes,
relationships between women buttressed the institution of marriage, even when they were themselves fraught with homo-
eroticism. By way of example, Marcus offers an incisive reading
of Charles Dickens's 1861 novel *Great Expectations* in which
she articulates the erotic longing texturing Miss Havisham's
obsession with her charge, Estella, whom she has instructed
to descend upon single men as a beautiful scourge, a siren
summoning them to ruin. Miss Havisham, decrepit and dis-
integrating, nonetheless burns with bitter voraciousness; she
is hungry for Estella and for what she believes Estella can
do: "Miss Havisham's enjoyment of Estella is inseparable from
her keen awareness of Estella's power to inflict pain, not only
on others but also on Miss Havisham herself. Miss Havisham
never exempts herself from her mission to make Estella ir-
resistible, and the love she lavishes on Estella resembles her
self-sacrificial affection for her faithless former lover."[3] On her
own, Miss Havisham is a fascinating embodiment of excess—a
moldering body being eaten by its own unreturned desire and
yearning for revenge. Here, as Marcus observes, she provides

a stunning counterpoint to the protracted conceptual opposi-
tions of male and female, heterosexual love and homosexual
love. There is perhaps no more iconic figure of unrequited
heterosexual love than Miss Havisham, and yet she navigates
her suffering through queer fantasies.

Miss Havisham is an extreme, and admittedly bonkers, example, but there are countless others: more explicit than Miss
Havisham and Estella, and less deranged, too, these same-sex intimacies flourish in Victorian fiction without, to our knowledge,
stirring suspicion in even the most conservative corners. Wilkie
Collins's novel *The Woman in White* (1860) depicts the passionate
devotion shared by half sisters Marian Halcombe and Laura Fair-
lie, who bemoan their imminent separation due to the latter's
marriage. "Poor dear Laura hardly leaves me for a moment, all
day," Marian narrates, "and, last night, when neither of us could
sleep, she came and crept into my bed to talk to me there. 'I
shall lose you so soon, Marian,' she said; 'I must make the most
of you while I can.'"[4] Yes, Laura crawls into bed with Marian
to talk, but Collins implies that their emotional closeness cannot be parsed from their physical affinity—to "make the most"
of Marian communicates a full-bodied relationship: one shaped
by caresses and love-flush, hushed tones.

Christina Rossetti invokes nearly identical language in her
1862 poem "Goblin Market": an intensely homosocial and
dizzyingly synesthetic portrayal of a young girl who, after being
seduced into eating deadly magic fruit, idles at the edge of
death. She attains salvation by lapping up the juice that streams
down her sister's face after a confrontation with the goblins
(emphasis mine):

She cried, "Laura," up the garden,
"Did you miss me?
Come and kiss me.
Never mind my bruises,
Hug me, kiss me, suck my juices
Squeez'd from goblin fruits for you,
Goblin pulp and goblin dew.
Eat me, drink me, love me;
Laura, make much of me;
For your sake I have braved the glen
And had to do with goblin merchant men."[5]

Although "Goblin Market" ends with the abrupt and san-
itized moral, "For there is no friend like a sister," the poem
carries a visceral physical charge. Laura clips a lock of her own
golden hair to pay for the goblins' fruit, a significant gesture because hair, both as an image and as a literary figure, evoked female sexuality. Victorian readers would have understood the act
of cutting one's hair as a mark of lost innocence. When Lizzie
angers the goblins by resisting their overtures, she withstands
their brutal attack and commingles the pleasure of renunciation
with near-sexual violence. And, of course, the sisters' intimacy,
like that of Laura and Marian, is rooted in deep physicality—
"Laura, make much of me," Lizzie exclaims, as she drips head
to toe with pulpy juice. Some illustrators have even interpreted
"Goblin Market" as pornographic. But as scholar Dinah Roe
observes, Rossetti "disguised Pre-Raphaelite realism with allegory and fantasy, thereby avoiding the critical outrage"[6] that
attended others' work—like, for instance, Rossetti's brother,
Dante Gabriel. A painter and poet, Dante Gabriel Rossetti,

together with those who shared his creative philosophies, met with scorn from Victorian critics, including Charles Dickens, for his keen sensual depictions of the day-to-day, on the canvas as well as on the page.

And of course, there's the famously melancholy scene in Charlotte Brontë's *Jane Eyre*, in which a young Jane crawls into bed with her dearest friend, Helen Burns, who is dying from consumption. It brims with the tender, unabashed love of two little girls who have been permitted so few choices and such skimpy happiness in their short, beleaguered lives. But for a slip of time, in the midst of suffering's shadow, they are free to adore one another:

"Jane, your little feet are bare; lie down and cover yourself with my quilt."

I did so: she put her arm over me, and I nestled close to her.

. . .

"How comfortable I am! That last fit of coughing has tired me a little; I feel as if I could sleep: but don't leave me, Jane; I like to have you near me."

"I'll stay with you, *dear* Helen: no one shall take me away."

. . .

She kissed me, and I her, and we both soon slumbered.[7]

There is no template for friendship, but this compassionate exchange between Jane and Helen—a declaration of love, and a farewell—has always seemed to me an antidote against the rhetorical scourge lambasting the too muchness of earnest, devoted companionship. Outside of heteronormative romance, we're taught to be embarrassed to love one another this way; it's the stuff of childhood fancy. As adults, we must renounce maximalist gestures before we commit ourselves as disciples to the temple of irony, where we filter so many of our most meaningful sentiments. Had Helen lived, she and Jane would have dedicated themselves to each other fully, just as they do in girlhood and perhaps even more so. But then, Victorian culture accommodated the maturation of female friendship, so long as it was not a hindrance to hetero-domestic affairs.

My friendship with Leigha was only a hindrance to my relationship with Nick because, as I contemplated my affections for her, an inconvenient possibility gripped my brain: maybe I simply didn't love my fiancé enough to marry him. Maybe I wouldn't revel so desperately in this love for my best friend if I also found romantic solace in the person to whom I had pledged myself.

I suppressed these prospects with all the violence of someone who knew them to be truths.

Years later, after I was divorced and remarried to my husband Paul, this lesson was substantiated, albeit elliptically. One sultry June night, I received an email from Amy, a dear friend from college, who informed me that she could no longer tolerate our friendship—could no longer, as it felt, tolerate me. In many ways this was my doing. Amy was smart, the sort of smart that's sharp and urgent and that makes me fall in love with a woman before I've thought to say hello. She was an early champion of my writing career—and more confident in my abilities than I was able to be; I'd grown increasingly dependent on her for guidance and validation as I picked through the mire of my insecurities and, all too often, fretted the way so many of us do that I was an abject impostor. Amy became a gleaming target for my lifelong impulse: to find an outside authority on my life, and to trust them in lieu of myself.

In the meantime, my mother had been diagnosed with stage three ovarian cancer—a week and a half before my wedding to Paul, in fact—and I found myself bewildered by these circumstances. Since graduating college I had both propelled and leaned upon a very specific narrative of myself: that I would complete a doctorate in English literature; that I would write predominantly in the service of highbrow academic pursuits; that my mother would witness this life I had determined as my destiny.

Suddenly, I was suffering pangs of vexing recognition: I no longer wanted to pursue an academic job, or to even complete my dissertation—or, more precisely, I did not want to complete my dissertation so much that I was willing to sacrifice even an hour of my new, fledgling writing career. And my mother—how much longer would she live? I reeled in this paucity of information and confidence. My selfhood, comprised of an acolyte's devotion to the ivory tower, and of my imperfect but fiercely hewn relationship to my mother, was cracking open in protracted, sometimes exhilarating, and often terrifying ways. I turned to Paul, as always, and to Leigha. But I wanted Amy too, with a need that unsettled me, particularly as I began to discern her burgeoning irritation. I suspected that I asked too much of her—that she bear witness to my proliferating existential fears and reassure me of my capabilities and, whatever annoyances I engendered, that she treat me like a convalescing kitten. Yet I couldn't stop.

I'm too sensitive to plead ignorance of my own desires; all the same, I'm impressively adept at tucking away scraps and shards of recognition—a thump in my gut or a fizzle in my upper chest or words, like fluorescent lights sizzling inside my head, "Kiss them!" "Kiss them!"—as if they had never manifested. Yet I knew that I had been attracted to Amy since college, although it had never occurred to me to say anything to her. At the time I had been in a relationship with the person who would become my first husband, and I was invested in maintaining what struck me as a reasonable and wise course. Because the information had never seemed relevant, and because I'm especially disinclined toward romantic rejection, I pretended to myself, my audience of one, that these urges I had noticed were misinterpretations. But as my queerness asserted itself as an inviolable aspect of my identity, it became increasingly difficult to dismiss it as an insignificant personality wrinkle, although I knew there would always be limitations to my experience. Once I knew I wanted to spend my life with Paul, who is cisgender and straight, my interest in other genders struck me as little more than untried fruit on a platter, one that, when it sailed past, I had rejected by choosing something else. Still, sometimes, when Amy visited me, or when I sat close to her in a bar or a theater, I would consider, a little sadly, how any romance between us likely would have been a full-scale disaster, but that if she had been game, I could never have said no.

When Amy ended our friendship, everything I had always known and soundly ignored cackled in my face like a hyena. As far as she knew, she was rejecting my—admittedly imperfect—

companionate affection. But it seared marrow-deep as a repudiation of unconfessed love. It didn't matter, I realized, that I had always shied away from pursuing a relationship with her—that I had, ultimately, wanted Paul more. I had loved her too, as a friend, and as someone I had desired: mourning her, I realized, would be a wretched ordeal.

And so it has been. So it is. Losing her has been one of the great heartaches of my adulthood: exponentially more painful than leaving my first husband and, in some ways, more humiliating. I've cultivated something of a smugness about my performance as a friend: I always assumed myself to be an excellent one. When friends thanked me for my steadfastness, I was grateful, but I also lapped it up like a parched cat, delighted that I could continue to treat my fantasies as fact: I was Rachel, the Good Friend. The *Best* Friend, even. The Best Fucking Friend.

I am, mostly, a good friend. I'm reasonable enough to understand that the women in my life have saved me every time I've foundered, and that without them I would be a howling misery. I am empathetic, generally. I am loving, nearly always. But I was an inconsistent, sometimes greedy friend to Amy, and whether this unspooled from silent romantic affection ultimately doesn't apply to the case. What I tried to be was a platonic friend, and when she judged me on that basis—when she considered how I measured up against what she wanted— Amy felt compelled to let me go.

In my more tempestuous moments, I've raged to Paul and to Leigha about how Amy treated me as Too Much, and how unfair it seems, how hypocritical when she knew and supported the premise of this book in its earliest stage. When she was, in certain ways, as Too Much as me. Once in a while I lapse into self-castigation and call myself a chump for struggling so in the wake of a lost friendship that, by now, has calcified. Sometimes, mercifully, I forget about Amy. Often enough, I remember her with something like empathy and sad acceptance. But every now and then, I feel a fool. I ought not—I know this. We have all shit the friendship bed at some time or another. But too muchness is already such a painfully stigmatized quality: when it becomes the grounds for rejection, we are predisposed to slip into self-loathing. It's what society has tacitly asked of us, after all, in the interest of our rehabilitation. And yet I am fortunate. In the face of these sputtering waves of shame, for some, I have always been just enough.

———

As we contend with the juggernaut of heteronormativity there has been a fissure—for many of us, it's not important that our relationships with women fit comfortably within that context. If "Goblin Market" were written today, Fox News would screech, "Incest!" When girls clambor into bed together on-screen, somewhere, an insecure buffoon crows, "Lesbians!" We are culturally resistant to the concept of continuums. Marcus points out,

> The received wisdom has been that all bonds between women are structured by the opposition between women and men, and therefore that women must either be rivals for men or comrades in the fight against patriarchy. In the latter view, friendship, erotic desire, and sexual

relationships between women are interchangeable, since
all three are considered subversions of a heterosexual order
that requires women to subordinate their bonds with one
another to the demands of men.[8]

Lingering anxieties that this is the case, that it's a cultural
hazard whenever women are more interested in one another
than in having sex with men, propels the impulse of social
surveillance: to ruminate over feminine intimacy, to represent
them in ways that shore up heteronormative male-centered
institutions.

In cinema, Noah Baumbach's *Frances Ha* departs from the
premise that female friendship is uniquely and independently
sustaining and provides an innocuous but tellingly prescriptive
cautionary tale against prioritizing one's friendship with a
woman and—this is the reasonable part of the film's warning—
losing one's selfhood in another person. The titular character
(played by Greta Gerwig) flounders precisely because she attempts to carve out a narrative in which she identifies herself
through her best friend, Sophie (Mickey Sumner). When that
friend commits to a romantic relationship and, consequently,
distances herself from Frances, the latter teeters into an acute
crisis of identity. There is a useful moral here, of course:
don't treat your best friend as a mirror. But Baumbach depicts
Frances's desire to grow old with Sophie as immature and even
semidelusional. The movie does not merely imply that what
Frances envisions is too much for Sophie, but that it's too much
for any friendship (and we know this is not the case). Despite a
worthy message that we thrive best when our dreams and desires are not tied up in others' agendas, the film doubles down

on the importance of Frances quitting her romance with her dearest friend.

The beginning of *Frances Ha* posits Frances's unhealthy attachment as the result of tightly hewn intimacy that she cannot accept as rooted to a specific moment in female twenty-something adulthood. Early in the film, Frances and Sophie are cozied in bed. The light is dim; shadows brush across their faces like gauze curtains. Frances asks, "Tell me the story of us." The title character delights in the romantic plot Sophie proceeds to sketch because it promises to activate a grand narrative, one that sits in marked contrast to the protracted stasis that otherwise defines Frances's professional life. As a twenty-seven-year-old apprentice at a New York modern dance company, she cannot yet call herself a professional dancer; she is only "someone who dances." While Sophie has already begun to carve out a niche in publishing, Frances scrapes together teaching gigs for peewee ballet classes to make rent.

And yet, at the beginning of the film, Frances impetuously shrugs off these material concerns. She instead dwells in transient moments of shared intimacy with Sophie: roughhousing in the park ("Not the hair!" squeals Sophie, the more particular of the two); drunkenly popping a squat in the subway; acquiescing to Sophie's nightly demand that Frances sleep in her bed—so long as she removes her socks. Each woman has lovers, but committing to anyone but Sophie registers as far-fetched to Frances. And, for the time being, Sophie refers to her own boyfriend, well-moneyed dudebro Patch, with diffidence.

Reciting the Story of Us—a fantasy in which the two are wildly successful, regularly vacation in Paris, and choose lovers over husbands—slakes Frances's thirst for a life narrative that is, yes, immeasurably fulfilling but more vitally marked by lasting togetherness. It signifies a pact, both sacrosanct and noble, intertwining Sophie's life with hers. Ambitions, sex, love: these are threads woven through the grand tapestry of two women descending upon the world, arm in arm.

But the Story of Us is not, we quickly learn, the story Sophie actually envisions for herself. After Frances surprises Sophie with a romantic post-work picnic early in the film, the two board the subway, and Sophie's attention swivels to her iPhone. Her standoffish behavior prompts a chagrined Frances to ask, and ultimately insist, that she be privy to the conversation. And so we learn: Rather than renew her lease with Frances, Sophie wants to move to a swanky Tribeca neighborhood ludicrously out of her best friend's price range, and she has waited until the day before confirming to tell Frances of her plans (this is a shit move on Sophie's part). And so, the ur-text of their friendship rendered obsolete, Frances must rummage and fumble to assemble a different life than the one she anticipated. Her plot points, once fixed, are now scattered and roving, simultaneously throwing into question who Frances will be if not, first and foremost, Sophie's friend.

Thus the film begins to chronicle Frances's process of relinquishing a bundle of dearly nurtured fantasies, most of them tethered to Sophie. And when Sophie moves to Tribeca and becomes goopy-syrupy monogamous with Patch, Frances must come to terms not only with Sophie's abiding absence, but also with the fictions that have propelled her faith in their shared future.

"We're the same person," Frances says of Sophie to her new roommates, Lev and Benji.

Later, her voice laced with thinly veiled anxiety, she tells Sophie, "You and I are both undateable. We're gonna end up spinsters." Sophie, who has since cultivated an air more sophisticated and bored, merely replies, "You better break that to Patch."

There's a certain pleasure in determining that we are "the same person" as our best friend, particularly for those of us who regard our friendships as romances. Often we are propelled to such vows when we find unevenly shaped pieces of ourselves in one another. But these moments, however vital, are only a nuance of a larger, fundamental drive to enlace oneself so tightly with another that all boundaries fizzle away. To assert that two are one is to defy tenets of logic on the hallowed principle of woman's intimacy—to desire spectacular manifestations of one's closeness because platonic romance is as vast and boundless as anything sexual.

And yet under different light this hyperbole emits a more somber hue. When Frances declares that she and Sophie are the same, she yearns to steady herself through identification. All of the questions that make us squirm in the twilight of our twenties—am I pursuing the right career? Should I commit to this person? What, precisely, do I *want?*—lose their charge when we decide that our best friend's life narrative validates our own. When Frances aligns herself with Sophie—Sophie, who has both a job and parents successful enough to fund a move to Tribeca—her increasingly disappointing dance career becomes, not a professional misfire, but an incontrovertible plot thread of their larger Story. Her choices are rendered valid, and unambiguously so.

After Sophie moves out of their apartment, however, her presence becomes more peripheral and laden with caveats (she can't hang out all day; she promised to meet Patch by five). Though Frances continues to tell people that she and Sophie are the same person, this description of their friendship begins to read more as a desperate grasp at an unraveling narrative and, critically, at her cherished perception of Sophie, who has never been her double.

Even at its most feverish, closeness is a vague, protean sensation, one we can experience even when we do not fully know the person catalyzing it. It's unclear exactly why Frances does not know Sophie the way she purports to—why she must learn just how little she knows. But this much is clear: Frances—out of fear of loneliness, insecurity, or immaturity—has been unwilling to interpret Sophie on Sophie's terms. We see the expanse of this gap during what amounts to the film's climax. After a fight with Patch, a liquored-up Sophie crawls into Frances's bed, and she murmurs everything Frances's basest self aches to hear—boozy promises of reunion and a resurrected narrative: Sophie's going to leave Japan, where she now lives with Patch, and, more crucially, she's going to leave Patch himself. She will return to New York City with Frances. The two fall asleep as Sophie intones, "I love you, Frances."

Sophie does love Frances; of this, we are never in doubt. However, when Frances awakes the next morning, it is not beside a Sophie committed to relinquishing her new life, but rather to the sound of Patch's car pulling away, her best friend in tow. Their night together was not a return for Sophie, but a retreat—retreat from commitments and change that have been far more overwhelming for Sophie than Frances has previously understood. Nonetheless, these are the commitments, and abiding changes, that Sophie has embraced.

One evening, in the midst of her estrangement from Sophie, Frances dreamily describes to fellow dinner party guests her conception of purest romance: a shared look across a crowded room that communicates one essential fact: we are each other's person. "That's what I want out of a relationship," she concludes. With Frances's remarks, we understand two things: this is what she wants from her friendship with Sophie. And she wants it precisely because they have never experienced it. In spite of affection, attachment, and intimacy, they have not quite grasped how to see each other.

But they learn. At the end of the film, Frances and Sophie beam at each other across the expanse of a reception. Frances has just showcased her first work as a choreographer. Sophie has married Patch. And as Frances basks in the pulse of that warm glow, indiscernible to the rest of the crowd, she finally understands whom it is she sees. It is not another manifestation of herself. It is not the embodiment of some predetermined life. It is Sophie, her best friend.

———

Baumbach's film delivers an insidious edict against women cultivating romances with one another, apart from men—one couched in cogent messages of independence and honesty. It's not an altogether alarmist cultural artifact, but a more muted representation of our milieu. Peter Jackson's 1994 film *Heavenly Creatures*, based on actual events, peddles in blatant fear-mongering. Purporting to convey the natural conclusion of unchecked female intimacy, the film chronicles the increasingly obsessive bond between two teenage girls unhappy with their familial circumstances. Ultimately convinced that one of their mothers is determined to separate them, they orchestrate and carry out a scheme to murder her in cold blood. The through line is clear: young women are prone to excessive attachment that can yield unthinkable destruction. Moreover, the film's evident lesbian panic intensifies the anxiety surrounding romantic female friendship, insinuating a more primal concern that men lack the organic pull on women's desires and affections that they've been taught to expect. Too Much friendships rail against this expectation, while refusing to account for an attraction that, for all its potency, cannot be read according to heteronormative discourse.

In 1953, Pauline Parker and Juliet Hulme[9] met in Christchurch, New Zealand. Before long, the two girls grew so attached it frightened their parents. The Hulmes made plans to remove Juliet to South Africa, indefinitely separating her from Pauline. But Juliet, fifteen at the time, and Pauline, sixteen, were determined not to be parted. Identifying Pauline's mother as the primary obstacle to their scheme, the girls resolved to murder her and frame the deed as a tragic accident. They arranged an outing to Victoria Park on June 22, 1954— Pauline recorded it in her diary as "the day of the happy event." After tea, they lured Mrs. Parker to a secluded hillside and, wielding a brick inside a stocking, bludgeoned her to death.

Pauline's diary—the source of the narration for *Heavenly Creatures*—was discovered during the investigations, its contents revealing the girls' intentions. Both Pauline and Juliet were brought to trial, found guilty, and imprisoned. They were released five years later, purportedly on the nonnegotiable condition that they never reunite, never reignite a friendship whose intimacy begot insatiability, a love dipped in terror. Pauline and Juliet are a case study of panic: the legible lesbian panic in their parents' desire to separate them, and born from their motivation for killing Mrs. Parker. There's panic whenever young girls reveal their capacity for bloodlust. And panic wraps itself around the center of Pauline and Juliet's bond; they fear being alienated from each other and will do anything to avoid it.

Jackson's film features the debut performances of Melanie Lynskey (Pauline) and Kate Winslet (Juliet). Lynskey's Pauline scowls from beneath a mop of brunette curls, her face softening only when she looks at Juliet, near-idolatry engulfing her eyes. In turn, Winslet's Juliet basks in this bald adoration. Chin aloft, she speaks deliberately, accentuating her English accent as a mark of superiority among the New Zealanders. She lords over Pauline too, partly because it's her natural inclination and partly because Pauline is a happily rapt devotee.

Together, Lynskey and Winslet perform this barbed, mutual love—one that can never satisfy. Both of them, since childhood, have been working around a deep-seated dread of isolation. When she was a child, Juliet's frail health inspired her parents to send her away to warmer climates. Now as a teenager, living with her parents again, she grasps for their elusive attention. Pauline barrels through the school halls, head down, keeping a brisk pace that beclouds the thickened epidermis of her solitude.

The two girls first encounter each other in the classroom, where Juliet's irreverence draws Pauline's attention, sparking a fantasy that's crystallized at the first sight of the Hulmes' splendid Christchurch residence. Pauline halts her bike, dazzled first by the house and then at the sight of Juliet on a bridge, sun-dappled and laughing as she flings petals into the stream beneath her. She's dressed regally—gauzy gown, crown atop her head—but Pauline, her face rinsed with enchantment, registers Juliet's play as authentic. We understand that, for Pauline, Juliet will henceforth exist as a fairy princess trapped in reality's squalor.

So often we think our interpretations are fact. In Jackson's scheme, the light that bathes Juliet functions as metaphorical illumination, a kiss of truth that transforms her into some splendid creature only Pauline can recognize. There's nothing especially bizarre about this dynamic: literature is dotted with women who seem exquisite byproducts of luxury—and, as a result, bewitch the lesser at their feet. In Jane Austen's *Emma*, Emma Woodhouse exerts deleterious influence over pretty, dithery Harriet Smith. Dainty, coddled Ash Wolf elicits Jules Jacobson's love in Meg Wolitzer's *The Interestings*. That affection is barbed with jealousy and covetousness—but it never approaches the cathexis of *Heavenly Creatures*, where a girl is inspired to crush her mother's skull.

The film's basis in a real-life narrative makes it even easier to wonder what went wrong. To cherish one girlfriend better than everyone else—to fall extravagantly in love with her—is no crime. But how could Pauline and Juliet possibly glorify their love, and each other, to the extent that other humans seemed to live only for and at their mercy? Then again, it's not worthwhile to plot cause and trajectory on a movie or on real life. There's never total coherence, no meaningful tipping point. We can't pause on the timeline, point a knowing finger, and say, "Here—here's where the bloodthirst became possible, when she finally knew she'd strike."

Murder, like love, exceeds the sum of the evidence. As she

narrates, Pauline even articulates their motivation, but we can never grasp what transforms an instinct into an event, how impulse mutates into brutality. The obscurity surrounding murder is terrifying in any case; what's often illuminated is ultimately just our prejudice about what sorts of people commit crimes. The mythology surrounding the Anglo-Saxon schoolgirl renders Pauline and Juliet's capacity for violence unthinkable. The schoolgirl is archetypally sweet, naïve even at the first blush of sexual awakening. If she is dangerous, that danger inheres in her desirability, perhaps even in her awareness that she has been objectified. Schoolgirls giggle mischievously, as Pauline and Juliet do; they might even traipse through the woods in their underwear, or assemble a shrine to their most cherished Hollywood celebrities (Mario Lanza, in this case). No matter how brazen the fantasies, the schoolgirl friendship never fully sheds its mantle of innocence: fresh curiosity and saddle shoes, fullhearted earnestness and notes on loose leaf. We know these clichés are false; that's why pop culture is always dismembering them.

Pauline and Juliet are rendered as most unusual in the voracity of their love, one plagued by endless need—for each other, and for refuge in a world of their own creation. Dissatisfied with their circumstances and stymied by parental limits, they create and cultivate the kingdom of Borovnia, populated by hedonist characters they sculpt together out of Plasticine. The girls spin a mythology that grants them access to this fantastic world, permitting pleasures alien to good Christian schoolgirls. And with this perceived supernatural mobility comes self-deification. The human world refuses to "appreciate [their] genius," Pauline writes, and so their intimacy serves as a means of worshipping themselves. The line from which the title comes is telling: "Tis indeed a miracle one must feel that two such heavenly creatures are real."

The fantasy may be alluring, but its atmosphere is porous. When Pauline travels to Borovnia, her fears and vexations dog her. Bored during a mundane sexual encounter, she hurtles her consciousness inside Borovnia's castle walls. Pauline is enthralled by the company of her Plasticine characters— now life-size—and tickled when her lover appears (also rendered in Plasticine), and is brutally sliced in half. A moment later, she gazes into a far corner where one figure transforms into bright, laughing Juliet. They share a flushed look of mutual admiration, but after a moment, Pauline's eyes brim with tears.

Even here, in this fantasy, Pauline cannot disentangle her love of Juliet from her tragic awareness that she will always be chasing after her, perched on the brink of loss. However fervently they intertwine their lives, Pauline is mired in unshakable anxiety. Safeguarding this relationship is not simply a function of love, but of a wretched, fundamental knowledge that it is too good to be true, too precarious to endure. Juliet is as much fantasy as flesh. Pauline, unaware of how strongly Juliet's father dislikes her, even daydreams in black-and-white of racing into the embrace of Juliet and her parents, who beam with pride as the two girls share a deep kiss.

These are not just desires for intimacy, but for a new origin story that absorbs Pauline into a refined world full of intellect and art. In more tempered varieties, these fantasies have never been uncommon among best friends. When I read the Baby-Sitters Club series as a child, I relished the plotline of Mary Anne and Dawn, girlfriends who become stepsisters and housemates. Even those of us fortunate to have a happy home couldn't help but dream of a different family, one that we could inhabit while retaining aspects of our own. But it's in the nature of a dream to exceed the possible.

And so Jackson's film runs on pursuit. Pauline's first visit to Ilam, the Hulmes' homestead, leads to a chase sequence throughout the grounds. Daytime frolics throughout the woods surge into playful games of tag. When Pauline indulges in the far-fetched, cherished vision of joining the Hulme family, it begins with an eager race down a ship's deck. The girls are locked into a ceaseless chase, never allowed to catch their breath. Seeking more than can be found in a single person, they can never be satisfied by what they share. And, as youths suspected of a so-called unnatural attachment, their parents' suspicions keep them from inhabiting their friendship in peace. Pauline is forced to visit a doctor who, with gravest solemnity, diagnoses her as homosexual. Disruptions in the Hulme household—plans for divorce, Dr. Hulme's dismissal from the college in Christchurch—inspire Juliet's parents to leave. For Juliet, the plan is unfathomable: her parents are abandoning her—again—while demanding that she forsake Pauline.

Their togetherness in jeopardy, Pauline and Juliet seek satisfaction one night by making love the way they imagine their favorite celebrities—those they worship as "saints"—do. It's erotic, but the girls are young; it's not difficult to read this relationship as one that eschews the strictures of heterosexuality without applying the totalizing stamp of "lesbian." It is one matter for the girls to characterize their intimacy on their own terms and another for outside observers to categorize it as if puzzling over the genus of a strange animal. We are eager, always, to make intimacy legible, but all bonds often veer into unplottable territory.

Despite the matrimony-centric schema ordering their perspectives on female friendship, the Victorians nonetheless depicted a sweeping calico of bonds between women. Charles Dickens's 1865 novel *Our Mutual Friend* includes among its vast cast of characters the devoted companions Lizzie Hexam, who, like so many Dickensian heroines, is beautiful, selfless, and long-suffering, and Jenny Wren, a disabled dolls' dressmaker who supports her alcoholic father and, though she seems whimsically idiosyncratic, refuses to suffer any man's tomfoolery, particularly where Lizzie is concerned. This pair of young women, snarled in poverty and all its accompanying plights, takes succor in small tendernesses. After long, laborious days, they unpin each other's hair by the fire, "it being Lizzie's regular occupation when they were alone of an evening to brush out and smooth the long fair hair of the dolls' dressmaker."[10] It's a sensuous and romantic ritual—two young women basking in their mutual physical charms, silken streams tumbling across shoulders and bosoms as a fire crackles in the dusk. And because Jenny Wren was accustomed to solitude before Lizzie came to live with her, it is fitting that she would revel in this companionship, determining that any husband would pale in comparison to her friend. "He couldn't brush my hair like you do," Jenny avows, "or help me up and down stairs like you do, and he couldn't do anything like you do; but he could take my work home, and he could call for orders in his clumsy way... *I'll* trot him about, I can tell him!"[11]

Jenny Wren speaks like a disenchanted personality from Mother Goose, and this is appropriate: Fanny Cleaver is her given name—one with a myriad of sexual implications—but, purportedly inspired by the English nursery rhyme, she rechristens herself. Her position in the novel is a slippery one—performative in a way that sometimes seems to resist her reduction to a disabled body. But then, Dickens's track record in writing female characters, not to mention nonnormative ones, is pitted at best; perhaps he means Jenny's sassy, hyper-girlish fantasies of a married future to be read as such: the adorably confident musings of a character who, as a result of her own, physical too muchness, has been altogether evacuated of sexuality, in name and in person (though she does, eventually, find a partner, and because this is a Dickens novel, he is disabled too). Regardless, Jenny's stern assessment of this lacking hypothetical husband lays bare a crystalline hierarchy: no man, according to her predictions, can soothe and delight her the way that Lizzie does.

But the friendship shared by Lizzie Hexam and Jenny Wren is a healthy one, unmarred by the panicked frisson agitating the bond between Pauline and Juliet. Intense homosociality abounds among women and girls in Victorian fiction, but rarely does it signal cause for alarm. After all, these women, even Jenny Wren, do not love their companions too much if they accept the heteronormative marriage plot as the template for their own timelines. Perhaps the most deadly female intimacy in Victorian literature occurs in Sheridan Le Fanu's 1872 gothic novella *Carmilla*, in which the titular character, an ages-old vampire, seduces and feeds on pretty, naïve girls. The story chronicles her pursuit of Laura, who is sweet, sheltered, and a bit dim; their quick intimacy, which confounds Laura; and Carmilla's eventual undoing.

But as the text takes great pains to emphasize, this parasitic relationship is not one shared by two girls, but rather a girl and a monster, the latter of whom must be divested of her femininity so that she can be butchered by a cadre of vampire hunters. In the aftermath, when Carmilla is dead—irreversibly dead, that is—Laura filters her experiences with the lovely and mesmeric vampire through the antiseptic rhetoric of dehumanization:

> The vampire is prone to be fascinated with an engrossing vehemence, resembling the passion of love, by particular persons... It will never desist until it has satiated its passion, and drained the very life of its coveted victim. But it will, in these cases, husband and protract its murderous enjoyment with the refinement of an epicure, and heighten it by the gradual approaches of an artful courtship.[12]

Queer women were not ubiquitously visible in Victorian England, but of course they existed, and were not necessarily in hiding: diarist Anne Lister, a nineteenth-century lesbian landowner who engaged in a string of liaisons and, later, married her wife, Ann Walker, with a ring ceremony, supplies just one example of a queer Victorian woman living with relative openness.[13] But Lister's marriage never received official sanction, and as Le Fanu's novella indicates, the notion of two women in love was, for many, perfectly unthinkable, so much so that a woman who loved another of her sex was no woman at all, but an unholy monster. This sort of paring, *Carmilla* insinuates, could only be the "resemblance" of real passion, a perverse, translucent imitation of sanctioned marital bliss—or, for that matter, of the chaste feminine bonds deemed appropriate by Victorian standards of etiquette.

To conceive of too much love, a "crime against nature," the Victorians unwomaned the woman. It's no coincidence that this kind of conceptual gymnastics also characterized nineteenth-century documentation of female murderers and their subsequent executions. In order to absolve the violence of hanging—violence visited upon a body that could beget and sustain life—lawmakers reasoned that the crimes that sent women to the gallows, often infanticide, evacuated them of womanhood, thereby, through ironic and brutal calculation, creating a warped form of equality between the sexes. Writes Laura Thompson, "The authorities executed women who had become 'unwomanly'; who had behaved in a manner so unnatural that it rendered them equal indeed with men, and obliterated any special privilege of gender."[14]

Heavenly Creatures might not divest Pauline and Juliet of their femininity, but it does insist upon the girls' self-imposed isolation, as if suggesting that a contorted friendship like theirs could only emerge like a virus sequestered in a petri dish, something impossibly rare and undiluted by the dross of the greater world. And it's certainly tempting, because their narrative is so bloody, to read Juliet and Pauline as exceptional, to believe that, like Carmilla or the impoverished baby murderers of Victorian England, they must be of a uniquely hostile sort, girls gone wild with bloodlust. But in many ways they are not. They are lonesome and dissatisfied and ravenous for mutual adoration. That night, with Juliet's departure imminent, they are merely seeking union—to glut themselves on another, to beat back what beckons next.

Killing Mrs. Parker, the girls reason, will ensure they'd never again risk separation. So, together, Juliet and Pauline bludgeon Mrs. Parker in the quiet of the woods. Her daughter strikes first, but each takes a turn crushing the brick deeper into the woman's skull. But with each ruthless thrust, they visibly come to realize that this botched and insufficient plan could only work in Borovnia, where desires can be witched into fact, ideas into events, where the world always aligns with your reading of it.

The film staggers to its bloody end: Juliet and Pauline, full of spite and desperation, complete their gruesome matricide. We return to the launching ship, the vision in black-and-white turned nightmare. Juliet stands on the deck, flanked by her parents, while Pauline is bound on land. And so, Pauline is left where she began that first day at Ilam, adoring her princess from afar, and this time knowing—wretchedly, definitively—that the gaping maw she sought to close was always determined to rip apart. Her chase is finished, but not because she's free. Out in front of her has always been futility; she only needed to acknowledge it for the race to be won.

———

It would be more comfortable for us to regard *Heavenly Creatures* as the far-fetched stuff of nightmares, to assume that the too muchness of Juliet and Pauline's intimacy is wholly unique from the relationships we navigate. Certainly, most of us are—thankfully—not in the practice of plotting murder whenever we're threatened with separation from a beloved companion. But that yen—to collapse into each other, to love and love and love without quotidian interruption, is also present in Baumbach's *Frances*. More recently, Robin Wasserman tackles the muddied boundaries between girl-love and girl-lust in her 2016 novel *Girls on Fire*. But rather than encourage panic, Wasserman interrogates patriarchal anxieties even as she draws out the teenage girl's capacity for violence. Yes, teenage girls love more fiercely—and are more powerful—than we might want to admit. They're capable of violence, and of bloodthirst, and maybe they'll chalk it up to the love of a girl. Maybe, like Carmilla, that love and the compulsion to gnash one's teeth are too tangled to parse.

But what is even more compelling than a bloodthirsty friendship is the particular terror with which we consider two girls willing to kill for each other, a fear so poignant we're quick to imagine it as an epidemic. Heteronormative ideology follows slavishly in the Victorian footsteps of Sigmund Freud: it presumes that without a civilization rigidly arranged around straight white men, women will mutate into Juliets and Paulines, gorge themselves on myopic girl-love, and brutalize anyone who raises an eyebrow. We will luxuriate in our so-called "hysteria," stoke its fires, let it burn. Or, at the very least, we'll stop paying attention to men's demands, gradually realizing that there is more freedom to be found in one another. That, like Laura and Lizzie of "Goblin Market," our salvation is located in the love of women, rather than in the grand erect institutions of men.

Nick was wrong to suppose that my friendship with Leigha damaged our relationship; in fact, her presence made my circumstances more bearable. And whereas Nick and I are now divorced, Leigha and I remain as close as ever. She and my current husband, Paul, get along swimmingly. It is Paul, in fact, who has soothed my devastation over Amy, who listened with patience and love as I admitted—to the two of us—the long history of my attraction, never doubting that I loved him less. We are hasty to pathologize intimate female friendships because such fervent same-sex romance seems irrevocably incompatible with heterosexual arrangements. But it's not necessarily; and even if it were, that question is beside the point. The pathologized Too Much friendship reminds us that we build lives with diverse people and in myriad ways. Heterosexuality's purchase on "normal" has been impressed upon us, not earned. We're at liberty to blur the lines and chase whomever we choose.

Chapter Five

PLUS

A week or two before my first wedding, Nick approached me with a frank request: After we were married, could I please not grow "fat"? He muttered his query through a bashful grin, acknowledging its distastefulness, but nonetheless conveying that he was in earnest. Nick remarked that he had observed a trend in which the wives of certain acquaintances had gained weight early in their marriages. He then articulated his wish that I would not lapse in a similar fashion; besides, he enjoyed having "the hot wife."

I don't precisely recall how I responded to Nick, although it would have been characteristic of me, at the time, to merely acquiesce, perhaps with a giggle that affected indignance. But I saw Leigha soon after, and when I mentioned it to her, she responded with bald disgust. How dare he, how objectifying and so forth. Yet we didn't belabor the topic for very long: I was going to marry Nick—the wedding gears were doggedly churning, seemingly without the opportunity for pause. His remarks were unfortunate, but at the time they didn't signal any worrisome traits—in part because I was disinclined to confront any indication that we were incompatible, but also because I was accustomed to monitoring my body with anxious and unforgiving scrutiny.

As a girl I was reedy thin and board-flat. When one of my friends began wearing a bra in fifth grade, I beheld my own nipples with despair: they were nearly flush with the rest of my chest and stomach. I feared that I was cursed to eternal booblessness. When—WHEN?—would my frame soften into those rounded contours that I so admired on my friend and on other, more amply developed women?

The answer, I would eventually learn, was high school. By ninth grade I had developed some semblance of a figure, enough so that when I tried on a skin-tight, powder blue dress in Guess, Mom refused to buy it for me, hissing, "Rachel, look at your ass!" (Unbeknownst to me, said ass had affixed itself, perhaps in the dark of the night.) For a year or two, my concerns with self-image, although pernicious, rarely extended beyond my face, which I believed to be a hodgepodge of abominations, most of which were located in my nose, pronounced and curved along its ridge. Since middle school my nose had prompted male classmates to make deprecating suggestions of rhinoplasty, and in sixth grade one boy devised for me the straightforward, if not especially inventive, moniker "Nose Girl." From time to time I would even catch my mother eyeing it while we were drinking coffee at the kitchen table. I would watch, as if in slow motion, her focus meander from the conversation and settle decisively on the center of my face. I'd squirm.

"What, Mom?" I would demand, already anticipating the answer. And so it followed.

"It could just be fixed *so* easily," she would respond, tracing in the air, as if on an invisible easel, precisely how a doctor could shave off wedges of bone and cartilage in order to resculpt my nose into something less conspicuous.

Each time our conversations took this agitating turn, I became immediately upset, sometimes tearful, and demanded to know why she didn't think I was beautiful just as I was.

"Oh, I do, I do," she would assure me. And I believed her—both because I wanted to and because, even then, I suspected that my mother's own preoccupation with aesthetic symmetry sprung from the ruthlessness with which she regarded her own appearance—and, yes, specifically her nose.

By senior year of high school, my face was no longer the prevailing site of my body dysmorphia; that feeble grace period concluded abruptly. I wavered between the American sizes four and six when the prospect of losing "five pounds"—an infamously ubiquitous aspiration—first reared its odious head. All at once, it was ever-present and unyielding, this new, nagging concern over whether my body was appropriately barren of fat. I began to compare myself to my friends: the circumference of my limbs, the curvature of my stomach. Meanwhile, Mom cautioned that if I did not take care, I would surely gain weight in my hips and rear end. I began to drink SlimFast shakes and fretfully grab at the fleshy slope of my abdomen.

Now, in my early thirties, my body is both healthy and, for

better or for worse, conventional. This is what I tell myself. However, it's not always what I am told. I have been sternly lectured on the necessity of a diet by certain well-meaning people, including one gynecologist who told me, as she administered a breast exam, that if I wanted to have children, my first order of business was tightening up. "Babies are wonderful, but we don't have them to improve our bodies," she quipped, her fingers padding along my bosom. Donning an oversize paper towel, my feet indecorously suspended in stirrups, I found myself ill-prepared to issue a suitable rejoinder. Instead, I gulped back tears.

In the course of my adulthood thus far, my body has enjoyed one brief respite from judgment. Immediately after leaving my first husband I received a bevy of compliments on my figure; even I had to admit that I was more lithe and taut than I had been since college. Six months prior, I had been hospitalized for a suicide attempt and had spent the months immediately preceding and following it plagued with stress-based stomach illness. Fights with Nick often culminated in bouts of late-night diarrhea.

When Paul and I began dating, my quotidian gradually smoothed and brightened, and my stomach regained its equilibrium. As a result, I gained weight. I worried quietly the way most of us do that the body I possessed was unacceptable because it was not some other body: one that is slimmer or that boasts more defined muscles or—irony of ironies—one that is less encumbered by breasts. Nonetheless, my social privilege is substantial because, in terms of corporate marketing, my figure isn't marked as excessive: I can locate my size in stores, although jeans are something of a gamble. My weight is rarely mentioned unless I broach the topic myself—the exception being when someone suggests that my health, or my author photo, would benefit were I to shed a few pounds. Painful moments, to be sure, and ones that have sent me reeling, but I know many women endure them—and I also know that these passing interventions could be far worse.

Still, the body image rigmarole has become wearisome: establishing a gym routine that is inevitably disrupted by a gaggle of deadlines; crying when Paul tells me that I'm beautiful because it has never been easy for me to trust in those words; ordering diet pills that I take for a week before confiding what I've done to Paul (he asked me to flush them, and I did); developing a healthy diet and telling myself that doing so is its own benefit—but as my figure abides, I grow aggravated. Even for someone like me, someone with a common and predictable body that is, if not glamorized, then tolerated, the demand to love oneself becomes a drudging game of whack-a-mole when everywhere present are prickling reminders that your body is too ample, too soft, and too unruly.

———

Female bodies have long served as battlegrounds for men's warring anxieties, although ideals of beauty have mutated over the centuries. But one of femininity's recurring ordering principles has been to limit and regiment the space we physically claim. Typically, we approach this conversation in terms of weight; and, to be sure, American culture has fostered a noxious environment for women of all sizes, especially those regarded as fat. "In Western society, fatness is interpreted as failure," writes Anne Helen Petersen in *Too Fat, Too Slutty, Too Loud*. "It's a health issue that's transformed into an ideological affliction...Modern capitalist society hinges on its citizens' constant drive to consume, but the successful American is someone who's able, whether through genetics or self-regimentation, to *contain* the effects of that consumption."[1] In all of its manifestations, too muchness is disparaged as a lack of control, generally the result of unregulated emotion. While the excesses of capitalism are accepted as part of America's ideology of progress, consumption—particularly female consumption— must never be rendered visible through embodiment. Those effects, as Petersen argues, must be rigorously circumscribed, the process itself mystified through whatever means necessary to maintain a female body that is unassuming in size and girth.

But whether we've directed our glare toward weight or muscles or thick thighs, Western society has always reduced women to their fragmented parts, and in so doing, has condemned our bits and pieces as criminally Too Much. The racialized, sexist ideology that scrutinizes women's body size holds true for conversations about hair, breasts, and even noses. A body without symmetry, or that defies patriarchy-approved measurements, is charged with wayward excess. After all, a body that reads as untamable or defiant dredges up anxieties over all that female bodies can do—and how little men understand them.

Weeks before Mom died, as we sat at the kitchen table— no coffee now; her stomach no longer tolerated it—I burst into tears. To be sure, crying when your mother is dying from cancer is not unexpected. During those miserable months I was always one gulp shy of a sob. But I had mostly avoided these emotional overtures when we were together because I didn't want her to feel guilty for circumstances beyond her control. This time, however, was different and propelled by greater selfishness. My sisters, both of whom are beautiful and fit according to socially accepted metrics, had briefly joined us, and they turned the conversation to exercise and weight loss. Meanwhile, my day-to-day had become particularly sedentary, as I struggled to finish a slew of freelance assignments while beating back anticipatory grief. When my sisters retreated to their rooms, I crumpled.

"Am I fat?" I choked out. Self-disgust burbled in the deep of me.

Mom regarded me gently.

"You are a little overweight, honey."

Another time, I might have sought to defend myself or yelled at her for harboring obscene expectations that were born from her own protracted sense of inadequacy—despite what others told her, I do not know that my mother ever realized she was a beautiful woman. Even in the midst of her cancer treatment, she would bemoan the necessity of—what else?—losing five pounds. It's not unlikely that her concern over my weight was partially residual projection, not to mention an index of her own anxiety about dying. For Mom, death meant the uttermost inability to care for us; it was forced abandonment.

I recognized all this and realized that I would have given a kingdom for the promise of Mom nitpicking over my appearance for another thirty years. So I hung my head in shame, a slumped white flag. Whatever I was—a little overweight, average, fat, fine—I felt as if I had failed her. I didn't ask for reassurances or for her to mitigate her assessment of me. Beyond this, my recollection of the remaining conversation is

muddy, save for a comment or two about the dangers of carbo-
hydrates and Mom's own confusion about my transformation
from scrawny girl to voluptuous adult—how had it happened,
she wondered. It was not the sort of conversation one hopes
to have with their dying parent, but then, it was comfortingly
consistent in its own warped way. She never meant to hurt me,
though she knew precisely how, and nobody loved me more.
Somewhere tucked into the exchange—I do not think I am
imagining this—her soft eyes sought my own, a gaze shadowed
by the fluffy turquoise beanie safeguarding her head from wisps
of cold.

"But you've always been beautiful, Rachel."

————

The Victorians certainly fretted over the female form, and
the masculine anxiety over its containment hung heavy in the
atmosphere, influencing contemporary literature and cultural
thought. *Alice in Wonderland*'s legacy, sprawling as it does across
cultural terrain, especially imbues this aggrieved preoccupation
with size. In the Alice books, the titular character is often hungry or thirsty, with a yen for tarts and puddings. As literary
critic Anya Krugovoy Silver remarks, Lewis Carroll's willingness to feed his heroine and to allow her to gorge differentiates
her from the female characters of other children's literature,
who are castigated for their delight in sweets.[2] But it's no surprise that Carroll's preferences for feminine bodies were luridly
specific: he fussed over his child-friends' diets, concerned that
they would overeat. In his estimation, it seems that this transgression was no less grievous than other fleshly misdeeds.[3]

Carroll was by no means an outlier in his privileging of thinness. Victorian heroines are typically sylphlike, and they rarely evince interest in food—rather, they're more preoccupied with nourishing others, "[serving] food for Victorian heroes" that they may handle but "not taste."[4] In Charles Dickens's 1855 novel, *Little Dorrit*, the titular character's slight, childlike frame is even delineated by her nickname—her first name is Amy—and she is self-sacrificing as a matter of course. With her ineffectual father, William, imprisoned for bankruptcy in the Marshalsea, Little Dorrit toils as a seamstress to maintain his comfort, as well as that of her elder siblings. And when her employer provides her with meals, she declines to eat with the household so that she can deliver the food to him instead. She is "apparently oblivious of her own hunger,"[5] as literary critic Helena Michie observes, and this methodical privation is conveyed as a defining attribute of moral virtue:

> She had brought the meat home that she should have eaten herself, and was already warming it on a gridiron over the fire, for her father, clad in an old grey gown and a black cap, awaiting his supper at the table. A clean cloth was spread before him, with knife, fork, and spoon, salt-cellar, pepper-box, glass, and pewter ale-pot. Such zests as his particular little phial of cayenne pepper, and his pennyworth of pickles in a saucer, were not wanting.[6]

The narrator's inventoried account of William Dorrit's dinner table, which directs our attention to small luxuries like a "little phial of cayenne pepper" and a "pennyworth of pickles," implies a gross asymmetry of circumstances. Little Dorrit does

not go hungry in order to feed her father, but rather to embell-
ish his meals, to approximate, to the extent that it is possible,
a gentleman's supper in the dank debtor's prison. It's moreover
evident that, upon returning home from a laborious workday,
Little Dorrit immediately begins these ministrations, her industry set alongside the indolent image of her father, who receives
his daughter's attentions in a derelict state of undress. This scene
is intended to stir readerly indignance: we are by no means supposed to approve of Little Dorrit's father, who reaps the benefits
of his daughter's drudgery but, at the same time, cannot bear to
hear of her working outside the home—after all, it's a reminder
of his own fallen state. But Little Dorrit's choice not to eat so
that her father may eat even more functions, for Dickens, as a
crystalline differentiation between someone who is selfless and
morally upstanding and someone who is a worthless louse. It is
wildly unfair and unhealthy, and yet we are asked to celebrate
our heroine because of this grandiose suffering.

Little Dorrit's martyrlike relationship with food not only
communicates her fundamental goodness, it moreover suggests
that she possesses both civility and high manners lacking in the
rest of her family. And although she is more modest than her
charming older sister, Fanny, self-renunciation reinforces Little
Dorrit's own physical delicacy. Skinny figures were not deemed
au courant with the pervasiveness that they are today, but being
slim—and, in particular, having a slender waist—became a far-
reaching concern by the mid-nineteenth century, magnified
by the near-liturgical emphasis upon feminine performance of
beauty.[7] Ideals of Victorian femininity were famously adopted
from the languishing tuberculosis patient, who, contrary to suf-
ferers of smallpox and cholera, were not disfigured by disease

but instead beautified. Dying from tuberculosis brought graceful, even exquisite refinement: a lean and pallid form, bright eyes, and flushed crimson cheeks and lips.[8] Cumulatively, these admired traits also fashion what Michie describes as "aesthetics of deprivation," in which signs of starvation—becoming weakened and pale—signified gentility. "'Ladylike anorexia' became inscribed and prescriptive as fashion began to decree smaller and smaller waists," writes Michie.[9] Corset laces were pulled tight, brutalizing women's internal organs to such an extent that, apparently, the uterus was sometimes expelled from the vagina.[10]

By 1873, two doctors, Charles Lasègue and Sir William Withey Gull, had separately diagnosed anorexia nervosa—although similar diseases had been recorded by physicians for years prior to that.[11] "Sitomania," or the fear of eating, emerged in 1859 when American doctor William Stout Chipley observed it in a patient, and French doctor Pierre Briquet remarked upon symptoms we associate with bulimia—women who purged every time they ate.[12] In fact, Silver argues that "anorexia nervosa . . . is deeply rooted in Victorian values, ideologies, and aesthetics, which together helped define femininity in the nineteenth century."[13] This is to say that Victorian womanhood was culturally organized by punishing, corseted discipline that manifested in most areas of middle-class Victorian life, especially where food was concerned. Being hungry and enduring that hunger while abjuring physical yearnings buttressed nineteenth-century understandings of what it meant to navigate the world in a female body.

Moreover, this rampant fixation with female physical control was witched into a morality lesson, one that was at times indistinguishable from superstition. Italian criminologist and physician Cesare Lombroso and his son-in-law, historian Guglielmo Ferrero, authors of *The Female Offender* (1898), seeking to locate the probability of social deviance in a set of physical traits, claimed that women of ill repute were more likely to be overweight. "Stature, stretch of arms and length of limbs are less in all female criminals than in normals," they write, "and, in proportion to the stature, the average weight of prostitutes and murderesses is greater than in moral women."[14] Met with the baffling and mutable machinations of feminine bodies, these men set about overreading them with dogged, near-fanatical persistence.

One year later, American writer Ella Adelia Fletcher published *The Woman Beautiful* (1899), a zealously comprehensive guide to personal upkeep in which no fragment of the body escapes the author's precise eye. Her book was by no means the only one of its ilk. Just years before, Frances Mary Steele and Elizabeth Steele Adams co-wrote *Beauty of Form and Grace of Vesture* (1892), and Mrs. H. R. Haweis's *The Art of Beauty* was published in 1878.[15] Fletcher, like so many of her contemporaries, is determined to advise women on how they may perfect every inch of themselves. Among her exhaustive set of chapters are instructions on the beautification of the hand, the eye ("the soul's window"), and of course a "woman's crowning glory," her hair. Chapter ten takes as its focus "the visible seat of emotion," directing women in the proper care of "the mouth, lips, teeth, nose, and voice." Fletcher, moreover, tutors her readers in how to wear perfume, how to properly walk and breathe, as well as how to bathe. It's almost impressively compulsive.

Of course, nineteenth-century conduct literature on

feminine beauty would never overlook physique, and Fletcher's comments on the issue of weight are predictably punishing. Emphasizing the importance of a trim figure through flagrantly racist rhetoric, she remarks upon "some tribes in Central Africa where the perverted taste for excessive corpulence is carried to such an extent that the 'beauties' have to be supported when they walk abroad, their flesh hanging like pendent bags from their arms and legs."[16] Remarks like these, in which people of color are rendered as grotesquely subhuman, served as instructive shorthand—oftentimes, they still do: to drive one's point, engage the bigotry and xenophobia of one's readers by emphasizing a particular aesthetic or practice as foreign. It then seems all the more distasteful. In this case, Fletcher suggests that accepting or, worse, honoring a fat body would be akin to savagery and fundamentally opposed to white genteel decency.

In a chapter entitled "This So Ponderous Flesh and the Opposite Condition," Fletcher embarks on a merciless crusade against the rotund, with the following thesis: "Every additional pound of flesh beyond that required to round out the form to artistic lines and harmonic proportions is a menace to woman's beauty and health and usefulness, and, consequently, to her happiness."[17] With vigorous condemnation, she declares the impossibility of living contentedly and in good health if one is obese, a term she unsurprisingly leaves to vague interpretation. "But obesity is not merely a beauty-destroyer," Fletcher avers. "There is a stronger charge yet to make against this most uncomfortable condition. Even roly-poly plumpness takes all the youth out of a woman's face and step; and every ten pounds added beyond plumpness ages her."[18]

But concerns over health provide a mere translucent mask

for the abject prejudice motivating so much of the ink spilled over weight loss. Even those who take to their soapboxes with good intentions—a committed interest in public health, for example—are influenced by a long history of regimenting women's bodies: how they appear, how they move, and what they ingest. The too muchness of a fat body, Fletcher argues, results from a predisposition to pamper oneself and a disinclination to submit oneself to a more rigorous diet:

> The phlegmatic temperament, however, which takes life easily, is oftener than not prone to self-indulgence, and therefore peculiarly exposed to be a victim of over-assimilation and mal-assimilation of food. If allowed to run its course the disease is one of constant encroachment and may bring in its train most painful complications.[19]

Decadence can only be overlooked if its effects are imperceptible. Although we readily impart shame upon those whose behavior is immodest according to convention's standards, we're generally more forgiving of bodies that conceal their participation in so-called excesses. It is therefore the fat body—the one that demands more space for itself—that is reliably accused of laziness and gluttony. But it is not enough to levy these charges against women who cannot or choose not to abide by these sermons of thinness. By way of warning, Fletcher maintains that any woman who is socially designated as overweight must necessarily be miserable, a conclusion evidently reached by way of her own disgust:

Could the woman who has let this monster of flesh over-
master her by such insidious degrees that she cannot
remember the simple joy of lightness of foot, but for a
moment change her corporal prison for the litheness and
freedom of the alert Diana, who chases balls over the golf
links, she would move heaven and earth and accept any
discipline rather than submit to such death in life, as her
imprisonment actually is.[20]

Language like this—so overblown that its cruelty is nearly
obscured—can be difficult to consider in a critical context. It
might seem so absurd that it could only be thought an outlier,
the musings of some unhinged jerk. But we know better than
that. We know how this rhetoric tucks into a Western lineage
of fat-shaming with disturbing facility. Bodies that demand
more from us, that compel us to interrogate our ideologies
of beauty and fitness and health, have long been pilloried and
treated as vicious social interlopers. And as far as Fletcher is
concerned, a fat woman is precisely that. "Wherever the fat
woman finds herself in a crowd—and where can she avoid
it in the metropolis?—she is in effect an intruder," she proclaims. "For, she occupies twice the space to which she is
entitled, and inflicts upon her companions, through every one
of her excessive pounds, just so much additional fatigue and
discomfort."[21] Per *The Woman Beautiful* we are not speaking
in metaphors when we refer to the space allotted to women.
When a woman gains more weight than is perceived as acceptable, she metamorphoses into an "intruder" who has not
only squandered her own life but also become a burden upon
others by encroaching upon space that ought to be available to

them. She is thus multiply diminished, primarily as a woman and as a public citizen.

This tirade takes a final manipulative turn as Fletcher bemoans her own helplessness in her campaign for women's beauty against the fat woman's fleshy protective shield:

> Too often, this so redundant flesh seems to serve as a bullet-proof armor, repelling all consciousness of the rights of others. The woman who makes a god of her stomach is incorrigible, and I fear no word of mine will avail to induce her to reform. She is the innately selfish woman who makes her very existence an offense.[22]

Perhaps this condemnation is meant as some ghastly form of reverse psychology—to spur women into action by relinquishing them as lost causes. But it seems just as feasible that this vitriol is only that: another hyperbolic call to alienate women whose bodies do not perform according to Fletcher's interpretation of beauty. We've long insinuated that heavyset or obese women ought not exist: by refusing to produce clothing in their sizes, mocking them on public transportation, and countless other infractions and aggressions. Fletcher opts instead for icy clarity: to live in a fat body is offensive, so much so that it would be better not to live at all.

Visceral attacks of this kind against fatness also surface in fictional venues, reinforcing the tacit cultural prejudice burgeoning across the nineteenth century. The narrator of William Makepeace Thackeray's *Vanity Fair* scarcely offers a kind word to any of the novel's characters—in fact, he's probably Victorian literature's bitchiest narrator, omniscient or otherwise. But his indisputable punching bag is Joseph "Jos" Sedley, the cowardly and doltish dandy whose obesity the narrator describes with painstakingly nasty particularity:

> He was lazy, peevish, and a bon-vivant; the appearance of a lady frightened him beyond measure . . . His bulk caused Joseph much anxious thought and alarm—now and then he would make a desperate attempt to get rid of his superabundant fat, but his indolence and love of good living speedily got the better of these endeavours at reform, and he found himself again at his three meals a day. He was never well dressed: but he took the hugest pains to adorn his big person: and passed many hours daily in that occupation . . . His toilet-table was covered with as many pomatums and essences as ever were employed by an old beauty: he had tried, in order to give himself a waist, every girth, stay, and waist-band then invented.[23]

Often read by literary critics as a queer figure, the narrator emphasizes Jos's more feminine sensibilities, particularly his shyness, his love of fashion and fine food. As critic Joseph Litvak argues, "the girlish Jos threatens to expose sophistication itself as already sissified."[24] Thackeray never explicitly suggests that Jos is gay, although he indicates that his desire for food outweighs his interest in sex, and in fact he typically derives his most sensuous exercise from gobbling his meals. But Jos, who purposefully orders his flamboyant, bedazzling clothes to be made too tight (something every fat man does, according to the narrator) and whose vanity is a platter of perfume bottles, cannot be tolerated as a legitimate presentation of

masculinity. Instead, the novel subjects him to all manner of in-
dignities, while simultaneously lobbing the greatest of insults:
that he behaves in an excessively feminine manner. We are always reminded that his nonnormative male presentation—his
femininity—is inextricable from his "superabundant fat," and
in fact he becomes the novel's embodiment of shame: a blushing, stuttering oaf who drinks too much and regularly bemoans
his fatness—but purportedly lacks the discipline to whittle himself down to a more conventionally attractive weight. It would
be facile to interpret Jos's character as an attack on women:
he manifests a host of anxieties regarding queerness and embodiment. However, the novel's implication is that fatness,
and the perceived emotional compulsion of gluttony, render a
man more feminine, which is to say that they are undesirable
qualities more expected in a woman.

Yet Queen Victoria, who reigned while Thackeray and Carroll wrote, grew visibly plump over the course of her reign—
the impact of bearing nine children over seventeen years. "It
is true she would never be a great beauty, and always wres-
tled with her weight," Julia Baird writes in her biography of
the monarch.[25] Of course, her royal status shielded her from
more direct intervention; moreover, as the sovereign of an empire, a full figure signified capacious strength: a body that could
and had produced British heirs to the throne and that com-
manded attention despite her short stature (she was barely five
feet tall). The Queen Victoria Memorial, located at the front
of Buckingham Palace, portrays her as maternity in marble,
stern and dumpling-faced, enswathed in billowing robes. Still,
contemporaries remarked upon her appetites for food and for
sex, neither of which were seemly in a Victorian gentlewoman,

but could not be refused to the Crown. In a malevolent and unethical turn, Victoria's obstetrician, Charles Locock, gossiped to female friends that, during pregnancy, "She will be very ugly and enormously fat...She goes without stays or anything that keeps Her shape within bounds;...she is more like a barrel than anything else."[26] Locock's nasty account of the pregnant sovereign—women had just recently been socially excused from wearing corsets while pregnant, although he clearly found her doing so ghastly—anticipates Fletcher's *The Woman Beautiful*, with its acidic accusations against plump women. In the eyes of her uncharitable beholder, Queen Victoria, like so many powerful women, appeared neither impressive nor even human. She was a thing to look at, an unpleasant, bulging splotch that offended precisely because it did not incur desire.

———

Across decades of fiction, female heroines possess birdlike bone structure, as if pieced meticulously together from willow branches. From the first lines of George Eliot's *Middlemarch* (1871), Dorothea Brooke—the beloved, moral linchpin of her community—is presented as singularly lovely, with "that kind of beauty which seems to be thrown into relief by poor dress." It's her "finely formed" hands and her "stature and bearing"[27] that render her all the more statuesque for being simply adorned, and the narrator often insists upon her ascetic vigor while simultaneously drawing our attention to her features which, enhanced by health, ironically acquire the consumptive pallor and rouge so prized at the time: "[There] was a gem-like brightness on her coiled hair and in her hazel eyes; there was warm red life in her lips; her throat had a breathing whiteness above the differing white of the fur which itself seemed to wind about her neck."[28] In the logic of the narrative, Dorothea's virtuous heart is evident in her beauty, which is to say that it is manifested in her slender, pale form. She is sometimes described as otherworldly, likened to the Virgin Mary or to a deity, a creature whose stunning allure transcends the mortal coil. Ethereality, even death, is entangled with Victorian notions of beauty: possessing porcelain skin, dazzling eyes, and rosy cheeks suggested one's genetic predisposition to tuberculosis.[29] Dorothea—any woman who claimed such attractions—is deemed desirable because, rather than being too much, her physicality evokes its absolute opposite: she is airy, angelic, weightless.

Just over a decade before *Middlemarch* was published, Eliot's novel *Adam Bede* (1859) introduced readers to Methodist preacher Dinah Morris, who, like Dorothea, is revered as something of a saint. Like Little Dorrit, she starves herself, choosing instead to feed more impoverished members of the community. Her aunt, Rachel Poyser, bemoans,

But as for Dinah, poor child, she's niver likely to be buxom as long as she'll make her dinner o' cake and water, for the sake o' giving to them as want...as I told her, she went clean again' the Scriptur, for that says, "Love your neighbor as yourself," but I said, "If you loved your neighbour no better nor you do yourself, Dinah, it's little enough you'd do for him. You'd be thinking he might do well enough on a half-empty stomach."[30]

This commentary from Dinah's brusque but affectionate relation is meant to be comical—certain characters find Eliot's heroine to be a bit much when it comes to self-renunciation. But there is little doubt that Dinah exerts an emollient influence over those she encounters, and it's through her utter lack of egoism, her willingness to absorb others' sufferings, that she becomes such a balm. Religious fervor and denial of the flesh might inspire gentle quibbles, but they are by no means disparaged as baleful excess. Yet if it's difficult, at times, to believe in such a person—if it seems that Dinah could not possibly be human, with all the messy desires bred by personhood—the text perpetuates celestial associations. Like Dorothea Brooke, she calls to mind the Madonna, and is depicted early in the novel "covered with her long white dress, her pale face full of subdued emotion, almost like a lovely corpse into which the soul has returned charged with sublimer secrets and sublimer love."[31] Neither Dinah nor Little Dorrit manifest awareness of bodily requirement, and as Michie notes, Dinah is particularly determined to divorce herself from the flesh.[32] To be figured as "a lovely corpse" reiterates the inextricability of her beauty with annihilating self-effacement.

When the women of Victorian novels, particularly love interests, are voluptuous, we are carefully assured that those curves exist in only the most desirable of places. Nonetheless, these plumper, more explicitly sexy women often eschew propriety and, rather than exhibiting robust morals, become fallen women. Hetty Sorrel, Dinah's conceited, petty cousin, is as extravagantly eye-catching as Dinah is chastely fair. Today she'd be considered a bona fide knockout, and Eliot's description portrays her as a Victorian pin-up girl:

It is of little use for me to tell you that Hetty's cheek was like a rose-petal, that dimples played about her pouting lips, that her large dark eyes hid a soft roguishness under their long lashes, and that her curly hair, though all pushed back under her round cap while she was at work, stole back in dark delicate rings on her forehead, and about her white shell-like ears...Hetty's was a springtide beauty; it was the beauty of young frisking things, round-limbed, gambolling, circumventing you by a false air of innocence.[33]

Eliot's narrator protests that these specificities are futile, that unless you are besotted the way Hetty's gaggle of idolizing devotees are, you can't possibly comprehend the potency of her appeal. But the pleasure others take in beholding Hetty is mimicked by the evident pleasure of writing about someone so magnificent. It brings more somatic delight, I would suggest, to introduce a reader to Hetty than to Dinah or to Dorothea. But in a Victorian novel, a lavish, no-holds-barred description like this almost guarantees trouble for the possessor of such bounteous charms. Hetty knows she turns heads; she revels in her power to do so, and worships herself like a work of art. In so doing, she forgets the precarity of her position as a young country girl with no money. She becomes pregnant after having an affair with a rich gentleman who forsakes her—and, whether due to her curvy form, her performance of innocence,[34] or some combination, nobody notices. She delivers the child, abandons it, and after it is found dead, she is convicted of infanticide. A body like Hetty's is reason for alarm and for vigilance: for to be so soft, shapely, and luxurious is to invite sin. Ginevra Fanshawe, Lucy Snowe's coquettish student in Charlotte Brontë's *Villette* (1853), is more worldly than Hetty, and perhaps for this reason her flirtations do not result in tragedy. But even more so than Eliot, Brontë inscribes her character's sexual indiscretions through voluptuousness, not to mention explicit gluttony. In her narration, Lucy recounts allowing Ginevra to eat her food, a ritual that satisfies each party in this bizarre symbiosis—she also observes, indulgently, that "Miss Fanshawe's travels, gaieties, and flirtations agreed with her mightily; she had become quite plump, her cheeks looked as round as apples."[35] Ginevra's weight gain coincides with her imminent elopement, and just as the buxom Hetty is tethered to images of butter and cream, Ginevra, whose impressive appetite Lucy notes, is inclined to swipe bread and milk from a forbearing Lucy.[36] There are no "lovely corpses" here, but rather two fleshy women utterly of the earth, who grow drunk on the sweetness of their charms and the rollicking desire they kindle in others. This vainglorious rapture generally demands a price: Ginevra may wriggle away more or less unscathed, but for Hetty Sorrel, it is her undoing. Better to feed on crust and water, to eye comfort with holy detachment, than to feast and glory in a body that—if you are not very careful—will summon hell on earth.

Even now, conditioning against broader, rounder embodiments begins young. Books like the wretched *Maggie Goes on a Diet* (2011) by Paul Kramer, featuring a cover with Maggie wistfully holding a tiny pink dress against her body, are targeted at little girls, although in this case, the titular character is fourteen years old. It's a familiar image, one that emphasizes the woman who spills out from the edges of a bite-sized, hyper-feminine garment—yet another corset, one presented as aspirational. In Kramer's book, Maggie slogs through a miserable and alienated adolescence until she begins to lose weight, at which point she is deemed worthy of female friendship and, ultimately, romantic male attention. I bought a copy of *Maggie Goes on a Diet* specifically as book research. The study of it was so blisteringly maddening that I've since contemplated setting it on fire.

And of course this preoccupation has long emanated from the nucleus of popular culture, palpating through the zeitgeist. Though some argue that Marilyn Monroe was hailed as a great beauty, curves and all, we must also remember that she was trained, even compelled, to appear docile and pliable. What's more, her clothes, which were custom-made, accommodated her striking hourglass shape, but according to contemporary sizing, might have, at most, run somewhere between American sizes 8 and 12—hardly "plus size."[37] While it's true that today's fashion industry scarcely tolerates these sizes, we continue to abide by warped logic when we attempt to render Monroe an icon for bigger women. Yet her fleshy too muchness was always subjected to inexorable scrutiny, her body eyed and strapped into the girdle that would package her, according to Hollywood's ravenous estimations, in the most befitting and lucrative ways.

The shape of the container may slightly shift, a membranous nip or tuck here and there, but it is always precisely that—containability—at issue: we merely treat it as a "new" problem, its novelty rendered through cultural amnesia. When Lena Dunham first got naked in HBO's *Girls*, hordes of viewers were outraged that someone larger than a size two would dare subject viewers to her flesh. After all, Dunham's body is not tame: it is tattooed, substantial, and rotund; most of us could not encircle her waist with our hands. She is, as Anne Helen Petersen argues, "too naked," which is to say, she refuses to tidy and burnish herself into a more palatable shape; she resists becoming the artfully restrained "nude." "The naked body is raw, without pretense, bare; the nude is nakedness refined: smoothed, proportional, pleasing," Petersen delineates. "Dunham becomes 'too naked,' then, when she refuses to turn herself into a nude, insisting on showcasing her body exactly as it appears."[38]

For a man to watch such a woman fuck is to confront aesthetic defiance—we were not made for you, and we don't care what you like—and, possibly, to contemplate the possibility of his own physical weakness. Here is a woman who is firm, thick, implacable. Try as you might to sidle next to her in a murky bar or tug her arm on a dance floor or nudge her to the side on the subway, she will not budge. In a similar vein, when Elizabeth Taylor, one of the Western world's most venerated beauties, gained weight in old age and illness, she became, with the swiftness of the public's tongue, a punchline. The erotic chasm between the trim, submissive body and one weathered and fat prompts uneasy laughter: how strange that this body has become illegible and wild, how unnerving that the woman has too.

———

Weight necessarily dominates this conversation but, in unsettling step with Lewis Carroll, American culture fears bodily fluctuations in most of their manifestations. If many of us yearned to fill our training bras, girls who developed breasts before junior high were swiftly reduced to the sum of their sexualized parts. A pubescent girl incites particular anxiety because her changes are swift and more visible; she is more liable to slip out of reach. On a man, a prominent nose might be conceived as part of his charm, even his desirability—in Darren Aronofsky's *Black Swan* (2010), Vincent Cassel is filmed from angles that render his schnoz almost phallic, particularly when he is grasping at Natalie Portman's quivering, sylphlike Nina. But Jennifer Grey, despite the walloping success of her turn in *Dirty Dancing* (1987), underwent rhinoplasty in the 1990s, perhaps concerned that her nose rendered her less attractive as a female lead. For all those who hail Barbra Streisand as a unique beauty, there are plenty who have ridiculed her appearance for its lack of symmetry. Every one of us is at liberty to modify our bodies in whatever ways make them more livable or beautiful or pleasurable to us, be it a nose job, liposuction, a breast reduction, or Botox. But we are always sifting through the dross, trying to discern what we are responding to at the bottom of our aesthetic desires. And regardless of what might motivate a rhinoplasty, echoes of racism and anti-Semitism imbue the discourse around noses; after all, prejudice and condemnations of too muchness often share a bed. Anything is too much for us when it is foreign or unfamiliar.

This discourse grows even more fraught around hair, and becomes especially steeped in racism. Perhaps one reason J. K. Rowling so easily envisions Hermione Granger as black is because so much negative attention is drawn to her "frizzy" mane. Harry and Ron only fully recognize her sexual possibility when she straightens it for a school dance: her overall appearance thus becomes tamer and more aesthetically restrained, a picture the heroic doofuses, salivating as they do over the modelesque Fleur Delacour, can better understand.

A black woman's natural hair, unchastened by products or flat iron, is bound to agitate racist bluster, and the Afro especially elicits glowers of suspicion. In the 1970s a sultry Pam Grier wore her Afro in so-called blaxploitation films, but these flicks were regarded by white viewers as trashy: fetish sites for people aroused by fantasies of asserting their power over black bodies. In stark contrast, Ali MacGraw became a symbol of romantic feminine fragility in *Love Story* (1970)—Hollywood cool embodied as white beauty with sleek, tamed hair. Although Faye Dunaway took on more daring female roles in edgy films like *Bonnie and Clyde* (1967), her hair was always perfectly coiffed and her body primly dressed and slim. Grier has long been regarded as an icon among black women, but the Afro—considered an aesthetic political statement in the 1960s signifying Black Power—has for decades been a focal point of discrimination, racially stigmatized as unruly against a sheaf of pliable Caucasian hair.

Prejudice against black hair endures as a rank and rampant presence, especially visible in bad-faith disciplinary measures. In May 2017 high school junior Jenesis Johnson was beset by both her teacher and assistant principal at North Florida Christian in Tallahassee, Florida, because her Afro was deemed inappropriate in a scholastic environment. According to Johnson, the assistant principal expressed her distaste blatantly: "She said, your hair is extreme and faddish and out of control. It's all over the place." It was, purportedly, a "distraction" that would merit dismissal from school if Johnson did not alter her style to something pronounced trim and sufficiently compliant by the school's administration.[39] It's an incident that is as discriminatory and shaming as it is commonplace: black students are charged with a litany of mythical offenses, for instance, wearing their hair in braids[40] or in dreadlocks. Each occasion reinforces the fact that when a marginalized person draws attention to herself with aesthetic decisions deemed conspicuous, white authority reels, thunderstruck at her audacious demand for visibility. It is too much, the bloom of an Afro, even if its wearer takes logistics into consideration and, like Johnson, ensured that she never obscured a classmate's view in class. It is too much, although an Afro is natural hair given space and permission to grow.

What is considered "natural" is so often at the crux when women are accused of too muchness, and in this case, there seems to be no winning. After all, long, ropey braids are verboten as well, precisely because they are so often comprised of hair extensions. What would be suitable—what would appease these school administrators—is the forced, and decidedly unnatural, application of Caucasian trimmings. Dorothy Dandridge's curls, black hair shorn to approximate the styles of other 1950s Hollywood starlets—that might be judged acceptable. As for Pam Grier's Afro: these schools protested, "Too much."

In the meantime, celebrities like Solange Knowles, Tracee Ellis Ross, Shonda Rhimes, and Uzo Aduba walk red carpets in their natural hair, a privileged space, to be sure, but one that nonetheless affords prime visibility in a fashion industrial complex enduringly obsessed with everything that is small and white. Beyoncé, in her 2016 single "Formation," also makes no apologies in her delineations of preference: "I like my baby hair, with baby hair and afros." And in 2019, Lizzo released "Juice," in which she joyfully, and with anthemic aplomb, declares that she will claim space as she pleases and rejoice in it. "No, I'm not a snack at all / Look baby, I'm the whole damn meal," she sings, exulting in her whopping femininity. Our culture of white supremacy might spit and sputter with indignance, but too many are intent that it should not prevail. Whatever the circumference of one's nose, one's thighs, one's hair—permission is irrelevent to the matter; it's merely a fiction born from power. There is always space, and it ought to be claimed.

———

Writing is a sedentary and vexed enterprise. I have always known this, although it became increasingly evident in graduate school, when I concluded each semester crouched over my laptop in the shadow of a gargantuan book cocoon. Now that I write for a living, it is something I know with confidence. I type across days and weeks and months; my body settles into the shallow dent of the couch cushion, flesh, stonelike, succumbing to its environment. By the evening my leg and butt muscles hum and the inside of my back seems to flicker, agitation born from inertia. Bone-tired and generally bewildered as to what sort of progress I'm making on my current project, I wallow, my brain seeking out nooks of displeasure. Always reliable is my persistent fear that I'm incapable of meaningful balance—of laboring and living in equal measure, of breaths of fresh air and walks around the block and the whole lousy catechism of wellness. I grab at my stomach, my thighs, and now and then I sob bitterly, although nothing about my appearance has meaningfully changed. I shriek to my husband that I am ugly and spent. I fall asleep in the same spot that I have spent the day writing until he gently nudges me to bed.

When I'm preoccupied by a grueling enterprise—drafting a lengthy essay or wading through extensive, mind-addling revisions—it evacuates me of disposable energy. I belong to a gym, but taking the time to go typically seems a temporal luxury. I've begun following YouTube fitness instructors, glaring at their velvety toned abdomens as I flounder through "quick sweat" cardio routines that I can accomplish within thirty minutes—my cat demurely overseeing my exertions from the couch. But like mold, Ella Adelia Fletcher creeps into my head: I am not the Woman Beautiful. I am the Woman Lazy and the Woman Neurotic and the Woman Out of Her Fucking Wits. I am the woman who, even though she has no children and *does* have a husband who coddles her, can only assume scattering responsibilities before abruptly ceasing regular personal maintenance.

Lately, in my distress, I'll long for my mother, only to recall that conversation at the cusp of her death, which traveled the topical route of weight loss. I am not angry with her for this, but the recollection of it unmoors me anew, amidst the ambient fog of stress, grief, and a body image that, always tenuous at best, sometimes has the tendency to rapidly deflate. The varying vectors of my too muchness—emotional, mental, physical— converge to produce a body dysmorphic mêlée, and I am undone as a result.

Here, another person might be able to supply a sunny summation to this testimony; I cannot. But if writing has, at times, whittled me down to my rawest self, it has simultaneously etched out a pathway to something better (I suspect this may be the paradox of creative endeavors). I see, in my purview, the possibility for what I know and what I feel to melt together and stiffen like a fist. Because I know that Ella Adelia Fletcher penned a truly monstrous tract of drivel. I know, too, that Little Dorrit ought to have eaten her own dinner with relish, rather than safeguarding it for her feckless father. And I certainly know that one should never model their aesthetic on a person suffering from an acute bacterial infection in the lungs. But when we are fat, when our hair defies gravity, when our noses are not perfectly pinchable, we're interpreted as wild and unruly, and often foreign. This—I know, I feel—is good. We remind all those buttressed and soothed by patriarchy that we cannot always be trusted to comply and, thus, we become threats, fuses primed to be lit.

Chapter Six

CRAZY

There is no looking glass here and I don't know what I am like now. I remember watching myself brush my hair and how my eyes looked back at me. The girl I saw was myself yet not quite myself. Long ago when I was a child and very lonely I tried to kiss her. But the glass was between us—hard, cold and misted over with my breath. Now they have taken everything away. What am I doing in this place and who am I?

—*Wide Sargasso Sea*, Jean Rhys

In many ways, singer Lana Del Rey's aesthetic cultivates a familiar and well-traveled celebrity image: white Old Hollywood glamour, feminine vulnerability that quivers like petals in rain, and luxuriant sex appeal. She sings with a sweetness that oscillates between girlish conspiracy and world-weary languor. But then, there's something else, too, something less expected. According to her lyrics, she's a little bit fucked up—not to an incapacitating degree, mind you, but enough to broadcast a tragically intense sensibility.

This is to say that Del Rey often refers to herself, sometimes obliquely but very often explicitly, as "crazy" or "insane." In the 2011 single "Born to Die" from her second album by the same name, she croons, "You like your girls insane," indicating through the song's romantic nihilist context that she is one such girl. On the same 2012 album, "Off to the Races" couples insanity with drunken vulnerability—Del Rey is the unhinged damsel in distress par excellence: "'Cause he knows I'm wasted / Facing time again at Rikers Island / And I won't get out / Because I'm crazy, baby / I need you to come here and save me." On "Cruel World," the first track on her 2014 album *Ultraviolence*, she spins a self-mythology of the sad party girl with these languid verses: "Put my little red party dress on / Everybody knows that I'm a mess, I'm crazy, yeah." (Contrastingly, the love interest to whom the song is addressed is "crazy for [her].") *Ultraviolence* especially trades in this variety of depressed chic, with songs like "Sad Girl" and "Pretty When You Cry"; the latter in particular exemplifies our cultural fetishization of feminine sorrow. No ugly crying for Del Rey, that's for certain, only elegant distress, free of snot and gulping sobs.

Still, her hyperperformative ennui is sly—Del Rey is never fully self-effacing, and her investment in the fantasy implies that it could be just that, a tongue-in-cheek presentation of eroticized sadness that has endured since Ophelia. To some extent, this is likely the case. And yet, because the nuance is not wholly perceptible, and ultimately dependent upon interpretation, the image sticks to Del Rey all the same, rendering her desirable through her specific hyper-feminine emotional fragility: a woman who, by her own account, is both fucked up and down to fuck; sad, but never too far gone to paint her pout into a deep crimson.

It's an option exclusively available to white women—to claim to be both genteel and crazy, delicate and ever so slightly unhinged. And when, on her 2017 album *Lust for Life*, Del Rey shifts—for the better, I would argue—toward more assertive emotional nakedness, the transition is amply oiled by her Caucasian beauty. Decisively embracing her melodrama is an alternative afforded to those whose too muchness is considered more socially palatable—to those who need not resist the stereotypes of walloping mental instability ascribed to people of color, particularly black women. Although "In My Feelings" seems like a sort of anthem to too muchness—Del Rey sings about crying into her coffee and in the middle of orgasm, only to demand, with sopranic defiance, "Who's doper than this bitch? Who's freer than me?"—it's white privilege that permits her to elude the gooey label of mental illness and rearticulate herself according to a new, more puissant interpretation. For that matter, it's that same privilege that enables her to claim a wild vulnerability as fortifying and empowered.

Modern Western society has for centuries pathologized women's mental health, medicalizing and stigmatizing any aberration from so-called psychological normalcy. Women have long been encouraged, through medication and sundry other means, to suppress the symptoms of mental illness into invisibility, grinding the serrated edges of our emotional expression into smooth, palatable visages. In the meantime, as Anglo and American culture have explored this capacious and unwieldy matter, they have both fetishized and aestheticized it, diminishing and refashioning psychological suffering as something cute, tame, and thoroughly whitewashed. In the broadest terms, mental illness is too muchness with a diagnosis. Of course, in an effort to butt against prevailing conceptions of mental illness, we should never present struggles with depression, anxiety, or any other psychiatric condition as uniformly positive phenomena. It is not for us to speak for others: too muchness, and what it means to inhabit it, can only be assessed by the individual, and experiences of it are endlessly specific. However, because it is already dangerous to live as an "intense" or emotionally voluble woman, the social atmosphere is doubly inhospitable to those who contend with chemical imbalances and the ways in which they manifest themselves. And because American culture shudders in the face of most visible feminine excesses, liberally affixing the label "crazy" to any socially inconvenient behavior, the labile boundaries between emotional intensity and diagnosable illness are always collapsing, rearticulated by hegemonic masculinity not as fundamentally personal experiences to be interpreted by the individual, but as conditions unworthy of distinction, significant only as symptoms that must be suppressed.

In some ways, cultural receptions of women's mental health can be understood as elaborated reactions to "ugly crying," a term coined by Oprah Winfrey and overwhelmingly tethered to femininity, which has taken on a life of its own. Superficially, it refers to crying with such gusto that one's face is slick with fluids and contorted in an unappealing way. Actress Claire Danes is often regarded as the patron saint of ugly crying (think of that tragic moment in Baz Luhrmann's 1996 *Romeo + Juliet* when she, the titular heroine, awakens to realize that her true love is dead and, before choosing death herself, heaves heavy, viscous sobs). There is, too, the ubiquitous Kim Kardashian meme in which her face is crumpled, mid-weep. But referring to crying as "ugly" gestures to a culture that is agitated by acute misery, that recoils at the illegibility of a woman's face when, ensconced in the depths of her distress, she does not, cannot, think about her impact on those around her. It registers as disgust and secondhand embarrassment, thinly veiled, masquerades as downcast eyes and about-faces, a retreat en masse from a woman wailing that she wants to die. Barring the instances where they coincide with "genius," struggles with mental health, in all their gnawing, raw reality, do not merely render a woman stigmatized for her illness, but for her deviation from sexual desirability and femininity. By gussying up the image of women's mental health, we have condemned anew the—so-called—madwoman to the attic.

Fictionalized representations of women's mental illness reveal the extent to which we circumscribe representations of suffering; even what is deemed appropriate to view from a safe distance is limited. Predominantly focused on white women's experiences, nineteenth-century Anglo culture's influence upon tacitly approved aesthetics for "crazy" women accounts for the endurance of these whitewashed narratives. Romantic and Victorian writers were fascinated by mental illness and by society's anxiety over its relative invisibility. At the time, perspectives were evolving regarding care for mentally ill patients: an 1845 article in the *Westminster Review* claims that "a pervading air of comfort and cheerfulness" circulates throughout institutions rather than buildings "erected after the fashion of prisons or dungeons" where "lunatics" were chained and whipped and altogether handled with brutality.[1] These were urgently necessary reforms. Nonetheless, it is un-surprising that nineteenth-century Britons, including authors, did not always convey sympathy for those who were variously afflicted.

In Jane Austen's 1813 novel *Pride and Prejudice*—and in its multiple adaptations—Mrs. Bennet's fretfulness is presented as comedic absurdity, an index of her dullness and incapacity for serious thought. For many of us, our image of the much aggrieved Mrs. Bennet is shaped by British actress Alison Stead-man, who performs the role in the BBC's 1995 miniseries with deft, whooping buffoonery. Austen likely would have been delighted by the performance and considered it a faithful rendering: after all, her narrator evinces precious little respect for the character. "*Her* mind was less difficult to develop," writes Austen of the Bennet matriarch. "She was a woman of mean understanding, little information, and uncertain temper. When she was discontented she fancied herself nervous. The business of her life was to get her daughters married; its so-lace was visiting and news."[2] The novel treats Mrs. Bennet not only as a simpleton, but also as a hypochondriac whose anxiety over her daughters' marital futures is both trivial and a fruit-less monomania. And yet, as a mother of five daughters and no sons in an era when women could not inherit property, her ru-minations over suitable husbands are not unfounded. Once Mr. Bennet kicks the bucket, the family home, Longbourn, will be wrested from them and delivered to his nephew, the simpering Mr. Collins.

As readers, we also have reason to believe that the Bennet

daughters have little to no fortune of their own. Their father, for all the disdain with which he regards his silly wife, is by no means as strategic as he might have been, having assumed that he would, at some point, sire a son. All this is to say that Mrs. Bennet's fears, albeit expressed with a certain trill vacuity and often without consideration of larger contexts, are fundamentally reasonable. And perhaps if she were depicted as possessing more grace and poise, the narrator might ask us to consider the burden of mothering a team of daughters with no means to care for them if she outlives her husband (Mrs. Dashwood of *Sense and Sensibility* is, for instance, treated far more kindly in similar circumstances). But we're meant to regard Mrs. Bennet as years past sexual appeal and almost pathologically foolish; her anxieties and hypochondria are only concerns due to their social ramifications. Her overeagerness to pair off her daughters, most particularly Jane, the eldest and prettiest, backfires in the most flamboyant ways when they're in polite company. Mrs. Bennet, to say the least, is not stifled by subtlety, and can cause the more reasonable members of her family acute embarrassment, particularly the novel's heroine and second eldest Bennet daughter, Elizabeth. We are concerned for the girls' welfare, to be sure, but not because Mrs. Bennet has sounded the alarm. And as for her motherly concern and the strife it engenders, we are hardly asked to consider it at all.

Although Austen gestures to mental instabilities in characters like Mrs. Bennet or *Sense and Sensibility*'s Marianne Dashwood, she is characteristically subdued and gracefully snarky, maintaining her focus on the comedy of English manners. By contrast, Victorian sensation novelists like Mary Elizabeth Braddon waded eagerly into the subject, and in so doing poked at the larger cultural solicitude surrounding the obscure diagnosis of "madness" and the fear that it would contaminate healthy minds like so much London smog. In *Lady Audley's Secret* (1862), her most famous novel, Braddon writes,

> Mad-houses are large and only too numerous; yet surely it is strange they are not larger, when we think of how many helpless wretches must beat their brains against this hopeless persistence of the orderly outward world, as compared with the storm and tempest, the riot and confusion within:—when we remember how many minds must tremble upon the narrow boundary between reason and unreason, mad to-day and sane to-morrow, mad yesterday and sane to-day.[3]

Lady Audley's Secret is a murder mystery, but it is above all a near-claustrophobic examination of the titular Lady Audley, or Lucy Graham, a young, somewhat trivial woman of mysterious origins who marries the gentle, middle-aged Sir Michael Audley and, soon after, is implicated in the disappearance of George Talboys, the dear friend of her husband's nephew, Robert Audley, who not a few believe to be in love with George: he ultimately marries Clara Talboys, who bears a striking resemblance to her brother. Robert embarks on a dogged search for his missing friend, and in the process learns that Lucy has, over the course of her short life, assumed multiple identities and committed a slew of crimes in order to achieve the comforts of wealth and to divest herself of her legacy: lunacy. The women in her family have suffered an unnamed but apparently severe mental disease, and her mother was confined to an asylum when she was young. Lucy's grandmother, we learn, died in a similarly unraveled state.

Lucy functions as both a vessel for Victorian domestic anxieties and as an avatar for the larger fears engendered by "madness." She does the unspeakable: abandons her child and husband and, through the allure of physical charms, achieves upward social mobility at a time when those with power and wealth relied on social hierarchies both for cultural coherence and as a means of ossifying their plush station above the unwashed masses. Lucy's mental illness, then, not only signifies the perils of female sexuality—and what it might conceal—as well as the instability of the female psyche, but also the contamination of the upper class by an unworthy interloper (aristocratic Victorians were not especially concerned with diversifying the gene pool). But Lucy's lifelong terror that she is, by virtue of her lineage, doomed to insanity evokes the marrow-deep terror among contemporaries that their own blood could be sullied and that they could therefore do nothing to prevent their own mental deterioration.

And say one did suffer from a psychological affliction—the stain of stigma upon one's family would be indelible. Moreover, though care for the mentally ill was finally becoming more humane, a Victorian asylum was by all accounts a dismal place, and in literature it is proffered as the ideal spot to disappear a person who is dangerous, or merely inconvenient. It was regarded as such beyond the page, too. In February 2019, letters revealed that Charles Dickens, weary of his wife, Catherine, attempted to have her imprisoned in an asylum. The couple had been wed for two decades, and Catherine had borne Charles ten children while he cultivated his literary celebrity. But Dickens was eager to persist in his affair with Ellen Ternan, a young actress, and Catherine Dickens was clear as to where she stood in her husband's affections. She confided in a friend, Edward Dutton Cook, that her husband no longer loved her and that he had exerted disturbing efforts to displace her. "He even tried to shut her up in a lunatic asylum, poor thing!" Dutton Cook wrote. "But bad as the law is in regard to proof of insanity he could not quite wrest it to his purpose."[4] Unquestionably, Dickens's treatment of his wife was atrocious—there's hefty evidence that Dickens was not an especially pleasant specimen of man—and it's fortunate that the law, so often the enemy of women, did not facilitate his lurid scheme. For, as Dutton Cook indicates, that was not necessarily a given. There's good reason that the "mad-house" lurks as an obscure menace in nineteenth-century fiction; it needles readers with two simultaneous fears: that they could be insane without knowing it, and, moreover, that they could somehow be wrongfully imprisoned, even condemned to madness through an erroneous life sentence—or, in Dickens's case, through a manipulative lie—in which they are locked up with "crazy" folks. Braddon's narrator could be considered empathetic—we're all mad here, as the Cheshire Cat tells Alice, and isn't it a beastly trudge when we're concealing a soul that's in turmoil? But Braddon's depiction of the easy slippage into insanity is almost certainly meant, first and foremost, to titillate, to remind readers that they could, unbeknownst to them, be walking among "mad people," that the symptoms are not always written on the body in a way convenient to those who wish to discriminate.

Disability, like any manifestation of otherness or marginalized difference, is habitually treated as a means of negative identification: we define ourselves against that which we are not, or more appropriately, against the things we fear or consider loathsome. Too muchness, while by no means synonymous with disability, typically yields a similar reaction. When we mark something as excessive, we shore up our confidence that we perform according to social metrics of appropriateness. We are neither too emotional, nor too talkative, nor too sexual, nor too agitated—and so forth. When it comes to mental illness, we're especially thirsty for clues that buttress our own normativity. "There's always a touch of fascination in revulsion," writes Susanna Kaysen in her mental illness memoir, *Girl, Interrupted*. "Could that happen to me? The less likely the terrible thing is to happen, the less frightening it is to look at or imagine. A person who doesn't talk to herself or stare off into nothingness is therefore more alarming than a person who does."[5] Braddon's titular character is the former—distractingly beautiful, harboring a disorder that is mostly imperceptible and, when it is revealed, vaguely, elliptically rendered:

> "I have talked to the lady," [the physician] said quietly, "and we understand each other very well. There is latent insanity! Insanity which might never appear; or which might appear only once or twice in a life-time. It would be *dementia* in its worst phase perhaps: acute mania; but its duration would be very brief, and it would only arise under extreme mental pressure. The lady is not mad; but she has the hereditary taint in her blood. She has the cunning of madness, with the prudence of intelligence. I will tell you what she is, Mr. Audley. She is dangerous!"[6]

This physician's diagnosis indicates a few things, first and foremost that he is shit at his job, or, to give him the benefit of the doubt: he is relying heavily on his misogyny in order to determine Lucy's condition. The novel has already revealed that her mother was confined to an asylum, and that because madness was ostensibly a fundamentally feminine condition, one passed from mother to daughter, Lucy has long assumed that she would one day meet the same fate. The physician echoes her own premonitions, his analysis buttressed by his sexism: she is indelibly stained by her mother's illness, assumed to be insane even when her deeds would not necessarily point to this.

Yet as critic Lyn Pykett remarks, many debate whether or not Lucy is, in fact, mentally ill, or instead a devious mind bundled away in an asylum in order to protect society from the mirage of her innocent comeliness. Then—and in many cases, now—"madness was used to label and manage dangerous, disruptive femininity in the nineteenth century."[7] But this question over Lucy's mental health, the possibility that she could be misdiagnosed or even lying, so subtle are her symptoms, renders her all the more frightening to behold precisely because her behavior cannot be differentiated and cordoned off as definitive signifiers of madness. "Someone who acts 'normal' raises the uncomfortable question, What's the difference between that person and me?" writes Kaysen, "which leads to the question, What's keeping me out of the looney bin?"[8] Kaysen suggests that our compulsion to stigmatize anyone who has sought treatment for mental illness is a method of bracing the illusion that sanity, rather than a naturalized construct, is something that can be clearly deduced—"a general taint is useful," she explains, in order to dispense with the hazards of nuance and instead rely on broad, stigmatizing generalizations, a paintbrush that delivers an indelible mark, at once a false exoneration for some—you are sane, you are pure—and damnation for others: you were never sane like the rest of us; you were tainted and weird and grotesque, and you always will be.[9]

The inheritance of female madness and its conceptual entanglement with moral dissipation emerges again and again across Victorian fiction, the most famous example being the vengeful Creole Bertha Mason who, in *Jane Eyre* (1847), serves as the obstruction to the titular character's happiness: she is Mr. Rochester's first wife, married because she was alluringly beautiful; despised because she was, allegedly, hypersexual and boozy; and ultimately incarcerated in his attic as a purported kindness because her mental degeneration would have otherwise required her to be institutionalized. The novel implicates her ambiguous heritage as fertile breeding ground for madness. Victorian readers would have understood the assignment of "Creole" as a marker of racial impurity, someone whose lineage intermingled European and non-European blood. The specificities of Bertha's parentage are obscure: her father was a European colonist in the West Indies.[10] Her mother was a native of the archipelago where Bertha was born, and she, like her daughter, was deemed insane. Ultimately, the specificities of DNA and psychology matter less than the beclouded assessments of British men like Rochester, who require very little information—only that she is neither white nor mentally normative—in order to distrust and disrespect her. Like Lucy Graham, it's unclear what, precisely, her diagnosis would have been; the novel instead seems to posit that mental illness comes as just deserts for those who indulge their too muchness—in Bertha's case, those who enjoy sex and libations and a good party. Rochester's account of her to Jane, meant to inspire sympathy, steams with racist loathing:

> I lived with that woman upstairs four years, and before that time she had tried me indeed: her character ripened and developed with frightful rapidity; her vices sprang up fast and rank: they were so strong, only cruelty could check them, and I would not use cruelty. What a pigmy intellect she had, and what giant propensities! How fearful were the curses those propensities entailed on me! Bertha Mason, the true daughter of an infamous mother, dragged me through all the hideous and degrading agonies which must attend a man bound to a wife at once intemperate and unchaste.[11]

The "infamous mother" to whom Rochester refers is labeled as such because—why else—she, presumably Jamaican like her daughter, is "mad, and shut up in a lunatic asylum."[12] Poor Rochester, bewitched by a woman of the island, was content enough to marry a person of mixed race when he was stupefied with wine and rich food and the dazzle of Bertha's wealth and charms. But as he wails to Jane, he was duped into wedlock with a woman "intemperate and unchaste," with "a pigmy intellect." To be clear, marriage to Bertha Mason doesn't exactly sound like a picnic; perhaps she was, as Rochester suggests, a woman motivated by lascivious cruelty and self-destructive indulgence. Perhaps, but that simply isn't what matters most. Just as Lucy Graham's

madness is an obscure condition easily conflated with her desire
for upward mobility and the sexual prowess that enables it,
Bertha's Creoleness and unapologetic desire are implied as the
soil that nourishes her own mental illness. A woman who
wants, who hungers—especially if she is a woman of color—
might as well be insane. Her temperament is in opposition to
the ideological structures, Victorian and present-day, that demand women who are silent, starved, and, in the face of it all,
complacent. How many mental illnesses have gone untreated
because they manifested in quieter, more discreet ways?

When Jean Rhys, a British author born on the island of
Dominica, wrote her novella *Wide Sargasso Sea* (1966), it was
meant as a corrective and a critique of *Jane Eyre*'s flagrant dehumanization and erasure of Bertha Mason. Focusing instead
on Bertha—or Antoinette, as she is called before her husband
renames her—Rhys reminds us that one vantage point blinkered by racism, misogyny, and a colonialist mind-set can utterly
deform a narrative and the woman thrust from its center.

Sections of *Wide Sargasso Sea* are narrated by Antoinette's
unnamed husband, whom we assume to be a young Rochester.
After they wed, he gazes with fatigue at the verdant Caribbean
landscape, its relentless vibrancy an extension of his trepidation
regarding his Jamaican wife:

> Everything is too much, I felt as I rode wearily after her.
> Too much blue, too much purple, too much green. The
> flowers too red, the mountains to high, the hills too near.
> And the woman is a stranger. Her pleading expression an-
> noys me. I have not bought her, she has bought me, or so
> she thinks.[13]

It's not unusual that an Englishman, accustomed to a muted atmosphere of porpoise-gray skies and the slump of fog, would be overcome by an island beaming with lush brightness from every corner. And yet, Rochester—we'll refer to him as Rochester for simplicity's sake—complains about the landscape as a prelude to his misgivings regarding Antoinette, which indicate on their own that she is "too much" for him, that her "pleading" visage broadcasts a glut of unreciprocated longing. As a child, Antoinette endures the teasing of village children who accuse her of madness because her mother has suffered an emotional collapse; the perception of mental illness as a feminine inheritance, Rhys suggests, is not exclusive to Western society. But if Antoinette loses herself by the end of the novella, it is through her husband's calculating barbarity: his insistence that she "be" Bertha instead of Antoinette, thereby negating her identity; his efforts to diminish her through performative infidelity—he sleeps with a servant where she can overhear; and his brash, racist cruelty within a community where, as a mulatta, her sense of belonging is already tenuous. He whittles her down, broad blossom to limp, broken stem, contesting every syllable that comprises her reality until, finally, he can bury her in an English manor attic where Antoinette's timeline slips away and she becomes a stranger to herself, lonesome and bereft of any anchoring selfhood.

Lady Audley's Secret, Jane Eyre, and, by extension, *Wide Sargasso Sea* convey narratives of mental illness that are steeped in gothic mystery, echoed by Charlotte Perkins Gilman's 1892 short story "The Yellow Wallpaper," which chronicles a woman's mental breakdown, sometimes interpreted as postpartum depression run amok due to the smothering and shoddy care of her smug husband. Gilman's story, told from the perspective of the unnamed woman, depicts the deleterious impact of a so-called "rest cure," prescribed by the narrator's physician husband, John. Monitoring and regimenting her every remark or twitch, John demands that his wife neither write nor visit with her family whose company she enjoys—activities that are designated as overly stimulating, and that she resist her urge to express to him the anxieties crackling inside of her head. With the rare exception of a severely circumscribed walk in the garden, the narrator is confined to a bedroom papered a ghastly yellow, tucked into a bed that is nailed to the floor. She harbors doubts that what her husband has ordered is at all helpful; in fact, she suggests at the start that this oppressive mental health regime will harm more than it remedies:

> John is a physician, and *perhaps*—(I would not say it to a living soul, of course, but this is dead paper and a great relief to my mind)—*perhaps* that is one reason I do not get well faster.
>
> You see, he does not believe I am sick! And what can one do?
>
> If a physician of high standing, and one's own husband, assures friends and relatives that there is really nothing the matter with one but temporary nervous depression— a slight hysterical tendency—what is one to do?[14]

Very often, women are not permitted to be sick—to experience pain—on their own terms, particularly in ways that would be received as illegible or queasy in their intensity. We aren't trusted to decipher the stimuli percolating in our brains or in our bodies. The narrator of "The Yellow Wallpaper" is, for all intents and purposes, forbidden from presenting symptoms that would contest her husband's diagnosis, or, at best, her accounts are discarded or recontextualized to suit the absurdly generalized, catchall description of hysteria. She writes on the sly, for "relief," but in particular so that she may assert the validity of her discernments, to carve out territory where they may exist without the threat of negation. "John does not know how much I really suffer," she confides. "He knows there is no reason to suffer, and that satisfies him."[15] The narrator understands all too clearly that she cannot trouble what John "knows" with the articulation of her own experience. His blinkered assumptions supersede anything his wife could discern by virtue of living in her body.

Even the inventions of her imagination, evermore feverish, become fodder for chastisement, rather than concern:

> I always fancy I see people walking in these numerous paths and arbors, but John has cautioned me not to give way to fancy in the least. He says that with my imaginative power and story-making, a nervous weakness like mine is sure to lead to all manner of excited fancies, and that I ought to use my will and good sense to check the tendency. So I try.[16]

The narrator's treatment, such as it is, is one of vehement intellectual and emotional suppression, in which both her creative inclinations and whatever distress she experiences—hallucinations, ultimately—are targeted as dangerous to acknowledge in the slightest. The impact, you will be unsurprised to learn, is that the narrator slides into a black muddle where, like Antoinette, she cannot distinguish herself from the phantom women she spies "creeping" behind the wallpaper and all throughout the secluded manor her husband has rented for her recovery. Gilman, who was hospitalized for "a severe and continuous nervous breakdown tending to melancholia," was prescribed a rest cure of this sort in 1887 and instructed "to 'live as domestic a life as far as possible;' to 'have but two hours' intellectual life a day,' and 'never to touch pen, brush or pencil again' as long as I lived...I went home and obeyed those directions for some three months, and came so near the border line of utter mental ruin that I could see over."[17] She penned "The Yellow Wallpaper" as a cautionary tale, and a plea to physicians, particularly the one that had treated her to the brink of insanity, to dispense with methods that, rather than engage a female patient's concerns, served primarily to buttress the cult of domesticity and quash men's nerves over mouthy women. Make her life small, and direct her to lock her brain in a vise. Toss her into prison, and when she protests, assure her that it's her sanctuary.

———

Today, we are quick to point to women writers who suffered from depression, anxiety, or schizophrenia as a means of creative affirmation—particularly Virginia Woolf and Sylvia Plath, who both famously suffered nervous breakdowns throughout their lives. But these literary celebrity comparisons have further focused the spotlight on white women of comfortable socioeconomic standing. Plath in particular adheres to idealized white girl femininity, with her beauty, voguish style, and fashion magazine internship—indeed, she is the very sort Hollywood would depict via Gwyneth Paltrow (and Focus Features did precisely that in 2003 with the biopic *Sylvia*). Those of us who have struggled with mental health are fortunate to find comfort in *The Bell Jar* and in Plath's poetry—she, like Woolf, was a masterful, visceral wordsmith who understood that living in the world can feel as nourishing as a rattling husk. But as we worship evermore feverishly at the temple of White Feminine Genius, she has become a Lana Del Rey-esque icon: fucked up, but beautiful and glamorous. Woolf, perhaps due to the esoteric tenor of her work, has not become quite so trendy, and yet she, too, has been co-opted as shorthand for the troubled but brilliant white woman creative. (A brief side note: the twentieth-century modernist was, unsurprisingly, sensible to the oceanic crash of too muchness—and its more distempering effects—particularly as she grappled with the demands of the literary profession. On Saturday, April 11, 1931, Woolf wrote in her diary, "But I have no pen—well, it will just make a mark. And not much to say, or rather too much and not the mood.")[18]

Repurposing women's mental illness as a signifier of genius enables us to bear witness from a cozier vantage point. Although few, hopefully, would argue that Woolf and Plath were brilliant because they endured sieges of the mind, we do seem to tacitly accept the inextricability of these attributes, to welcome others to suffer for the art we enjoy. I make no claims to the greatness of either Woolf or Plath, but I *can* state with certitude that I write best when I am regularly attending therapy appointments and adhering to my prescribed dosage of medications. Dark nights of the soul are creatively derailing, in addition to being positively miserable.

But we've long sought palatability and justification where women have anguished. Charles Dickens's heroines—generally pretty—are, accordingly, always pretty when they cry. As Elizabeth Gaskell's titular heroine *Ruth* (1853) succumbs to a bullyish hair-shearing after enduring the traumas of romantic desertion and childbirth out of wedlock, the elegant resignation of her visage, its beauty consistently emphasized, insinuates her moral fortitude. Her benefactors' housekeeper carries out this punitive crop in a shame-wielding thrust of power but, notably, doubts her actions after peering into Ruth's docile, finely wrought face. In George Eliot's 1871 novel *Middlemarch*, young doctor Tertius Lydgate proposes marriage to the pretty and snobbish Rosamond Vincy after encountering her in tears. Eliot's narrator indicates the folly of this union, but nonetheless, it illuminates the idealized manifestation of feminine distress: something delicate, trivial, and comely—a sight to make a man fall in love, or at least to turn him on. Eliot's narrator—who harbors precious little love for Rosamond—admonishes against both the fetishizing of a sad and beautiful woman, not to mention the assumptions we make about a person's inner life when their exterior is so aesthetically pleasing. But we cannot resist suffering made exquisite, and modern life has made gawkers out of the lot of us.

Yet for all our beauty worship, we are even more inclined to hanker after the grotesque—particularly when it emanates from someone or something who has heretofore excelled at the performance of conventional desirability. In the midst of a 2007 custody battle with ex-husband Kevin Federline, Britney

Spears absconded from rehab, walked into a hair salon, and, with purposeful promptitude, shaved her head. She was widely lampooned for the incident. Media outlets broadcasted images of her shorn and snarling visage to elicit, what else? Gasps of shock and, in the most uncharitable cases, laughter. There was, and there remains, lurid fascination in watching a bubblegum sex symbol shed her practiced poise, and the golden hair she saucily teased throughout her performances. A few days later, at a Mobil gas station in Tarzana, California, Britney, bald and donning rumpled leisurewear, slumped in the passenger seat of her silver Mercedes, Alli Sims, her second cousin twice removed at the wheel. While Sims briefly vacated the car, videographer Daniel "Dano" Ramos, together with a photographer from X17, descended upon it, the click of the camera tittering, a sonic curtain of opportunism rendering Ramos's queries laughable as he asks, still filming, "Are you doing okay? I'm concerned about you." In the fluttering light of the camera flash, Spears seems to dwell in the liminality of boredom and resignation. She rests her arm against the car window, casts her gaze beyond the flash, but—for now—she meets the paparazzi's dizzying deluge without detectable reaction or recalibration. Briefly, she seems a skewed reincarnation of Ruth, a melancholic beauty divested of her crowning glory, though of course Spears did not yield to another's razor. And before long, she reveals that she will not suffer this intrusion. When the crew continues to film Spears at a Jiffy Lube, she exits the car and, wielding a long, green umbrella like a spear, Spears rams it into Ramos's Ford Explorer as she yells, "Fuck you!" It's a hasty retaliation: after a few strikes, she drops the umbrella, trots back to the Mercedes, and she and Sims immediately drive away.[19] I can recount these details, of course, because Ramos's footage is available online. It will be retrievable, probably, until the internet implodes.

Spears later apologized for taking an umbrella to a paparazzo's car, and Ramos has even remarked in an interview that he and his colleagues were accustomed to working closely with her—that Spears was not averse to the attention. "Britney just loved it. She just enjoyed it, but there were times that it caught up to her. She didn't give us the memo."[20] The tangled and conditional relationship between a starlet and a coterie of paparazzi is by no means specific to Spears's variety of fame, and surely the opportunities and access attendant to celebrity breed certain aggravations (we are hasty to equivocate this way whenever we express empathy for a powerful woman). But if all of that is true, it's equally possible that Spears had habituated herself to a set of circumstances—in particular, vastly truncated privacy, compliments of the paparazzi—that she understood as her new, permanent atmosphere. The weather brought a perennial deluge of camera flash: perhaps the path of least resistance meant learning to welcome it whenever meddling seemed something akin to fun, or at least like savvy public relations.

In years prior, at the height of her bubblegum prowess, Spears telegraphed a divergent response to celebrity from the one Ramos suggests, one in which she is tolerant, long suffering, and tragically fatigued. In the music videos for her singles "Lucky" (2000) and "Everytime" (2003), Spears dramatized the glamorous depression that would later become intertwined in Lana Del Rey's persona: each performance, although gussied up with the trappings of popstar glitter, is unsettling in its vulnerability—Spears's doe eyes have always broadcast a resigned sadness, as if her hopes have been dashed. As Alice Bolin writes in *Dead Girls*, Spears sings "My loneliness is killing me" over and over in her first—colossal—single, "…Baby One More Time"—but we hadn't listened, not really.[21] And maybe we overlooked her anguished isolation in these videos, particularly in "Everytime," where Spears depicts the allure of death in the face of romantic misery and overexposure. We tie ourselves in knots in expeditions for authentic, wholly unmediated celebrity responses to the wider world, but the notion of personal authenticity is a red herring in any case. Still, the Spears who glides tragically through the videos for "Lucky" and "Everytime" seems to settle into the Spears listing against the window to her Mercedes, a warped metaphor if ever one existed: the automobile, so often advertised as the American symbol of freedom, becomes a gilded, wheeled prison where its occupant can still be hunted down like a dog.

The hair shaving and umbrella episodes sit alongside Spears's hyper-performed tristesse as contrastingly unfiltered, raw, and ugly: they shocked witnesses in ways that her gentle, carefully produced videos purposefully did not. And for that reason, maybe we admitted to ourselves a few twinges of guilty relief: watching a famous woman throw caution aside and, instead, hand herself over to too muchness, even in a way that bespeaks punishing turmoil, can act as a pressure valve by proxy. Imagine not holding oneself together, imagine saying "fuck it" to decorum, and deciding that for a spare few days, it wasn't worth trying. That, instead, the only thing left to do was fall. It's not the sort of lesson we ought to take from this story; there is no

deliverance in lapping up another's pain, even when it is resonant. But knotted within our overlapping cultural corsets we
can't help but admit it: for a wisp of a moment, Spears's rage
seems delicious.

Then again, we've cleaved to that moment, mulling it over
and meme-ing it and firmly fastening it within our cultural
repository of beautiful, distraught women. In a famous iteration
of the 2007 Britney meme, Spears's wild-eyed, growling visage
glares beneath her shorn head, with block white text marching
atop her photograph: "If Britney can make it through 2007,
then I can make it through today," it declares. The image
acknowledges Spears's personal trials, but any discernible sympathy is undercut through a cheap grab at freak-show humor.
The photo, now infamous, invites us to gawk at the spectacle
of Spears, as if she is a ghoulish hysteric trapped in the dim
halls of an asylum.[22] On February 17, 2017, media outlets celebrated the ten-year anniversary of the head-shaving event.[23]
But this feverishly commemorated incident exists as only one
glaring point on a timeline in which the ebbs and flows of
Spears's mental health have been weaponized against her, both
across tabloids and in more intimate contexts. In 2008, one
year after the incident, she refused to relinquish custody of her
sons to representatives of her ex-husband, Kevin Federline, a
conflict that led to a call to the police. They surmised that
she was under the influence of some undetermined substance,
and ultimately Spears was delivered, involuntarily, into psychiatric care, circumstances commonly referred to as "5150":
a reference to California's law code for involuntary commitment.[24] Swiftly, she was divested of her autonomy. In addition
to losing custody of her children, Spears was legally restrained

by a conservatorship—a form of supervision typically reserved for those who are impaired by age, infirmity, or acute mental illness and thus cannot act in their own best interests. Spears's father, Jamie Spears, and lawyer Andrew Wallet were named her conservators, although Wallet resigned in March 2019. To this day, Spears is constrained by the exacting terms of this guardianship. If she purchases something, it is documented. She is not permitted to drive a car or even to own a smartphone. She looms large as one of the world's most famous women, an icon of sugar-sweet, hip-flicking pop music, and she is strapped into the most bedazzled and inexorable of harnesses.

In 2018, controversy over Spears's sovereignty percolated anew when she unceremoniously withdrew from her Las Vegas residency and reentered psychiatric care. Ostensibly she vacated her Vegas spot because her father was ill and then sought care due to the stress engendered by his condition. But among Spears's most staunch fans, speculations meandered about foul play: many suspected that Jamie Spears had forced his daughter from her residency because she was neither taking her pre-scribed medication nor heeding the "no driving" regulation. Some said she was being held involuntarily. A hashtag cam-paign, "Free Britney," waxed across social media, and celebrities like rapper Eve and Miley Cyrus have taken up its mantle. It's unclear whether these rumors hold water—regardless, recent events have rekindled a long smoldering anger harbored among Spears's most devoted admirers, a vast indignation held in soli-darity over the way her father, and others, have whittled away at her personal liberties. "As far as we know," writes Josephine Livingstone, "she has no illness debilitating enough to warrant a conservatorship under the ordinary application of the law. She was once branded *crazy*, so *crazy* she remains: totally without autonomy, cut off from the world, at the mercy of people who control her access to her children. It's no wonder that the plight of Britney Spears continues to haunt us."[25]

Sometimes we covet celebrity gossip because it creates the illusion of access—for a moment, a kind of life utterly foreign to our own seems knowable. Spears's tribulations invoke another breed of fixation, not mutually exclusive from the other, but shot through with dread: the blot of "crazy," nearly as vague as the accusation of "too much," sticks to a woman's skin, leech-like and glaring and vigorous. We need only look to America's prisons—a carceral system of damnation—to understand that we have never been interested in rehabilitating the most vulnerable among us, of supposing something other than the worst when our inclinations wander into prejudice. Spears, of course, is not marginalized like a black woman locked away without due process: she occupies a singular space in which she is technically in possession of colossal wealth and fame, while also being deprived of access—to her sons, to purchasing power without oversight, to mobility—by those close to her. And as her father endeavors to amplify his influence by extending his conservatorship to three additional states, including Louisiana, her homestead, Spears is treated evermore as a modern-day madwoman, an incurable hysteric.[26] If Bertha Mason and Lady Audley were condemned according to archaic, anxious theories on mental health—a mother's madness all but guarantees her daughter's twin fate—then Britney Spears is subjected to an updated fiction in which she will always be imprinted by the cruelest aspersions, speculations witched into fact because when it comes to women living with mental illness, we are generally disinclined to be gracious. And assumptions, born from slips and scraps of information, become a feast ample enough to sustain her narrative, which, of course, has been snatched from her hands. A woman whose too muchness trickles into the realm of mental health is never granted the pen to her own story.

Spears's reactions to public ruminations about her life, whether on the "anniversary" of the head shaving or to the paroxysm of conjecture surrounding her personal affairs, are typically subdued. She chose to indirectly commemorate the ten-year head-shaving event with an Instagram post quoting Pslam 126:5, "Those who plant in tears will harvest with shouts of joy," indicating to her fans that she was not scrubbing the incident from her public narrative and was instead incorporating it into a story of religiously grounded recuperation. Perhaps some of the media attention she received for this vague acknowledgment was offered in good faith. But perhaps Spears—together with the aid of her handlers—recognized that she must seize the reins of this story before someone in the blogosphere did the math and broke it anew, particularly for younger fans who, in 2007, might have been too young to recall the media feeding frenzy: remember when our sweet pop princess lost both mind and mane as we swarmed her like flies in hot honey? And while it would be encouraging to believe that the story was one foregrounding emotional rehabilitation, we can only shit ourselves so much.

The "Free Britney" campaign prompted a more direct address from the starlet because, as Spears wrote in an April 23, 2019, Instagram post, "There's rumors, death threats to my family and my team, and just so many . . . crazy things being said." She explains that her former manager, Sam Lutfi—who must now adhere to a temporary restraining order taken out against him by Spears's legal team—misrepresented her circumstances years ago by writing fake emails purportedly from Spears, and that these recirculated missives, suggesting that the conservatorship is destructive, are false.[27] "I am trying to take a moment for myself, but everything that's happening is just making it harder for me," Spears writes. "Don't believe everything you read and hear. These fake emails everywhere were crafted by Sam Lutfi years ago ... I did not write them ... My situation is unique, but I promise I'm doing what's best at this moment." These comments are accompanied by a video that, while shorter, amounts to the same thing: a brief assurance that nothing is amiss. "Don't worry, I'll be back very soon," she emphasizes. Her voice, still candy-dipped and husky, like a sweet bourbon, is measured, matter-of-fact. She appears neither happy nor rested—understandable, after a volley of death threats to her family—but she addresses her audience's solicitude with calm.[28]

I don't count myself among the participants of the Free Britney campaign, but since 2007 I have spent unnecessary time worrying about her. It's difficult to resist: vulnerability has always been entwined with Spears's sex appeal. Her trademark look—straight ahead, eyes wide and mouth partly open, as if she thinks she might be in trouble—wafts through her oeuvre of music videos: after a head toss, or as she dances (and who could look away when she danced?). She seduced us while appearing to recognize something precarious in her midst. For my part, I revisit "Everytime," one of my favorite Britney Spears songs, and the video that most shocked me: it never occurred to me that this beautiful woman who, as a teenager, I had regarded as my absolute opposite, thought about death the way I sometimes did, as a refuge. It hadn't occurred to me that she might be sad, and I've been rattled by this sadness, which strikes me every time I see Spears or listen to her speak—but then, this might be my own variety of fetishization.

Whenever my mind totters over to this place where I think of Britney, and the loneliness that's killing her, I cannot help but feel silly. Because Spears is wealthy, famous, white, and conventionally beautiful, she recovered from her mid-aughts image crisis and public relations emergency, wherein the burden of emotional distress cracked the veneer imperative to anyone living in the glare of high visibility. She will, I hope, untangle herself from these new imbroglios in a way that privileges, rather than exploits, her mental health. It would be encouraging if, over a decade after the dramatized episodes of the shorn head and the umbrella, flagrant gawking at a celebrity— at anyone—so mired in suffering were not so explicitly tolerated. On the fifteenth anniversary, there might be think pieces admonishing against these lurid reminiscences. But with the crush of this new controversy—Free Britney—and the pathological ogling, the intrusions that seemed to motivate Spears's April 2019 Instagram message, I confess my pessimism. Too muchness is always treated as pageantry, and so we will watch.

In recent years, a variety of public figures including Jennifer Lawrence, Missy Elliott, Emma Stone, and even Oprah Winfrey have offered testimonials to their own struggles with anxiety. But of course testimonial offers a more innocuous kind of visibility than what Spears has endured, one less likely to garner stigma. There is no risk in referencing a private struggle so long as one's public image remains pristine. There is no threat of the lampooning directed at Fiona Apple in 2000 when, during a set at the Roseland Ballroom in New York, she had her infamous "meltdown," running offstage after only forty minutes[29] or the performative concern oozing from headlines after a concertgoer body-shamed her during a 2013 show, bringing her to tears.[30] And there is no hazard of the vicious scrutiny faced by the R&B singer Kehlani after she posted on social media about her suicide attempt, prompting—for whatever reason—singer Chris Brown, a suspect in various assault cases, to accuse her of fabricating the story, which then encouraged scores of others to do the same.[31] But although I feel gratitude when highly visible women lay bare their ordeals with mental illness, and empathy for those, like Britney Spears, who did not precisely choose to do so, I could never begrudge anyone for preferring silence. Too muchness has made it difficult, often insuperable, to conceal my serrated edges: my face speaks before I do. We do not, however, owe the world testimonies of our pain; we owe one another the willingness to bear witness.

Yet these are herculean lessons when our milieu repurposes women's mental illness as a gateway to men's emotional clarity. In twenty-first-century pop culture, mentally ill female characters shore up a fantasy of mental illness as a charming, whimsical trait possessed by rosy-faced white girls whose suffering has bestowed upon them a bone-deep wisdom. In *Garden State* (2004), Zach Braff brings us what Nathan Rabin coined as the Manic Pixie Dream Girl, but the film pays little attention to accurate depictions of mania. Natalie Portman's Sam lobs quips left and right, her mental illness indexed by compulsive lying, which is hardly interrogated, her presence in a psychiatrist's waiting room, and some adorable non sequiturs ("I can tap dance; wanna see me tap dance?"). Meanwhile, Tiffany (Jennifer Lawrence) from *Silver Linings Playbook* (2012) embodies excess that the film mitigates with her sexual desirability—Jennifer Lawrence, after all—and conveys emotional insight that, similarly to *Garden State*, shepherds male protagonist Pat (Bradley Cooper) back to a healthy life trajectory (and, of course, into her arms). In each case, the film's interest resides in the hero's journey, and in the case of *Silver Linings Playbook*, Cooper's performance as a man reeling from the one-two punch of divorce and a nervous breakdown is both sensitive and visceral. But Tiffany, a young widow who, like Pat, rails against the hell of her own mind, serves as a lesson in self-acceptance and resilience. She cannot be too "crazy" if she is to perform her role as a romantic and emotional restorative.

As a matter of fact, even Tiffany's too muchness is harnessed for the purposes of education. "You know what, forget I offered to help you," she snaps at Pat in a diner after weathering his condescension. "Forget the entire fucking idea, because that must have been fucking crazy, because I'm so much *crazier* than you...I'm just the crazy slut with a dead husband!" In some ways, the scene is pure delight: Pat, after looking askance at Tiffany's sexual history, is deservedly mortified by her wild, ferocious laughter and cyclonic departure from the diner—all of which looks cathartic, in its way. But the scene is meant as a lesson, an early entry in Pat's rehabilitative curriculum. Before long, Pat and Tiffany become friends as they practice for a dance competition—despite the former's monomania regarding his ex-wife—and he gradually enjoys what amounts to free, take-no-shit therapy masked by amateurish choreography. Tiffany's pain, as has long been the case, is treated incidentally, and is easily soothed by a promise of love. She is one more female character among scores of others who fall on swords for men, beating back, or even exacerbating, their own deprivations. We meet—extensively—with Rochester's rough, self-indulgent, but nonetheless genteel agony before Brontë reveals to us the full narrative of Bertha's imprisonment, that her mind creates its own hellish cage, trauma-born and unrelenting. *Lady Audley's Secret* treats the titular character's mental illness as, first and foremost, a hazard to the men in her midst. We hail from a tradition in which women's mental health is compulsively packaged as a male inconvenience, or worse. Physicians in the Victorian era were chronically reluctant to consider female suffering on its own terms. And still today, we do not take it seriously.

Accompanying this diminished, trivializing regard is a prevailing, bootstraps mentality dictating that women should be able to gracefully handle trials of any sort, come what may. But in nearly every corner of our lives, we are reminded that the world was neither built for our welfare nor our benefit. As a matter of course, we sometimes learn to self-medicate with the materials available to us: it's a numbing act of self-preservation, even survival. And certainly, it's no surprise that these practices are generally figured in terms of moral failing in the face of trying circumstances. Women are not simply dragooned into complying with society's dictates, but also compelled—no matter how archaic the expectation—to serve as exemplars of virtue and domestic femininity. Boys will be boys, and so their leisure and comfort has always been integrated into the cultural context: an intimate gathering to guzzle whiskey, inhale in public smoking rooms, and gawk and leer at strip clubs, the brunt of which are significantly reliant on women's labor. Even the opium dens of the nineteenth century were, however controversial, preserved as secluded, exclusively masculine spaces for indulgent repose. A little temptation never hurt a proper gentleman, so long as he was discreet in the appropriate ways. Women, on the other hand, have struggled to seek solace— from poverty, from sexism, from racism, from men—and have been condemned for the extreme measures they sometimes take for relief.

The lure and stigma of self-medication becomes all the more fraught for those who, even in a more egalitarian world, would struggle to wrangle their roaring brains or brimful hearts. After all, the use of any numbing substance can function as a palliative measure for the pains inherent to too muchness. At the end of my first marriage, exhausted and heartbroken, I began to drink heavily at night, always alone, as I padded across the cool floor of my studio apartment. Certain substance-based coping mechanisms might be unhealthy in any case, but for women they are damning. Leo Tolstoy's titular *Anna Karenina* misuses opium when she is plagued by the burdens of a nineteenth-century infidelity scandal, harpooning what little social dignity she has retained. It's dangerous stereotyping to imply that because a woman is passionate or inclined to intense emotional expression, she will be more likely to turn to drugs or alcohol, but Anna's increasingly debilitating paranoia and jealousy, coupled with her social isolation, render her vulnerable to any available means of relief. As for those witnessing her mental and emotional disintegration: they would just as soon turn a blind eye to her suffering.

We don't often read about Victorian women's substance abuse, and with good reason. In the nineteenth century, a temperance movement loomed large in Great Britain. Men who drank were considered lowlifes, but women who drank were nothing short of fallen, that is to say, abandoners of the virtuous life they were expected to diligently follow. Engravings like "The Clew,"[32] by Charles Keene, published in the March 8, 1879, edition of *Punch* magazine, illustrate with brevity Victorian society's condemnatory view of female alcoholism. Our eyes are directed to the diminutive and ragged figure of a little girl, her hair shorn haphazardly, as if someone had attempted to cut it while reeling in drunken delirium. She is barefoot and, based on the wrappings of those surrounding her, vulnerable to the English chill. What's more, Keene's shadowing seems to imply grime as much as it supplies dimension to her small person. A policeman, together with a small crowd of concerned passersby loom over her, their gazes re-emphasizing our focus on the little girl and the policeman who has bent toward her and taken her hand. The corresponding text reads:

> The child was evidently lost!—cried bitterly—could not tell where its Parents lived, or whether she was an Orphan, or what her Father was—or where she went to school.—Enter Intelligent Policeman.
>
> Policeman (in a friendly whisper). "Where does your Mother get her Gin, My Dear?"
>
> [And the mystery was solved.]

British cities, namely London, teemed with destitute children like the one rendered here, and to be sure, their plights—homelessness, the perils of factory labor, grave illness—were urgent social matters that demanded attention. And to a paltry extent, they did. In 1833, the Factory Act or Children's Charter[33] tightened child labor regulations so that children under nine could no longer work in factories, with the exception of silk mills. Children under the age of thirteen could work no more than nine hours a day, or forty-eight hours a week. Other similar reforms were devised during Queen Victoria's reign, and while they might have improved conditions that were previously even more ghastly, the strident poverty that made it impossible for Londoners to feed their children and brought about the alcoholism gestured to in "The Clew" ran evermore rampant through British manufacturing cities.

The caption to Keene's engraving assumes, without considering extenuating circumstances, that this child has turned street urchin because her mother, in taking to drink, has divested herself of maternal responsibility. Poor women are drunk women, it dangerously implies: they forget their children and dose themselves with gin until the pubs close. Abusive and neglectful parents have existed for as long as our species has procreated, and Victorian literature abounds with ill-treated children. But when it comes to considering mothers who were less responsible, or less kind, the emotional strains of privation go unmentioned. Indeed, this example urges an alliance between child and law enforcement that insinuates, however obliquely, that the gin-drinking mother belongs in jail and that the child would do better under institutional care. But in all likelihood, a child with parents too drunk to feed her would not have been spirited away by a benevolent bureaucracy; probably, she would have died in an alley.

Charlotte Brontë's biographer and fellow novelist Elizabeth Gaskell focused her novels more squarely on the working class of northern England, and in so doing attended to the consequences of lives strained by grim toil, punishing working conditions, and protracted hunger. In *Mary Barton* (1848), set in 1840s Manchester, Gaskell introduces us to a minor, albeit significant character, Esther—wayward aunt to the titular Mary. At the start of the novel, we learn that Esther has run away from home; later we learn that she had fallen in love with a naval officer she expected to marry, but who in short order impregnated and abandoned her. She turns to prostitution in a desperate effort to save her ailing baby, but to no avail: the child dies, and, bereft, Esther languishes on the streets of Manchester, oscillating between sex work and prison. As she explains to one character, she cannot merely return home, for her fall has been too definitive, not because of her sex work, but because of her burgeoned alcohol addiction:

> I must have drink. Such as live like me could not bear life if they did not drink. It's the only thing to keep us from suicide. If we did not drink, we could not stand the memory of what we have been, and the thought of what we are, for a day. If I go without food, and without shelter, I must have my dram.[34]

Gaskell's rendering of self-medication turned addiction is not wholly unsympathetic, but it reifies Victorian conceptions of fallenness: that those women who have resorted to prostitution or engaged in illicit affairs or premarital sex are either un-repentant or appropriately self-loathing. In Esther's case, she drinks because she cannot "stand the memory of what we have been, and the thought of what we are"; that is to say, her by-gone purity is intolerable to contemplate in her current, squalid circumstances.

Gaskell's narrator nudges us to be a little indulgent, but every bit as punishing as cultural gender expectations dictate: "Maybe I would drink too if I had become so filthy and hated myself so much." What the novel does not sufficiently acknowledge is that Esther's misery is largely manufactured by cruel, prevailing forces that deny a woman the right to make a mistake, espe-cially when that mistake is falling in love with the wrong person and even more so when, dazzled by that love, you become sexually intimate prior to the legitimizing bonds of matri-mony. And as literary critic Deborah Logan points out, despite this presentation of "extenuating circumstances," Gaskell pre-serves the "drunken-prostitute stereotype" by ignoring one key fact: gin, or the "dram" to which Esther refers, cost far less than bread. One could also acquire it more easily, and rely on it to stave off hunger for longer periods of time. "Thus," Logan posits, "alcoholism, like prostitution, among the poor and working classes was generally more a matter of economics than of sensuous self-indulgence or inherent moral depravity."[35] But what if there were "sensuous" enjoyment in drunkenness after a chilly, starved night? In our perpetual quest for the Good Victims, we are determined to rewrite marginalized narratives so that every act of desperation is neither motivated by a de-sire for pleasure nor productive of it. We want to believe that Esther drinks not because she likes it, but because it ushers in a welcome impassivity in the face of her dismal circumstances and, what's more, offers the deranged practicality of cheaply safeguarding against hunger. She cannot, after all, be a victim if she smiles, if she for one evening does not grapple with remorse, or with the desire to escape the life that now unravels before her like tar-soaked cloth. It's seductive—the possibility of smudging out the day and all its discontents. After all, this world was not made for us, and it can be a damned bitter task to live in it. But this existential incompatibility has never been considered a sufficient "extenuating circumstance." We cannot accept respite unless it manifests in its most virtuous forms, unless it abides by the ideological notion that indulgence—particularly in alcohol or drugs or other items marked as "unhealthy"—is always an index of moral weakness.

In the context of a novel, we typically understand and are frequently encouraged to sympathize with a character as she self-destructs. But without a narrator reminding us of context, we're often inclined to isolate drug use and alcoholism, rather than treating them as symptoms of impossible circumstances. And when it comes to addressing substance abuse as a broader issue—the "war on drugs," as Richard Nixon pronounced it in 1971—we're also far more likely to target women of color. Unlike white women, whose too muchness is stigmatized only when it manifests through action, the distorted light of prejudice proffers women of color as excessive according to fundamental racial attributes. Held in suspicion by default, the American criminal justice system is ever ready to pounce. As Andrea Ritchie reports in her book *Invisible No More*, "Black, Latinx, and Indigenous women make up a grossly disproportionate share of women incarcerated for drug offenses, even though whites are nearly five times as likely as Blacks to use marijuana and three times as likely as Blacks to have used crack."[36] These shamelessly racialized disparities are provoked by the illusory but damning stereotypes that not only yoke drug use to poor, nonwhite femininity, but also deny them the paternalistic coddling that is more often afforded to white women who break the law. Too muchness is thrust upon women of color as a stigmatizing, permanent condition before they have the opportunity to claim it as something less vituperative. And so, we fling assumptions—self-indulgent, outsize cravings for drugs and sex—and punish extravagantly. As Ritchie argues,

> Law enforcement interactions with women of color are informed by perceptions of their bodies as vessels for drugs ingested, swallowed, or concealed and of women of color as "out of control" unfit mothers, community members dependent on drugs and men, or coldhearted "gangsta bitches" prone to inhuman violence.[37]

In America, the "war on drugs" has not been waged in affluent fraternity houses or in the homes of flush white executives who celebrate a weekend in the Hamptons with lines of cocaine. Rather, Ritchie reminds us, it has ravaged the communities of impoverished people of color, resulting not only in wildly skewed statistics, swollen with racism, but in assumptions of guilt based upon the landscape and the lurid character sketches that censure women of color for their behavioral excesses whether or not they have ever resorted to substance abuse. In a white male-dominated society that purports to diagnose the reasons for racialized poverty without shouldering any blame, women of color become the focal point of condemnation. And there is no space—no sympathy—to be supplied if a woman claims her right to indulge. If she drinks a vodka tonic after a backbreaking, miserable day, she fails as a maternal figure and is, on the contrary, an "'out of control' unfit mother." Hegemonic forces might argue that she neglects the burden of hoisting her community from poverty. Her vulnerability is thus interpreted as a racially specific moral failing, one that will confine black and brown children to poverty in perpetuity. Like the fallen women of Victorian fiction, she is execrated as irredeemable, but not merely for her own alleged shortcomings. Instead, the fallen women of color is weaponized as both thesis and justification: the particulars of her life explain, according to a specific, prejudiced logic, the degradation of an entire race while divesting complicit systems from social responsibility. If she is beyond hope, so must her children be.

Hollywood's overwhelming whiteness has resulted in most famous depictions of impoverished, addicted women of color being crafted by white people. But in 2016, director Barry Jenkins intervened with his semiautobiographical film *Moonlight*, in which Naomie Harris performs the supporting role of Paula, a mother struggling to raise her son, Chiron, as she succumbs to the unremitting wrench of a crack addiction. Harris's Paula is terrifying and feral and, at times, ruthless, but she is never, as others have observed, a pat trope. K. Austin Collins writes, "Paula is not merely a 'crack-addicted mother,' as the stereotype typically goes, but a fully imagined woman who loves her son and tries to hold down a job and to raise him, even as she struggles with addiction."[38] Her maternal affection and her suffering are as visceral—and demand the same attention—as her drug-addled rage. As Paula, Harris dares viewers to reduce her to a fallen woman, someone who is only deserving of censure, to whom the luxury of empathy ought not be extended.

When Juan (Mahershala Ali), the crack dealer who has become something of a paternal figure to Chiron, chides Paula for her addiction, the film presses upon its resistance to easy assumptions. It's funny, in its gloomy way, for a dealer to scold a potential paying customer, but as Paula defends herself, her throaty drawl crackling with hostility, she spits Juan's condescension in his face while simultaneously reminding the audience that she cannot be flattened into that ubiquitous type: the addict mother who loves getting high more than she loves her son. "Who the hell you think you is? Huh?" she demands of Juan. "What, so you gonna raise my son now?... You ever see the way he walk? You're gonna tell him why the other boys kick his ass all the time? You ain't shit." Paula may not be the mother she hoped to be to Chiron, but she sees him with lucidity—she pays attention. "By the end, we've been reminded," Collins concludes, "[that] she's Chiron's mother. And Juan is no better than she is."[39] Paula is not inured to her responsibilities as her son begins to navigate the world as a gay person, even if her addiction yanks her off course. And the only person to whom she ultimately holds herself accountable is Chiron, with whom she reconciles after getting clean. Together, Jenkins, Harris, and playwright Tarell Alvin McCraney give body to a character who will not be interpolated as this or as that: the business of apprehending and naming her excesses— and they are deadly excesses—is hers alone.

―――――

So-called "troubled celebrities" like actress Lindsay Lohan and pop star Demi Lovato exist at the opposite end of the privilege spectrum from women like Paula, and the impoverished alcoholic women of Victorian narratives, but their respective examples of addiction elaborate upon the cultural reception of women's substance abuse. The media has pilloried Lohan for her drunken antics since they first began circa 2007, when she was arrested for multiple DUIs. She is the child star gone wrong par excellence, the sweetheart swallowed whole by Hollywood's hedonism—a fall that has lately become increasingly complicated by her culturally and politically tone-deaf behavior.

Certainly Lohan's wealth and fame have affected her use of influence and platform in some gruesome ways, from her reckless habit of driving while intoxicated to deeply ignorant outbursts in the face of Middle Eastern refugees. But whether or not Lohan is a sympathetic case—or, for that matter, a decent person—it's notable, if not surprising, that the larger response to her struggles with alcoholism has been one of scornful amusement. A sexist logic motivates this reaction: we delight in "messy" female celebrities with an affected knowingness, as if their strife was somehow predictable, that their moral weakness, their too muchness, has merely risen to the surface. We elide discussions of mental health and mystify Lohan's famously difficult childhood in condemnatory discussions of her addictions. The media seems particularly eager to lampoon former female child stars like Lohan who struggle to maintain emotional equilibrium. They perform sympathy, but it's drenched in derision.

As a result, a famous woman who publicly narrates her addiction must perform the struggle in a diligently precise way, so as to circumvent widespread mockery and her reputation's ruin. Singer Demi Lovato, who, like Lohan, is a child star and Disney alumnus, was drawn in by Hollywood's ready offerings of cocaine and booze. She claimed to give it all up, only to later reveal that while shooting the 2012 recovery documentary *Stay Strong* she had been using cocaine. It seems as if she did break with substance abuse not long after that point, but relapsed in August 2018, at age twenty-six, after six years of sobriety.[40]

Lovato's fans learned the news not because of a panting TMZ report, but because she announced it by releasing a new single, "Sober," and, to the extent that she could, grabbed the narrative reins before they fell into the grasp of bystanders and speculating bloggers. The lyric video, which she posted on her Instagram account on June 21, 2018, recreates the sizzling granular snow of a broken television, the verses spelled out against its backdrop, like a retrieved epilogic message. At its beginning, oversaturated footage of Lovato flashes before us, spliced with, among other items, closeups of a liquor bottle, a dingily impersonal hotel room, and a pair of strappy stilettos toppled to the side, like hope overturned. All of this is evidence, the video seems to indicate, and it is also the past. The song's premise is stated quite plainly, but in the chorus, Lovato makes no bones about what she needs to express: "Momma, I'm so sorry I'm not sober anymore / And Daddy, please forgive me for the drinks spilled on the floor." It wasn't long after releasing "Sober" that Lovato overdosed: thankfully, one of her assistants found the singer passed out and, though she was initially feared dead, swift action revived her. Lovato entered rehab, and on August 5 posted again to her Instagram account a brief note, now deleted, the first paragraph of which read: "I have always been transparent about my journey with addiction. What I've learned is that this illness is not something that disappears or fades with time. It is something I must continue to overcome and have not done yet."

To my mind, Lovato's candor on such a swollen topic indicates genuine bravery. "Sober" is a devastating wallop of a confession, one that is honest without being totally overblown or platitudinous. But what might have been cathartic and, frankly, lucrative for Lovato would likely be for another public figure an insurmountable ask, a demand for emotional labor when they simply aren't interested in nurturing, or drawing support from their relationships with fans and admirers. A famous woman like Lovato or Lohan must recognize that while she can ask for and strive for total privacy, she cannot ensure it. She is also not required to care about the feedback she receives about aspects of her life unconnected to content production. But public opinion is a maw as exacting as it is ravenous. When women stumble on that great, hot-lit stage, their recovery is endlessly, and searingly scrutinized.

Lovato has been received relatively gently. Still, responses to "Sober" and to her overdose have laid bare how stringently we assess women's vulnerability, how the search for the Good Victim, a fundamentally bad-faith effort, is in fact a blanket demand prescribing the way women perform their weaknesses. The lyrics to "Sober," after all, fulfill expectations of penitence: Lovato apologizes to her parents, intimately referred to as "Momma" and "Daddy," insinuating the self-expectation that she fulfill the domestic role of an obliging and successful daughter. She even addresses "my future love," with an apology "for the man that left my bed / For making love the way I saved for you inside my head"—a nod to heteronormative expectations of propriety, the illusion that we must "save ourselves" for one particular person, as if our identities are wholly absorbed by our sexual decisions. And, perhaps most crucially, she mourns her inability to be an example to her fans: "I wanna be a role model," she sings, "but I'm only human." In these verses Lovato implies the impossibility of role models—that the demand for pristine example is wholly at odds with the tumult of being a person in the world. Still, she expresses a yearning to be this fantastical creature, indicating that she has, to some extent, internalized the behavioral standards for public women. "I don't know... why / I do it every time / It's only when I'm lonely," she pleads, suggesting that at the base of her addiction is depression, that she hadn't necessarily been having a good time. And so, in a meager way, Lovato has been rewarded with a relatively unsullied reputation. There is perhaps nothing Western culture laps up more readily than a woman who seems ashamed of herself.

Neither Lovato nor anyone else should be maligned for their struggles with addiction. And my views on Lohan, influenced though they may be by some of her behaviors, are not tainted by judgment regarding her own bundle of personal struggles. I suspect, however, that if she had narrated the trials of her substance abuse in a way more similar to Lovato, with regret and self-castigation—and, of course, if she had not revealed a penchant for driving under the influence and thereby putting others' lives in danger—she might not be regarded as a punch line, as a tawdry cautionary tale for our amusement.

———

Although women's mental illness has been vilified and di-minished and banished to moldering attics, we are, gradually, slouching to the right side of things. The glacial shift toward more heterogeneous cultural representation breeds more fine-spun, empathetic portrayals of too muchness in all of its forms, particularly in the arena of mental illness. The series *Crazy Ex-Girlfriend*, which premiered in 2015, is one of the most re-cent compelling depictions of a woman's borderline personality disorder, and the 2019 animated series *Tuca and Bertie* illumi-nates the quiet horror of generalized anxiety. In the former, Rachel Bloom's character, Rebecca Bunch, digs her heels into behavior that's often mortifying in its resonance: she is self-destructive, selfish, exasperating, and she is tangled in a thicket of pain. *Tuca and Bertie*'s creator, Lisa Hanawalt, allows her lead duo, voiced by Tiffany Haddish and Ali Wong, respectively, to be both ribald and utterly gross within a textured narrative of compassionate female friendship. Marvel's *Jessica Jones* intro-duced us to a traumatized alcoholic who is also, despite some of her worst inclinations, a deep-hearted hero. Gradually, mentally ill characters emerge who are fleshy and difficult and extraor-dinary. They rely on antidepressants, like *One Day at a Time*'s Penelope (Justina Machado). It's a herculean task, leaving the Victorians behind: to take a wrecking ball to the dank, panop-tic asylums and to rip apart the yellow wallpaper. We struggle, still, to perceive Bertha Mason and Lady Audley with clarity, to unsnarl the conceptual knot that distorts mental illness as monstrosity. These muddled pathologies have long suffused our thinking, urging us to regard our pain and our instincts with the most uncharitable suspicion. Mainstream Victorian culture would have women villainize ourselves at every turn: It would recklessly conflate too muchness with mental illness, rather than understanding them as interlaced and staunchly tethered to the way one lives in the world. It would diminish our too muchness—all that's glorious and the parts that trouble us—as the squall of crazy bitches. We do not choose the brains that spark inside our heads, lifting us into bliss, bearing us across a placid sea, and then, without warning, casting us into hell. My mind, sometimes fevered, addled, other times perfectly unextraordinary: I must take it as it is and grapple with it however I can. Sometimes it's too much. I would not choose otherwise.

Chapter Seven

CUT

I have neither a voice nor hands, nor any friend nor a foe;

    I am I—just a Pulse of Pain—I am I, that is all I know.

    For Life, and the sickness of Life, and Death and desire to die; —

    They have passed away like the smoke, here is nothing but Pain and I.

—Amy Levy, "Felo de Se"

Bodies that can beget new life are cursed to be ravaged. Puberty startles us in late childhood, when our abdomens throb with the tremors of menstruation. Those who bear children stretch and vomit and tear, bodies gyrating into vicious agents of vitality. Some pain chooses us more than we choose it.

And then sometimes those boundaries are too fickle to discern with confidence. Sometimes, by way of compulsion, an urge murmuring beneath the skin, we demand and negotiate our own physical afflictions. We tug at shirt hems to conceal the slender path yielded by a razor's slice. Our thighs blister with the hissing kisses of cigarette butts. Underneath long sleeves, red blossoms unfurl from a scissor's decisive twist. To inflict self-harm is not necessarily a means of courting death—it never was for me—but it's a glutting of vicious impulse that, however paradoxical it seems, brings a ghoulish sort of quietude. Pain shocks us into pause, and sometimes we yearn to be still.

When I was twelve, I might have told you that I cut myself because I was ugly (I believed that I was, anyway, and that is all that matters). Or, maybe I cut myself because I had earned a B-plus on an algebra test: imperfect results that demanded a different, more visceral, kind of lesson than whatever the quadratic formula had failed to illuminate. But these episodes, however clear the trajectory seemed from mishap to masochism, grew from a recalcitrant, gut-level sense of my own essential superfluity. By pre-adolescence, I learned that my too muchness extended beyond a social and familial inconvenience. I had absorbed biting feedback, both from people who loved me and those who didn't, and it swelled from within my chest, flush and acidic. I wanted to be perfect—comely, charming, and beloved—but it seemed that others found me excessive. And all at once, I decided that they were right, and for more reasons than they knew. This matter of being so distended with feeling, of flinching against the gravelly scrape of criticism, even when it was light and well-meaning—it had become unbearable. Something gelatinous seemed to consume me from the inside, harboring in its mass every crime for which I had indicted myself: being too sensitive, too gawky, too inclined to tears. It *was* too much—being like this, feeling this way. I felt myself tumbling against the world, knocking against it at every turn, the jelly mass that burgeoned from my chest ballooning, quivering urgently, inexorably. It seemed ever-ready to pop, and yet refused, choking me instead with its precarious, taut bulk.

Given these intense conditions, and the extremity of my makeshift solution to them, you would be reasonable to assume that I remember my inaugural cutting episode. But I don't. From the first time—it was seventh grade, this much I recall—they conjoined as moments of ritual, one hardly discernible from the other because the effect was much the same: a thickening in my brain, a demented serenity as I meticulously scratched parallel lines along my torso. My tool of choice was a pair of purple scissors that commingled innocently among pens, clips, and other small tchotchkes, all stuffed into a hand-painted clay pot my mother had bought for me when I was little.

The scissors hid in plain sight, whimsical tools for my amateurish craft projects—cutting out celebrities from teeny-bopper magazines, mostly—until they were repurposed for more macabre aims. Sometimes, after looking at my face in the mirror, I would unravel into gasping fury and apply the blades with less care, impatiently enclosing them on a pinch of skin, then pressing and twisting. Once, after a fight with a friend, I carved the word "FUCK" into my forearm. I always took care to conceal my work, but in that particular case, a classmate spied the angry red scrawl and, unbeknownst to me, called my mother from school. When I slipped into the passenger seat during carpool, she turned to me, exasperated and accusing: "Let me see it. I know it's there."

My parents already knew about this habit of mine; I told

them after an especially miserable weekend during which I had foraged for bottles of Tylenol and Advil and Motrin, lined them up on my bedroom floor, and contemplated them, little pharmacological pawns at the ready and willing to provide. (Years later, I would learn that this particular poison, while thankfully allowing me time to think better of my actions and seek help, resulted in being force-fed a bowl of liquid charcoal which is, to say the least, fucking disgusting.) After a bout with the purple scissors, I swallowed six Tylenol, not because I thought it would have any effect, but as a bizarre practice round for the main event that, every now and then, penciled itself between the lines of my school planner. Then I clambered to my feet. This was an awfully lousy pastime, cutting myself and dwelling on a slew of fatalistic musings, primarily among them: "If I kill myself, the boys can't laugh at me when I pass them in the hall." During seventh and eighth grade the tormenting and behind-the-back whispers could send anyone home in tears, but I feared—often believed—that what my schoolmates had to say about me was true, and I loathed myself for it. I loathed myself, but I didn't want to, and I didn't want to die, not really. I wanted to believe there were other possibilities, that the tunnel cowering over me concealed, somewhere, a small, but traversable, passage of light.

Timidly, I padded downstairs. My father's parents were staying with my sisters and me while our parents traveled, and I found my grandfather in quiet repose on the couch, watching television. I sat next to him and promptly began to sob. His face folded into worry, and he put his arm around me as he summoned my grandmother. They listened, gently prodding here and there, as I confided everything: how I had been cutting myself for months, how sometimes death presented itself as a seductive option, how, despite my desire to be otherwise, I was colossally, achingly sad. That night, when my parents returned, my grandmother organized a family meeting and asked me to tell them what I had expressed earlier that afternoon.

My parents were, unsurprisingly, troubled. They were also, I think, frustrated, and a little angry. I can't imagine anyone would like being ambushed with such news after a weekend away: Surprise! Your twelve-year-old daughter, whom you love and have given every advantage, is super bummed and has taken a fancy to self-injury! They interpreted my circumstances as a result of narcissism: I spent so much time wallowing—what if I considered those who didn't enjoy my same privileges? It made sense: I was, after all, thinking about myself a great deal. But those thoughts were not deliberate mental pathways; rather, they were compulsive, unproductive circuits of self-abuse. When I began volunteering at a food bank, my mind was no less inclined to declare war on itself. Any moment of pleasure would be swiftly harpooned by dark, boring, but insistent vocabulary: ugly, undesirable, unwanted. And then, the old refrain sounded out: Cut, cut, cut.

I couldn't tell my mother or father because I didn't know how to apply words to this new habit that had become so corporally tempting. I knew it was a punishment of sorts, although I'm not sure I ever articulated that to anyone besides my therapist, the one found for me soon after I confessed my self-harm. As with most experiences, it registers more clearly in the rearview mirror: cutting became my means of self-regulation and conditioning, a way to snip away at my superfluity and trim my edges. I was learning, obliquely, that too muchness could be as dangerous as it was integral to my disposition. I was cellophane, punctured and ripped by a world that could not accommodate my need for softness. It seemed to me pathetic, this inability to countenance my bratty classmates, my reflection, or a perplexing algebra problem, without regarding life as a catastrophe. I didn't understand why I was always spilling everywhere, my emotions too mammoth to remain packaged and kempt: instead, my insides sloshed out like an intestinal flood, disgusting everyone with their red vulnerability, and rendering me ashamed and bent with self-loathing.

The conundrum, of course, was that my solution only exacerbated the symptoms I was so desperate to conceal. I undertook cutting with the same precision that guided my schoolwork and my writing, and when the exercise held me in its thrall, I didn't cry; I was silent and stony-faced—the way I most desired to be. Self-harm was a pressure valve as much as it was a form of discipline, and in its screwy way, it worked until I disclosed the activity to my parents and until, sometime later, my classmates learned my secret through the junior high gossip grist mill. Cutting contained a lucid kind of logic to me—emotionally, it kept me in line—but to others, it was wild, a certain mark of insanity. I became a punch line; one fair-weather friend referred to me in a tirade as "Suicidal Rachel," which is not especially creative but conveyed the sentiment. Cutting, the very thing that I had resorted to in order to curb my too muchness, became its principal evidence. What reasonable girl would do such a thing, after all? My parents suspected that I was overly dramatic and obsessed with myself; my classmates considered me—when they considered me at all—a flagrantly unbalanced nerd. In the meantime, I had handed myself over to the regimen of addiction. I didn't consider the whys or what-fors: I only knew I wanted to keep cutting, and so I did.

———

Every woman- and girl-identified person who self-harms experiences pain and its associated rituals with fundamental specificity. It's a practice, often an addiction, as it was in my case, undertaken for a myriad of purposes and in response to all manner of impulses. But what we do share is the restive, tapestried history of female self-inflicted pain. In an attempt to make sense of my own inclinations toward masochism, I've muddled through the sandy borderland between socially sanctioned mutilation and stigmatized mental illness. And I've learned, as most girls do in their youth, one of the guiding lessons of femininity: that the world does not want our anguish. It would sooner smother it—us—and for centuries has done just that.

Our suppression of female self-harm manifests itself across Western culture, where mutilation emerges primarily, and most prominently, as a masculine mode of self-purification. We often see it occur in fiction: a man, often a blatant misogynist, resorts to self-harm in an attempt to cleanse himself from unholy erotic desires. In *The Scarlet Letter* (1850), certain adaptations of the *Hunchback of Notre Dame* (1831), *Brave New World* (1931), and in *Sweeney Todd: The Demon Barber of Fleet Street* (1973), women are figured as corrupting forces, engendering lust that must be extinguished. Arthur Dimmesdale, the craven minister who abandons his lover and their daughter in Nathaniel Hawthorne's novel, self-flagellates as a ritual of penance and spiritual cleansing. Meanwhile, he allows his lover, protagonist Hester Prynne, to be shunned by their claustrophobic Puritan community, forced to wear a crimson "A" on her dress to signal her sin of adultery. Hester, through this public shaming, is divested of autonomy and reduced to a hieroglyph, becoming a mere signifier of the temptations for which Dimmesdale self-indulgently performs penance.

The elderly Judge Turpin in *Sweeney Todd* similarly mistakes righteous self-pity for repentance. After making a habit of spying on his ward, Johanna, his voyeurism leaves him undone by desire and contemptuous of the girl's alleged "mockery" and "temptation." Like Dimmesdale, he whips himself to expel his fleshly yearnings, all the while dwelling in an egomaniacal enactment of self-loathing. For these men, shame is sexualized, and intertwined with the misogynistic blame they direct at the objects of their sordid passion. What they most seek is neither humility nor forgiveness, but rather to reassert patriarchal power—over their desires and over women—through the brutality of their masochism.

These Western narratives are, collectively, an index of the broad, cultural interpretation of women as ministers of male pain—women's suffering is always relationally subordinate. However, the men from each of these narratives vary broadly in disposition and ethos. For instance, John the Savage, from Aldous Huxley's dystopian *Brave New World*, engages in self-flagellation not merely as a reaction to sexual longing, but due to a larger existential horror born from his experiences in a spiritually and culturally barren society. As John wrestles in torment, his snakebit romance with Lenina Crowne looms large, but she is one, albeit consequential, example of the moral corruption he rebuffs. Nonetheless, in each text and script women are posited as pain emissaries—in some cases as Jezebels brandishing their bodies to tempt and tease—and these designations obscure their own agonies. When John attacks Lenina, when Claude Frollo witnesses Esmeralda's hanging in *The Hunchback of Notre Dame*, their demented logic substantiates: any woman who propels me to masochism ought to suffer. Her own devastated body atones for mine.

But we might argue that, more than anything else, female self-mutilation has been integrated into cultural narratives in a way unique to the gender. That, in fact, it has been hiding in plain sight as rituals of religion or of beauty. In the Middle Ages, female martyrs like Saint Wilgefortis starved themselves to secure their chastity in the face of eager suitors. Wilgefortis, ultimately, grew a beard, and the rest of her body sprouted a sort of pelage that disgusted her wealthy gallant. Roaring mad at her defiance, her father sentenced her to crucifixion. Certain accounts also tell of the young and avid Saint Mary Magdalene de' Pazzi who, in the seventeenth century, followed Saint Wilgefortis's example. By age ten, she secretly donned a crown of thorns and whipped herself, both practices of self-abnegation. By age twenty, she had joined a convent, where she limited her diet to bread and water—a dictate from God, she claimed—and coaxed the novices to both whip her and to stand on her mouth. She also continued her ritual of self-flagellation, often in public view, which she undertook to exorcise the demons rollicking inside of her. She died at age thirty-seven, refusing, while on her deathbed, any physical contact from the other nuns, lest they be stricken with erotic desire.

Centuries later, women continued to brutalize themselves,

although the aim, rather than blessed transcendence, was profoundly material. Victorian fashion strapped women into corsets, seizing ribs and lungs in an effort to abide by grinding beauty dictates. They gulped pills containing tapeworms in order to facilitate weight loss (a so-called diet that has not been fully abandoned even today). For hundreds of years women have been grimly disciplining and disfiguring their bodies, shattering their bones, in the service of sexual desirability. But these customs, while violent, are unique and by no means equivalent to masochistic impulse. Moreover, the way a woman chooses to express herself through physical presentation is strictly her business—that she possesses the choice is the paramount matter. Still, we must recognize one bald fact: while women's bodily suffering has been policed and disregarded, and our grapples with mental health stigmatized, we have always been encouraged to wreak havoc upon ourselves, so long as it is in the interest of male desire.

In an interview from 2000, critic Elaine Scarry positions suffering and creation as "radical opposites."[1] Hegemonic gender edicts have indeed stipulated our unmaking—our suffering they have brushed aside. In the meantime we have mutilated ourselves, whittling down our bodies according to au courant beauty metrics. And we have been not so much congratulated as admonished against respite. Destroy your body, and perhaps you might live.

These are socially sanctioned forms of self-harm, acts taught and committed in docile compliance. A woman's body punished her for donning a corset; nonetheless, the precious resource of cultural capital triumphed over fleshly discomfort. But in the late nineteenth century, doctors took notice of a more singular and specifically masochistic variation of female self-harm—pain inflicted methodically, purposefully, and for its own sake. At the time women's pain was often—and is still—regarded as a biological and even moral necessity, but when Too Much women regulated their sensorial experiences in such strident ways, the medical institution was baffled, and rather tantalized. Women who intentionally harmed themselves were regarded as sites of sexual excess; in the Victorian era, a time equally infamous for extreme repression and unflagging fascination with sex, medical journals puzzled over the "Needle-Girls" phenomenon—"a peculiar type of selfmutilation... sometimes seen in hysteric persons"[2] wherein women began pricking themselves with their sewing needles, even threading them into their skin.

Of course, not all of these so-called "hysteric persons" used needles as their implement of choice. In 1896, for example, physicians George Gould and Walter Pyle published their observations of one thirty-year-old woman in New York in *Anomalies and Curiosities of Medicine*, noting that she had "cut her left wrist and right hand" in late September of 1876. Three weeks later, after being refused opium, she reportedly "again cut her arms below the elbows, cleanly severing the skin and fascia, and completely hacking the muscles in every direction." She continued this pattern of self-mutilation at intervals of a few weeks, sometimes inserting objects like shards of glass and splinters into her wounds. (According to the article, the woman cut herself for the last time in June 1877.)

Contemporary medicine diagnosed these women as hysterics, their self-harm a symptom of their femininity and, thus, their fundamental emotional surfeit. For articulating their suffering they were branded with hysteria's stigma. Many were unnecessarily bundled away in asylums, deemed irreparably ill because their words went unheeded. In L. E. Emerson's 1914 *The Case of Miss A*, a psychoanalytical study, he endeavors to understand a twenty-three-year-old patient referred to as Miss A, who told doctors that she had cut herself "twenty-eight or thirty times." He recounts her history, one fraught with the trauma of sexual assault and its stigma: For "many years (five or six)," she was sexually abused by an uncle and, years later, one of her cousins attempted to sexually assault her as well. Finally, she was abandoned by a suitor after he discovered she wasn't a virgin. The suitor called her a whore, Emerson writes, and pierced by this rejection, she later carved a "W" into her leg.

Emerson remarks upon "the sexual nature of her acts," noting that the "relationship to Hawthorne's *Scarlet Letter* is interesting." Operating in the Freudian school, he deduces that there were numerous motives for her self-mutilation: The first was that "cutting was a sort of symbolical substitute for masturbation." Miss A was also propelled by "a desire to escape mental distress" and a longing to punish herself. Emerson moreover surmises that she intentionally drew her own blood out of "a desire for regular menstruation." While his interpretations may not be entirely wrong-headed, they are narrow, almost foregone conclusions in an age when women's suffering was conceived simultaneously as a medical oddity and a gendered imperative, filtered through psychoanalytic discourse that saw women as fundamentally deficient with constitutions too histrionic for measured self-expression. What might these women have said for themselves if male physicians had not been so hasty to speak for them?

———

"Pain—has an Element of Blank—," writes Emily Dickinson in Poem 650, "It cannot recollect / When it begun—or if there were / A time when it was not—." "No Future—but itself." Pain, as Dickinson imagines it here, is the alpha and omega of a spontaneous universe created with its first throb. It is not deliverance, per se, unless blankness is what you seek, but it is a state that is both complete and transient. There is no evidence to be had that Dickinson was contemplating self-harm when she wrote these verses, yet however unintentionally, she captures a state, an episode I've chased like a darting light: it looks like a summons, it seems like a promise, and yet it always slips away, a thingless mirage that tantalizes a nd vanishes.

I didn't know Dickinson's poem when I was twelve and had begun to rush toward pain as a way of harpooning the mass of my emotions. But, always one to seek liberation through words, I hungered for any narrative or scrap of verses that I could interpret, however broadly, as literary companions to my own overwhelming unhappiness. I scrounged and hoarded these lines and passages like treasures: lyrics from a Tori Amos song—I had just discovered Tori and considered her my personal savior—the alienating tragedies of a Cynthia Voigt novel, or harrowing narratives like William Styron's *Sophie's Choice*, *The Diary of Anne Frank*, which I read and reread, and Nien Cheng's memoir *Life and Death in Shanghai*. Books like the latter three felt instructive in their engendering of deep humility: I would never suffer anything like these women, real and fictional, and because my father's family descends from Eastern European Jews, I was aware that people quite close to me, whom I would never know, had endured and died at the hands of evil that cast my own emollient circumstances as shamefully soft. In these ways, the written word provided solace, but elliptically, or, in the latter cases, they supplied that old, treasured idol: perspective.

But if there were many nonvictimizing narratives about self-harm when I was a young teenager, I did not know them. I did, however, know girls like me, who cut, and when we found each other it was exhilarating, like locating another member of some twisted secret society, the banner of which we had previously carried furtively, and alone. Because cutting was not necessarily a pathway to suicide; it could be managed, concealed, and shared as common, sacred terrain. It served us as a pressure valve for too muchness—a physiological transference. We compared methods and tools, which varied: I preferred scissors; another friend, one of my dearest, hid shards of broken CDs and glass in her bedroom. One night, when I was sleeping over at her house, she retreated to her bathroom to cut in the wake of a romantic disappointment.

The glass slipped, I think. It sliced her fourteen-year-old skin with more severity than—I hope—she intended. I was anxiously awaiting her return when she burst into her room, slick red blood scribbling down her leg. We huddled together in the dark as she summoned the courage to clean the wound, two quivering figures on the kitchen floor. I was worry-stricken and wanted to tell her to stop—I knew we both ought to, that the monster we indulged only proffered the illusion of a tamer beast—but I also knew that I wouldn't. And why, in that case, should she listen to me?

Throughout the rest of junior high and high school, I

continued my scissor ritual, intermittently swearing it off forever, but gradually slouching back into the same miserable but
reliable practice. I discovered Francesca Lia Block's novel *Violet
& Claire*, perhaps the first time I encountered a reference to
cutting on the page, not to mention a female intimacy that
seemed as passionate as the love I harbored for my closest
friends. When I read Stephen Chbosky's *The Perks of Being a
Wallflower* I relished its sentimental maximalism, its depiction
of teenagers who sought the "infinite"—big, wide-eyed moments, the possibility of feeling everything—in the context
of a visceral story of trauma and mental illness. Books could
not cure me, and I didn't expect them to, but the shame that
churned inside my gut whenever I hurt myself or caught a
glimpse of the aftermath peeking from beneath my sleeve or at
the lip of my shirt began to ease in small but meaningful ways.

And yet, writing about self-harm as a distinct practice, one
undertaken for its own sake, remains relatively spare. By the
1960s, "confessional" poets like Sylvia Plath and others had
thrust mental health into Western cultural discourse. Plath only
seems to have written about cutting once, but her work renders
with unflinching precision the experiences of mental illness and
women's psychiatric care. (Her novel *The Bell Jar*, published in
1963, is the most famous example and is rightly admired as a
triumph of the genre.) Joanne Greenberg's semiautobiographical
novel *I Never Promised You a Rose Garden* (1964), written under the pen name Hannah Green, is another rare, mid-century
text that depicts self-harm. These are important and devastating
works. But because Plath died tragically, by suicide, her per-
sonage too often becomes obscured by the froth of mythos.
Americans do love their sad, sick girls, especially posthumously.

Plath's 1962 poem "Cut"—spare, yet visceral—was published in her renowned, posthumous volume *Ariel*. The title
implied rather than stated, we encounter the speaker in medias
res, as she observes the pulse of her fresh wound: "A flap like
a hat / Dead white / Then that red plush." "Cut" evokes an
aspect of self-harm that most confounds the cultural imagination: that someone—in this case a cutter—might regard her
gruesome act with bemusement, wonder, or even relief.

By puberty, the experience of inhabiting my body had become nearly insupportable, like a top-to-toe experience of
staring at the sun. Feeling had become too pronounced, almost
synesthetic, and so it was through turning on myself, staging a
physical confrontation, that I managed, however fleetingly, to
detach from it. Briefly, I could shift the pronouns and transform
my body into a depersonalized collection of parts: my torso
became a torso; my wrist was merely a wrist. "A million soldiers run / Redcoats, every one," Plath's speaker remarks as the
blood spills. But this rush, born from the act, is accompanied by
curious detachment. "Whose side are they on?" she wonders.[3]
I chased this ambivalence—to both live in my body and to not
care about it, to not even entirely register it as my own, this
was exhilaration. The next day, as my skin began to knit itself
back together, I would examine the wound as if I had happened
upon a blossom or bush that someone else had recently planted,
and which I had only just noticed.

The parameters of self-harm are capacious, so much so that
representing it can be a tangled business. Sometimes its circumstances are tethered to a death wish, but not exclusively.
Some cutters adopt conventions that they follow with liturgical
care, and yet urge triumphs over ritual: if, for instance, I was

overwhelmed by the impulse at school, I would surreptitiously scratch my wrist beneath the desk until my nails were wadded with skin. Often enough, cutting doesn't suit as an accurate depiction of the masochistic practice. And so, within this web of self-harm practitioners, we have few emissaries—people to whom we can turn for resonant testimonials in a similar way to seeking guidance from those in recovery from addiction or those who live with various forms of mental illness: self-harm, after all, generally incorporates both. But representative figures require an element of specificity—they must be remembered for something definitive, an action rounded off with a period, rather than a protracted ellipses. Self-mutilation, cumbersome term that it is, fundamentally defies particular designations. But then every experience of mental illness is a symphony of pain, and though we have sought and appointed ambassadors as a route to understanding, much of our discourse remains reductive, limiting, with so many narratives thus far unheard.

It was not until the 1990s that the American cultural imagination indicated a degree of readiness to face the severe phenomenon of self-harm. This particular decade saw an uptick in teenage suicide,[4] which surely explains the catalyzed social investment. 1994 was also the publication year of Dr. Mary Pipher's *Reviving Ophelia*, a book that briefly claimed eminent authority on the fraught experience of adolescent girlhood. At the same time, young women living with mental illness found a surrogate in Elizabeth Wurtzel, author of the juggernaut 1994 memoir *Prozac Nation: Young and Depressed in America*. Were self-mutilation to choose a poster child, Wurtzel would likely be assigned that grim title. Now something of a celebrity after *Prozac Nation* was adapted as a film starring Christina Ricci,

Wurtzel has published a number of other books and written for a slew of publications. But in the early nineties, *Prozac Nation* offered many female readers a familiar but elusive narrative: it chronicles Wurtzel's experimentation with cutting.

In *Prozac Nation*, Wurtzel depicts self-harm as a mode of negotiation, an attempt to harness intangible shitty feelings. This impulse is familiar to me. When my own anguish or shame or self-hatred broiled with overwhelming ferocity, I sought to temper it by giving it a body—my body. It provided me with the illusion of control; after all, it is far easier to assume sovereignty over something we can touch. If the female martyrs rendered themselves whipping posts, flesh to eviscerate as a means of transcendence, Wurtzel employs the body as a canvas with powers of emotional transfiguration:

I did not, you see, want to kill myself. Not at that time, anyway. But I wanted to know that if need be, if the desperation got so terribly bad, I could inflict harm on my body. And I could. Knowing this gave me a sense of peace and power, so I started cutting my legs all the time. Hiding the scars from my mother became a sport of its own. I collected razor blades. I bought a Swiss army knife, I became fascinated with the different kinds of sharp edges and the different cutting sensations they produced. I tried out different shapes—squares, triangles, pentagons, even an awkwardly carved heart, with a stab wound at its center, wanting to see if it hurt the way a real broken heart could hurt. I was amazed and pleased to find that it didn't.[5]

Here, finally, was sustained attention to cutting—perhaps one of the first instances in mainstream culture and one not exclusively framed as a prelude to suicidal ideation. Taken together, Plath's "Cut" and Wurtzel's account of her self-harm rituals gesture to the paradoxical yearning so fundamental to cutting: to at once be fully inside one's body, but also floating above it, an observer whose interest has been strangely piqued.

Yet, because the brutalized female body has been so fetishized, depicting female pain in all its visceral nuance can be tricky. Gillian Flynn's first novel, *Sharp Objects*, adapted as an HBO miniseries in 2018, introduced a wide audience of readers to one interpretation of female self-harm through its protagonist, Camille Preaker, a journalist who returns to her claustrophobic, Confederacy-bent hometown in order to cover the murders of two preteen girls. The sadism visited upon the young victims, their bodies warped into sites of suffering and horror, sits in restive tension with Camille's own topography of pain: since adolescence, she has carved words into her skin as a means of creating permanence out of the ephemeral:

All I know is that the cutting made me feel safe. It was proof. Thoughts and words, captured where I could see them and track them. The truth, stinging, on my skin, in a freakish short-hand. Tell me you're going to the doctor, and I'll want to cut *worrisome* on my arm. Say you've fallen in love and I buzz the outlines of *tragic* over my breast. I hadn't necessarily wanted to be cured. But I was out of places to write, slicing myself between my toes—*bad, cry*—like a junkie looking for one last vein. *Vanish* did it for me. I'd saved the next, such a nice prime spot, for one final good cutting. Then I turned myself in.[6]

It's fitting that Camille, who from childhood can depend on so little, would obsess over the possibilities of endurance—the things we can keep. The conditions of her upbringing render her perpetually bereft, with a mother who does not love her, a father she has never met and whose identity is impossibly smudged, and a stepfather who is uninterested in cultivating their relationship. The younger sister she adored also slips through her fingers, dying in childhood. There is "safety" in wounds and the scars they breed because they supply evidence—that we are here, that we can act, that we can, at least sometimes, choose what we feel.

In the miniseries, Amy Adams delivers a performance as Camille that is both tender and unyielding. Her character's history of self-harm is not applied as a hackneyed narrative device, diminished to allegory as is so often the case with women's suffering. Instead, viewers are confronted with the gut impulse to fling oneself toward violence. Through Adams, we witness, albeit through the indirection of theatricality, the yen for one's own blood, the inexorable urge to visit physical destruction upon oneself because the mere act of living in the world is, often, too much. To the extent that self-harm is a punishment—and I would not presume that everyone sees it that way—it illuminates a visceral fact of patriarchy: to exist as a woman or femme can feel untenable, but we are taught that every difficulty demonstrates our own insufficiencies and weaknesses. We are instructed, through every possible socio-cultural channel, to hold ourselves accountable for the slog of matriculation in a country that doesn't especially care about or respect us. When ensnared in a trap, an animal, left with no other recourse, will eventually gnaw at its own limb in a bloody ploy for freedom. Here's the paradox: sometimes we cut ourselves in order to survive.

———

With the exceptions of *Prozac Nation*, *Sharp Objects*, and *Girl, Interrupted*—Kaysen makes reference to her inclinations toward self-harm late in the memoir—nonclinical writing on female masochism is sporadic. We have seen these narratives surface in the early aughts, but their entrance has been halting and timid. Yet, in *The Empathy Exams*, Leslie Jamison tenderly and tenaciously considers the subject while supplying one potential reason for this dearth: it's a dilemma of representation. How do we authentically depict female pain in a milieu that has long fetishized it? "The hard part is that underneath this obscene fascination with women who hurt themselves," she writes, "…there are actual women who hurt themselves."[7] Young adult literature has also engaged the topic, with conspicuous titles like *Cut* by Patricia McCormick and *Scars* by Cheryl Rainfield. Research has indicated that self-mutilation serves as a form of punishment for girls more often than for boys, and that, in the meantime, girls are more likely to perform stability and competence. To be sure, my aim was foremost to mete out retribution, whether motivated by an unfriendly mirror or a B-plus. This inclination to absorb one's own rage bears out in studies on prisoners: women are more likely to harm themselves—men, each other.[8]

And so bearing witness is our recourse, our one tool to chisel through our own myopic self-absorption. Pain grows like fungus; it insists on our company. "You can't live without me," it chides, and I suppose it's right. We won't eradicate suffering—it's a consequence of breathing—and we almost certainly cannot eradicate self-injury. I've not fully extinguished my own inclinations; I doubt if ever I will.

But I am better, and I am happier—not always, sometimes only barely. Although nearly dormant, the urge to self-harm will find its open doors. When I grow angry, my first impulse is to strike myself against the side of my head as hard as I can, again and again and again. Paul rushes to stop me before I grow too violent and unwieldy, before the slaps begin to feel ludicrously insufficient and I must seek severer methods. Years ago I might have fought him, wildly; sometimes even now I struggle against him at first, before I realize that I feel something else: relief.

It saddens me at times that after over twenty years, I haven't managed to fully relinquish my long-held ritual. A confession: I cut myself in the midst of writing this chapter, old habits quickened, I suppose, by the barb of memory. I am still learning that self-harm is not narcissism. A woman who is cutting is not indulging; she is carving out a route to survival, the only one that's perceptible to her. And although she is no culprit, although she owes neither defense nor apology, she is already ashamed.

Chapter Eight

HORNY

One humdrum winter afternoon, during winter break of my freshman year of college, I sheepishly tucked myself into bed, accompanied by a woebegone McDonald's Happy Meal toy. This plaything—a small car—held no emotional significance for me; on the contrary, I had seized it in a fit of sexual desperation: when packing for vacation, I had forgotten my vibrator, which was, as a result, sitting uselessly—maddeningly!—inside my dorm room. At first, I suffered only minor concern: surely I could survive a month of fumbling with my bunglesome fingers. But two weeks of gravely unsuccessful endeavors into digital masturbation rendered me bereft—bereft, and very, very horny. I was single, but while relatively free with my kisses, I was, at the time, less inclined to become intimate under casual circumstances. I also didn't have my driver's license, so I couldn't drive independently to Nancy's Nook, Virginia Beach's trusted source for erotic paraphernalia—and while my mother and I were close, asking her to accompany me was decidedly out of the question. Besides, in my state of erotic derangement, I required immediate satisfaction.

I had seen *American Pie*, and I knew that in the quest for an orgasm, necessity often bred creativity. Surely there was a tool somewhere in my family's house that I could repurpose, one that wouldn't be missed or ruined by my meddling. And so I rummaged through bins of cheap old toys, primarily the spoils of yesteryear's kids' meals, all long abandoned by my sisters and me. I examined each one, contemplating their respective capacities for clitoral stimulation. Mostly, I was disappointed. And then, finally, I happened upon a toy car with rubbery, rotating wheels: it wasn't much, and yet, perhaps, just perhaps, if I were inventive and patient, ecstasy awaited.

But let's not tarry on delusions: it won't surprise you that my efforts were an utter failure, and that after roughly thirty minutes of masturbating with a Happy Meal toy, I was forced to abandon the project. Thankfully, one male friend was in town with whom I'd shared a couple of very casual interludes, and I determined that the urgency of my carnal requirements outweighed the embarrassment of asking him to drive me to Nancy's Nook. He kindly agreed, and at last, I was delivered to my trusted hanky-panky retailer, where I surveyed their vast and comprehensive wall of dildos and vibrators. Preferring simplicity, I selected a violet and white striped dildo with modulated speeds. I'm happy to say that we enjoyed several years together before she ascended to the sex toy shop in the sky.

———

My forays into the wide world of battery-operated stimulation, while eager, did not start until late in teenhood, when I received my first vibrator as a gag Christmas gift. Until then, I indulged in fantasies of my own design, navigating sexual desire as a preadolescent through erotic world-building. I fantasized while skating at the roller rink, adopting a ritual wherein during each excursion I requested that the DJ play "Slide" by the Goo Goo Dolls. Then I zipped along, my thoughts efflorescing into a twelve-year-old's version of sexy musings. Too naïve to understand the song—that it narrates a man's reaction to his girlfriend's pregnancy—I fixated on a scrap of lines from the chorus: "Oh, May, put your arms around me / What you feel is what you are and what you are is beautiful." To feel beautiful, to understand it as personal truth, was a sensation so foreign as to seem exotic—and as for being told that a beloved someone found me so, well, I couldn't fathom it. But music provided the soundtrack to my burgeoning erotic awareness, and when I glided through the rink in my plastic Rollerblades, speed and melody transported me from my gawky pre-adolescent body; I became an airborne essence capable of inhabiting another reality—one in which I was May: who was beautiful and, according to the man who loved her, could, however faintly, perceive that beauty as her own.

In junior high, what struck me as most climactic was not intercourse, the mechanisms of which still confused me, but instead the possibility of reciprocal, lustrous longing, of being touched—anywhere—and the passionate kisses that illuminated the desire for so much more than my uninitiated mind could comprehend. In the dark of night, huddled under the covers with my Walkman, I began touching myself, but with the bashful timidity of a girl intimidated by her own depths. When I discovered Sarah McLachlan's album *Fumbling Towards Ecstasy*, the title seemed a canny summation of my circumstances.

I think that I sensed, in my early adolescence, that sexual yearning, like my other physiological experiences, would be, for me, something both colossal and untamable. I sought out music that expressed my wellspring of longing, glomming onto sweeping, womblike melodies and self-serious, nearly liturgical instrumentals. I taped Sarah McLachlan singles off the radio: "Possession," of course, as well as "Sweet Surrender" and "Building a Mystery." I swiped my mother's Loreena McKennitt album *The Book of Secrets* (1997) so that I could act out the part of the sacrificial lover in "The Highwayman," and I lay prone on the floor as "Dante's Prayer" swam inside my ears. I imagined losing my virginity to half of the Pure Moods compilation, and could hardly listen to Enigma's "Sadeness" for fear that the rapid breaths at its middle—heady and urgent—would unspool me like thread. At age twelve, sex's significance lived in its proximity to mortality: in fantasizing about it, I was imagining a love so tectonic it knocked you to your knees, a person so adored that you would sacrifice yourself to spare them. These, of course, were the fancies of a spoiled girl who, because of her penchant for melodrama, tended to imagine her first sexual encounter taking place inside of a temple, preferably on an altar of some kind.

Over the course of teenhood—after I had kissed boys and begun to understand the rapture of mutual arousal—the oceanic pull of desire continued to rise up in my chest and throat, unwieldy and, I feared, hazardous. Still a virgin, and still relatively inexperienced, I was never concerned about what I might do, but instead what these feelings implied. My fantasies were imbued with the shame of too muchness, by then a familiar and diligent attendant. By senior year of high school—after I had been gifted my first vibrator—worrying over being too much meant, for me, fretting over my avid masturbation habit and my enjoyment of pornography, which I would download on the trusty and legally dubious platform Kazaa and then, after satiating myself, delete in embarrassment. Would lovers find me grotesque? Would they think my carnality indelicate and, thus, unfeminine? To this day, I have difficulty invoking the word "horny"; it is so contextually tailored to male desire, to say nothing of its phallic imagery, that it seems to condemn any woman to whom it is applied.

Of course these insecurities are culturally manufactured. Women, after all, are not supposed to be "horny"—at least not in ways deviating from the illusions proffered in heteronormative, male-directed pornography. The word, crass and imperious, connotes a desire that is, fittingly, unselfconsciously demanding. Even now, Western culture condemns these experiences when made manifest by women. Significantly, the word also calls to mind the term "cuckold,"[1] a mocking name for a man whose wife has been unfaithful. In both art and literature this disgrace was sometimes designated with a set of horns to be worn by the unlucky husband. To be a "horny" woman, then, is to be sexually unruly, with an appetite so excessive it yields crimes of infidelity and perversity—and, most notably, male sexual humiliation.

For women to celebrate their horniness nakedly, and on their own terms, is an act of necessary sexual resistance, but one that stigmatizes and even endangers its practitioners. American culture mystifies female self-pleasure and even intense sexual longing, occasionally essaying a vibrator joke, but pussyfooting (no pun intended) around feminine erotic desire. Most women need to get off, and some more often than others. Centuries of misogyny have normalized the perspective that women who engage frequent sexual partners and—crucially—do not conceal it are sluts. And now, as we navigate the brambles of the #MeToo movement, conservative obsession with female purity virulently persists, an organizing principle for continued efforts to manage women's desire. But sexual too muchness does not merely comprise the resulting action; it also includes the originating drive: we're just as fidgety when women speak openly about wanting to fuck. A horny woman is always a desperate woman, a figure of fun and a punch line. Sometimes, if we squint, it may seem as if we've traveled miles from the intense Victorianesque slut-shaming of previous decades, but the conversation has in fact taken the form of a false binary: a woman is either a slut or she is a joke—and in many cases, she is both.

———

The myth of Victorian prudery is one of the prevailing misconceptions about nineteenth-century culture. We've adopted an understanding of Victorian culture as systemically excising sex from every corner, muffling sensuality into repressed silence. French philosopher Michel Foucault refers to this theory as "The Repressive Hypothesis." But as he explains, this notion of prudery is an illusion—the Victorians were *always* talking about sex; they were simply doing so in accordance with very specific and regimented provisions:

> Yet when one looks back over these last three centuries with their continual transformations, things appear in a very different light: around and apropos of sex, one sees a veritable discursive explosion. We must be clear on this point, however. It is quite possible that there was an ex-purgation—and a very rigorous one—of the authorized vocabulary ... [But there] was a steady proliferation of dis-courses concerned with sex—specific discourses, different from one another both by their form and their object: a discursive ferment that gathered momentum from the eighteenth century onward.[2]

For Foucault, whose philosophy was rooted in the study of power structures and how individuals are shaped by the larger forces that control them, the "proliferation" of sex talk in Victorian society is less significant than the matter of who had the authority to speak about it, the positions and viewpoints from which people spoke about it, and the institu-tions that prompted people to speak about it, as well as how that information was dispersed. The motivations for power and knowledge, he claims, cannot be extricated from one another—power is amassed through knowledge, and in accu-mulating knowledge, we become more powerful.[3] But make no mistake: for those who possessed power—members of the church, medical doctors, the criminal justice system—there was pleasure in having the authority to control and moni-tor sex, and in coming to possess knowledge about it too.

For example, different hegemonic structures scrutinized sexual "perversities"—same-sex desire, for example—because they were attracted to the possibilities of seizing that knowledge and enticed by the very content itself. Foucault also explains that those who fled from these multifarious, searching entities gained pleasure through that act of circumvention or, in other circumstances, by confessing their so-called sexual perversities. Both parties, the seeker and the sought, found satisfaction in their role within this coiled game of cat and mouse, a self-reiterating process that Foucault refers to as the regime of "power-knowledge-pleasure."[4]

Alas, Foucault didn't have much to say about patriarchy or where women fit into this paradigm, which, while limited, is a useful one. But it will be no surprise that it was men who wielded power in terms of sexual discourse, including writers whose work fell under the so-called realm of perversity. Between 1879 and 1880, Victorian pornographer William Lazenby published the underground erotic magazine *The Pearl: A Magazine of Facetiae and Voluptuous Reading*,[5] which included titles like "Miss Pokingham; or They All Do It," not to mention a prodigious amount of flogging content (it was shuttered by authorities due to its obscenity). Poet Algernon Charles Swinburne is thought to have contributed to the periodical and to have authored the anonymously published *Whippingham Papers* (1887) which, as the name suggests, is entirely devoted to flagellation. Female characters were present in this literature, with names like Miss Tickletouch and Miss Latecome and Miss Switchem, but their exploits, however lusty, were almost certainly penned for male pleasure. A brief play, entitled "A Visit to Miss Birch," opens with the impressions of a young voyeur,

Sally, who is titillated by the sight of one woman whipping—
or "birching"—another:

> Where is my spying-hole? Oh, here it is. Now for a
> full view of the exhibition that is going on. Oh, there
> stands the mistress, with rod in hand, ready for the attack,
> and my little blubbering lady is lifting up her petticoats.
> There they are tucked up about her waist—and now she
> is loosening her drawers. I declare—down they go, sure
> enough. Now she is horsed! The mistress takes up her
> shift, and shows as pretty a bottom for a girl of fifteen as
> could well be seen. Now she begins to give it to her...I
> am delighted with it. Oh! Dear, quite delightful. How
> charming it must be to give a pretty girl like this a good
> whipping. I should like it of all things in the world.[6]

In the book's preface, the author notes the ubiquity of flagellation in English society, positing its presence as a larger cultural
fascination, a site of eroticism within the commonplace. And
while that may be true, monologues like the one delivered by
Sally are the Victorian rendition of faux lesbian pornography
even as they satirize the sadomasochism of quotidian discipline.
Sally is turned on by the clandestine experience of seeing a
pretty girl whipped, and the reader in turn is offered not only
a careful account of the encounter, wherein Sally stands in as
their surrogate, but also the pleasure of imagining one woman's
desire nourished by an intimate encounter between two others.

Yet these characters and their exploits are written not to
argue for female sexual agency; on the contrary, their excessive
lust and penchant for BDSM are presented as almost

buffoonish. That said, the *Papers* also includes the incestuous ballad "Reginald's Flogging," in which Reggie confides his fear of being flogged by his schoolmaster to his father and brother—they are both eager for the boy's bottom to receive a good birching—and then, ultimately, suffers at the hands of his teacher. And what a flogging it is, as his school chums can attest: "'Oh, many's the bum I've seen swished since / I've come / And many's the swishing I've had / But I never saw yet, and I ne'er shall forget / Such a swishing as that of this lad, I trow, this / yellow-haired rosy-cheeked lad.'"[7] Although no explicit confirmation exists, à la Oscar Wilde, there's considerable speculation that Swinburne's sexuality was fluid, and his blisteringly erotic work implies the same, particularly this relentless poem in which poor Reginald's bottom is whipped to a pulp. Yet Wilde once remarked of Swinburne that he was "a braggart in matters of vice who had done everything he could to convince his fellow citizens of his homosexuality and beastiality without being in the slightest degree a homosexual or a bestializer."[8] Maybe he was hiding in plain sight or maybe he delighted in being a provocateur in an age when weird carnality made grand old conservative gents especially squeamish.

But Swinburne's queerness may also have inspired him to seek out the work of other poets who expressed unconventional desires. "Anactoria," a dramatic monologue that takes as its inspiration Fragment 31 by the Greek poet Sappho, indicates, in fact, a less punishing view of intense female desire. Written from Sappho's perspective, Swinburne imagines the poet's anguish as she beholds her former lover, the titular Anactoria, marry a man. Sappho's pain is somatic, wrecking: "I feel thy blood against my blood: my pain / Pains thee, and lips bruise lips, and vein stings vein / Let fruit be crushed on fruit, let flower on flower / Breast kindle breast, and either burn one hour / Why wilt thou follow lesser loves? are thine / Too weak to bear these hands and lips of mine?"[9] The speaker positively gnashes her teeth with vicious longing. Swinburne's word choice is both violent and fleshy; in this moment of anguish, Sappho seems to relive her most intimate encounters with Anactoria in a sort of ecstatic mourning. These are not, however, gentle verses; in fact, so brutal is Sappho's lust that she imagines consuming her lover so that she may become a corporeal tomb housing her forevermore: "That I could drink thy veins as wine, and eat / Thy breasts like honey! That from face to feet / Thy body were abolished and consumed / And in my flesh thy very flesh entombed."[10] When it comes to the too muchness of erotic yen, the urge to mutilate and eat one's lover may take the cake. Of course, "Anactoria" is more than an explosion of romantic jealousy: it's a contemplation of loss and legacy—Sappho asserts that she, unlike her lover, will be remembered because of her poetry—but it imagines female desire, lesbian desire, with an explicit ardency that was, to say the least, peculiar for the nineteenth century.

And yet, whatever Swinburne's motivations might have been, he was still a man, with all the trappings of Victorian male privilege. Employing the poetic form as a kind of drag, he imagines what a queer woman from Greek antiquity might have felt as she watched her beloved abandon her for a more conventional romantic arrangement. Suffice it to say that a woman poet would not have enjoyed Swinburne's popularity had she written about feminine desire with such visceral sinew. For all the controversy it stirred, *Poems and Ballads*, the collection containing "Anactoria," was widely read. And in the meantime, much of Victorian literature, when it gestured to female sexuality, did so amidst a flurry of patriarchal anxiety.

Bram Stoker's *Dracula*, for instance, published at the fin de siècle in 1897, intertwines female erotic longing with actual monstrosity. The vampire's first victim, Lucy Westenra, is characterized as a sweet-hearted flirt who, upon receiving three marriage proposals, wonders why "they can't let a girl marry three men, or as many as want her, and save all this trouble?"[11] (Generally, when a woman in a Victorian novel makes this sort of remark, she's toast.) Once Lucy has become a vampire herself, she transforms from a naïve, boy-crazy peach into a dark-haired lascivious demon, whose thirst for blood is conflated with a hunger for sex:

> When Lucy—I call the thing that was before us Lucy because it bore her shape—saw us she drew back with an angry snarl, such as a cat gives when taken unawares; then her eyes ranged over us. Lucy's eyes in form and colour; but Lucy's eyes unclear and full of hell-fire, instead of the pure, gentle orbs we knew. At that moment the remnant of my love passed into hate and loathing; had she then to be killed, I could have done it with savage delight. As she looked, her eyes blazed with unholy light, and the face became wreathed with a voluptuous smile . . . She still advanced, however, and with a languorous, voluptuous grace.[12]

In life, Lucy's sex appeal was decorously packaged. But her vampiric body, as Dr. Seward, one of her rejected suitors, remarks, oozes at once with hellish brutishness and sensuality. Together with his band of vampire hunters, one of whom was Lucy's betrothed, the doctor laments how her "sweetness was turned to adamantine, heartless cruelty, and the purity to voluptuous wantonness."[13] As if to emphasize the point, her fair hair has grown dark (it's always the dark-haired women in Victorian literature who find themselves in the most trouble). Seward's urge to destroy her is galvanized by what he sees; his horror at her vampirism cannot be parsed from his disgust— and, to be clear, arousal—at her naked lust. This misogyny is borne out in the elderly Van Helsing's plan to eliminate her. He says, with all the casualness of a doctor suggesting a dose of Tylenol, "I want to cut off her head and take out her heart."[14] After the men have staked Lucy—her former fiancé does the honors in what becomes an absurdly homosocial ritual of mutual male pleasure—Seward and Van Helsing carry out this plan with antiseptic brutality: "the Professor and I sawed off the top off the stake, leaving the point of it in the body. Then we cut off the head and filled the mouth with garlic."[15] In the world of *Dracula*, a female body so consumed with sexual wantonness becomes inhuman—demonic—and must be annihilated. Excessive lust is punished with excessive violence, a body torn apart so that she may no longer tantalize the men who, when she lived, desired her so feverishly.

The Victorians must have regarded vampirism as a convenient way to discuss female sexuality, because *Dracula* is not the only narrative of its ilk. Published in 1872, predating Stoker's novel by over two decades, *Carmilla*, a novella by J. Sheridan Le Fanu, chronicles a love story between two girls, one of whom happens to be an ages-old vampire with designs to feed upon her mortal companion. Laura is conveniently dim and so while she regards Carmilla's affection as peculiar, she is slow to understand the supernatural threat being visited upon her:

> [My] strange and beautiful companion would take my hand and hold it with a fond pressure, renewed again and again; blushing softly, gazing in my face with languid and burning eyes, and breathing so fast that her dress rose and fell with the tumultuous respiration. It was like the ardour of a lover; it embarrassed me; it was hateful and yet overpowering; and with gloating eyes she drew me to her, and her hot lips travelled along my cheek in kisses; and she would whisper, almost in sobs, "You are mine, you shall be mine, you and I are one for ever." Then she had thrown herself back in her chair, with her small hands over her eyes, leaving me trembling.[16]

In response to these ministrations, Laura asks Carmilla, "Are we related?" which, frankly, is very funny, especially when Carmilla reacts with frustration in the face of her mark's towering—and obstructive—cluelessness. For Le Fanu makes no bones about the intensity of Carmilla's desire: the yen for blood and for intimacy are, as in the case of Lucy Westenra, indistinguishable and incandescent in their power. Her attentions remind Laura of "the ardour of a lover" because, in essence, that is what they are, although it's entirely possible that Carmilla is more interested in acting as a sire to Laura—that is, turning her into a vampire—rather than merely feeding on her, which she could do easily, and all at once. This act would establish an eternal bond; as she exclaims, "You and I are one forever." But even if she were to kill Laura, as she has done with previous girls, the protracted ritual of smaller, steady attacks mimics a clandestine romance where lovers unite in the dark, commingling and entangled. What Laura does not understand is that she has already become a part of Carmilla: her blood flows through her veins, together with the life force of other past conquests.

Carmilla, like Lucy, is tracked and destroyed by those determined to prevent her from wreaking further destruction. Her desires, of course, are all the more pungent to the men who eventually kill her because they are, as the Victorians would say, "against nature"—of a same-sex persuasion. Ultimately, Carmilla, revealed to be the anagramic alias of the ancient Countess Mircalla, is discovered inside her coffin, "floated with blood, in which to a depth of seven inches, [she] lay immersed."[17] The text luxuriates in the image of a porcelain-skinned demon drenched in crimson; so does it also, with near eroticism, narrate the process of her staking and beheading, a young woman's body torn apart for its sins of the flesh:

> Here then, were all the admitted signs and proofs of vampirism. The body, therefore, in accordance with the ancient practice, was raised, and a sharp stake driven through the heart of the vampire, who uttered a piercing shriek at the moment, in all respects such as might escape from a living person in the last agony. Then the head was struck off, and a torrent of blood flowed from the severed neck. The body and head was next placed on a pile of wood, and reduced to ashes, which were thrown upon the river and borne away, and that territory has never since been plagued by the visits of a vampire.[18]

In case there's any question, I do not support vampirism; it strikes me as quite an unhealthy way of life. But this caveat aside, what Stoker and Le Fanu reveal, through the metaphor of monstrosity, is a searing intolerance of flagrant feminine wantonness. Lucy and Carmilla both articulate and embody their desires without shame, a form of sexual audacity that is judged intolerable. Victorian vampires, particularly those coded as feminine, are generally motivated by arousal; the text presents them as endlessly libidinous, ravenous for the bodies of their victims. Victorian culture, however clandestinely it might have been titillated by women, could not conceive of them expressing such unruly desire; the cultural understanding of femininity foregrounded dispositions both docile and self-denying. To imagine a woman otherwise, to imagine her lascivious and hungry and ready to fuck, was to imagine nothing less than a bloodthirsty monster.

———

Thankfully, literature has supplied us with women's narratives in which erotic desire is celebrated and nourished as something fundamental and sustaining. We are not so Victorian that it has been impossible to carve open these spaces for freer discourse. In addition to *The Awakening* (1899), which glares unflinchingly at the domestic constraints of fin-de-siècle female sexuality, Louisiana writer Kate Chopin also composed erotic fiction. Early in the twentieth century, Virginia Woolf gestures to the potency of desire between women in *Mrs. Dalloway* (1925), and a few years later crafted a gender- and genre-bending romp of a novel, *Orlando* (1928), which is at its heart an affectionate missive to her lover, fellow writer Vita Sackville-West. Los Angeles memoirist Eve Babitz penned *Eve's Hollywood* (1974), *Slow Days, Fast Company* (1977), and *Black Swans* (1993), all of which are flush with heady sexual interludes involving men and women alike. From girlhood, French-American writer Anaïs Nin was an avid diarist, often recounting her varied romantic relationships, although *Delta of Venus* and *Little Birds*, collections of short erotic fiction, were both published posthumously.

Audre Lorde's love poetry, as well as her "biomythography" *Zami: A New Spelling of My Name* (1982)—a lyrical meditation upon her relationships with women—insists with particular incandescence upon the undeniability of black lesbian desire, but also recounts, tenderly, the fledgling erotic experiences of youth. Lorde's memory of helping her mother make the Caribbean dish souse commingles the synesthesia of her African heritage—accessed through the physicality of cooking—and the masturbatory pleasure she discovers in using a mortar and pestle:

Without even wiping it, I plunged the pestle into the bowl, feeling the blanket of salt give way, and the broken cloves of garlic just beneath. The downward thrust of the wooden pestle slowed upon contact, rotated back and forth slowly, and then gently altered its rhythm to include an up and down beat. Back and forth, round, up and down, back, forth, round, round, up and down... There was a heavy fullness at the root of me that was exciting and dangerous... That invisible thread, taut and sensitive as a clitoris exposed, stretched through my curled fingers up my round brown arm into the moist reality of my armpits, whose warm sharp odor with a strange new overlay mixed with the ripe garlic smells from the mortar and the general sweat-heavy aromas of high summer.[19]

Coming of age, being shocked into a glimmering awareness of one's own body is, by Lorde's account, both extraordinary and commonplace, a startling event and a moment that swims into the everyday, the practices of workaday life. The exquisite too muchness of mounting pleasure, the escalation toward climax, and our relishing of these fleshly experiences, cannot be emblazoned with the stigma of excess when our lives are punctuated this way—by the little ecstasies and the big. To lust is not, as the Victorians posited, to be a monster, but merely to discern the world in all its sensuous particulars and to take it into oneself. Lorde's prose is all the more radical because she dares to demand a black queer woman's right not only to pleasure, but to openly articulating it.

For, even now, feminine lust is treated as an exclusive privilege, accessible to only certain bodies, while the rest are presented as grotesqueries. The 2011 comedy *Bridesmaids* supplies just one exemplary case in Melissa McCarthy's character, Megan. McCarthy is an extraordinarily talented comedian, which she makes clear in the film, but its focus is myopically fixated on her too muchness. She's outspoken, exuberant, fat— and she's lusty as hell. The running gag regarding an erotic conquest is not written as empowering, or even as typical. The foundation of the joke, in fact, rests in Megan's sense of sexual entitlement. She's rendered as lascivious and dogged in her pursuit, and her nonnormative body emphasizes the "comedy" of her horniness. Isn't it hilarious, the film asks, that this character who shits and farts in abundance and dresses with frowsy tomboyishness would also want to have sex? It's so often the fat woman, or the conventionally "ugly" woman, or the elderly woman, who makes the dirtiest joke in the film. After all, these are "safe" characters whom we don't imagine as belonging to the sexual circuit anyway: we don't need to fear for their chastity or, in the case of older women, fight to protect it.

Even the HBO series *Sex and the City*, hailed in the early aughts for its frank discussions of masturbation, tea-bagging, and female desire in general, implies a "norm" in terms of how horny we can be without slipping into aberrant territory. Samantha Jones (Kim Cattrall), we are meant to understand, is an anomaly both for her intense desires and for her openness in articulating them. *SATC* does not, like so many other instances in popular culture, imply that her desires paradoxically render her undesirable. In fact, it's quite the opposite. But in this case, her glamorous beauty points to her as an exception—and we're meant to chuckle when she indicates, reluctantly, that she's a decade or so older than her friends. Her storyline is also arguably the most fanciful: while she is not a punch line, per se, we are often meant to laugh at her antics. She'll fire an employee and then immediately fuck him on her desk, and wait out a hundred women in a restaurant to ensure she is the one to bed the waiter. It's unsettling that her sexual fluidity is placed in the same domain as these endeavors. She is, after all, the only one of the four to date a woman; Carrie Bradshaw (Sarah Jessica Parker), on the other hand, evinces acute biphobia. If you were the so-called "Samantha" of your college friend group, then you were likely dubbed the "freaky" one, someone vulnerable to slut-shaming by those intolerant of intense female desire.

Many of us related instead to Charlotte York (Kristin Davis), or we told ourselves that we did—and I would argue that we are encouraged to do so. Her storyline, though meant to trouble the obsession with searching for the ideal husband, nonetheless follows a common trajectory. A preppy, Connecticut-bred art dealer, she enjoys the privileges of a blue-blooded upbringing as well as those dealt to a comely, white brunette. She dates rigorously, and with hawk-eyed focus, marries, divorces, marries again, and then attempts to become pregnant. (The narrative of her infertility is, on the other hand, a foray into urgent, under-discussed territory.) But when it comes to sex, only the extreme circumstances of forced abstinence drive her to hormonal distraction. Unhappy in her first marriage, her self-imposed decorum breaks when she lapses into a bout of savage screaming at a Kappa Kappa Gamma luncheon over her longing to be good and fucked: a scene played for laughs rather than resonance, because Charlotte has broken the tacit gentility agreement of this notoriously well-monied sorority. And unlike Megan from *Bridesmaids*, Charlotte's urgent horniness is charming precisely because she is culturally coded as such: thin, sexy—but genteel and well-dressed. It's okay to love sex, *SATC* says, it's natural, and it's healthy! But the contingencies the show imposes on ultra-horniness, embodied by Charlotte, suggest its plumb absorption of cultural mores.

While we do see efforts to combat this narrative, the labor is often performed by women of color. Rapper Lil' Kim emphasized the priority of women's sexual sovereignty in the 1990s through her sartorial decisions and in her music, as did Foxy Brown. Salt-N-Pepa released singles like "Shoop" and "Push It"—"Can't you hear the music's pumpin' hard like I wish you would?" they rap in the latter—that delight in the expression of unbridled female desire. As the AIDS epidemic ravaged marginalized communities across the United States, the late Lisa "Left Eye" Lopes of the R & B trio TLC donned a condom as an eye patch to broadcast to her fan base the importance of safe sex. In the early aughts, rapper Khia's 2002 single "My Neck, My Back (Lick It)" announced itself with a salaciously matter-of-fact demand for men's attention to female pleasure. Over the course of her career, Missy Elliott, too, has recorded music that unapologetically showcases her stipulations for any person she takes to bed. More recently Nicki Minaj, Megan Thee Stallion, and Cardi B have asserted themselves in wardrobe and in their lyrics as assertively sexual. Minaj, for instance, raps confidently about who wants to fuck her and who hasn't, and what she demands from a lover in the bedroom. The track "Only," from her 2014 studio album *The Pinkprint*, opens with an especially audacious declaration: "Yo, I never fucked Wayne, I never fucked Drake / All my life, man, fuck's sake / If I did, I did a ménage with 'em / And let 'em eat my ass like a cupcake." Both Lil Wayne and Drake appear on the track after Minaj's opening verse as rejected suitors who emphasize their unceasing devotion to her.

Model and actress Amber Rose has taken an especially keen approach to challenging the extant diminishing perceptions of female sexuality. In 2015, she introduced SlutWalk as a yearly event that recognized the systemic shaming women endure for expressing their sexualities, raised awareness for domestic violence, and called for the abolishment of rape culture, as well as general inequities of sex and gender. The event was successful while it lasted—Rose canceled it in 2019 for personal reasons[20]—nonetheless, Rose, like Lil' Kim, Minaj, and Cardi B, remains a target for her sexual assertiveness. Similarly to *SATC*'s Samantha, few would argue that these women are unappealing for rapping about or discussing their relish for explicit sexual acts, but as women of color, their sexuality is already coded as excessive, hazardous. They are fundamentally vulnerable to attacks of lewdness that white celebrities more easily eschew. Decades before, Madonna—now anointed as a national sex symbol—confronted similar, though less virulent, protestations after filming controversial music videos for "Justify My Love" (1990) and "Erotica" (1992) and, in 1992, after publishing the coffee-table book aptly titled *Sex* (the book contains footage from the latter music video). But Madonna has always been legible to the mainstream palate: even when her videos are challenging or nearly pornographic, her careening melodies and soprano voice mitigate any perceived aggression. She knows how to deliver a hook and a chorus— how to package a song so that it is widely digestible. And, for the most part, especially as she has reinvented herself time and again as a pop genius, a guru, and as a mother, she has been treated as an exception. If both your commercial and physical desirability are not in question, you may not escape the stigma of sexual too muchness, but you won't be lampooned.

Combating deep-seated, culturally sanctioned shame is already a complex business, particularly when it comes to younger girls. And at present, intense sexual drive is still coded as shameful, if not explicitly then implicitly. We praise women like Nicki Minaj and Amber Rose for their unrepentant sexuality with the recognition that we do not have their celebrity, their bodies, or their access to a glamorous lifestyle in which one is paid to be beautiful. We also recognize the condemnation directed at them for defying fixed ideals of feminine decorum. We're offered the binaristic possibilities of *slut*—as it is hegemonically defined—and *punch line*. Neither are culturally attractive options. We are taught to strive to be Charlottes or, if we must, Samanthas—never Megan from *Bridesmaids*. There is nothing so embarrassing, Western culture admonishes, than female horniness unrequited. And as for Carmilla, who stalks her girlishly naïve conquests in the night, well—get thee behind me, foul lesbian vampire. Be the chaste girl who spends her Friday night swapping benign pleasantries on a Tinder date— not the one ensconced at home masturbating in her underwear, as pornography blares its telltale dirty talk from the computer screen. Yet I'd protest that with access to the right materials, the latter is a perfectly delectable way to kick off the weekend.

Chapter Nine

CHEAT

Those of us who choose to marry and represent that bond with a set of rings know the soft anxiety of a ring fitting. One tries to determine aesthetic and tactile preferences in a context leaden with both cultural and economic heft, all the while fielding a volley of questions, the practical jumbled with the existential. "How does the size seven feel? Now try the six and three quarters. Better? Do you want it to feel loose or snug? Remember, your comfort is the most important thing. Do your fingers expand in the summer? What sort of wedding do you want? Are you planning to have kids soon?"

It's preferable to avoid selecting a ring so small it throttles your finger, but that's a far less disquieting possibility than the alternative: a wedding band that's too loose. A wedding band, slightly slicked with hand cream, that flees your finger with a flick of your hand. A wedding band that—in the perfect convergence of circumstances—transforms an afternoon into a cliché by bouncing off your finger onto the sidewalk and then clinking tragically down a storm drain.

A lost wedding ring, beyond the distress it engenders, carries an ominous symbolism. It implies the fallibility of an institution: one that has, historically, been relied upon to fasten society's hold on women's bodies and freedom. Bulky with long-cherished ideals, not to mention anxieties and hopes, a wedding band encircles not just a finger but a selfhood. After all, when we finally settle on the precise measurements, tentatively shake our hands once or twice to ensure minimal wiggle room, we are not merely demonstrating that we fit inside its perimeter. We are promising our partner, ourselves, and the institution of traditional marriage that we are the sort of women who can abide by matrimony's dictates, that we—for better or for worse, 'til death do us part—can conform to the ring's smooth but unyielding contours.

For many women, this transition is a joyful, easy one. Marriage is one form of commitment among a platter of options, and if it seems most personally suitable, then there's no reason to reject it. But our fetishization of marriage—in no small part manifested by the industrial complex buttressing it—can muddy the boundary between want and obligation. Someone who has never had cause to doubt the logic of marriage is likely to assume the mantle more willingly and with less agitation. And yet there are thousands of women who marry, happily, only to realize that the constraints do not suit them, whether due to a shift in their relationship or simply because they find themselves disinclined toward institutionalized monogamy.

There are women who shift restlessly beneath traditional matrimony's burden, try as they might to acclimate to it. Desire, they find, is not some malleable clay. When we promise to always want the same person, and all that accompanies them, we are throwing dice that will not necessarily land where we intend. Or perhaps we have taken a gamble on ourselves, only to realize that when we are shoved like fingers into wedding bands, we begin to throb under the constriction.

Sometimes these women fuck up: we have one-night stands or protracted affairs or perhaps kiss a random person in an out-of-town bar. Whatever American culture would have us believe, infidelity is not necessarily a relationship's death knell. But sometimes we realize that, rather than recalibrating as a couple—reconciling, and returning, newly penitent—we long for emancipation.

A woman who cheats, especially a woman tethered to a conventional marriage, knows all too well that the only act more egregiously selfish than infidelity is abandonment. To be clear, there are certain specific extenuating circumstances: we are more inclined to exonerate a woman fleeing an abusive marriage or a philandering spouse. Without these caveats, any woman serving divorce papers suffers leery, sidelong glances, sometimes even outright censure. Before Cheryl Strayed finally declared, under the alias of Dear Sugar, that "wanting to leave is enough,"[1] women had only been supplied with liturgy to the contrary; a liturgy that continues to ensnare unhappily married women in the familiar haunts, whether church, family, or one's own carefully learned, internalized shame.

And for an adulteress to leave her marriage, well, that's altogether worse. It means wearing one's sin like silk lingerie, reveling in its pleasures and daring others to protest. Demanding a divorce after committing infidelity implies the latter's legitimacy. Women are supposed to be humbled—shamed—by the emotional and sexual excesses that render us incompatible with a measured life. And when we sleep with the wrong people, uttered apology is not sufficient. Our lives, even our sexual sovereignty, must serve as apology.

But for all the bite of its condemnation, Western culture has something of an, ahem, "love affair" with adultery, and more specifically with adulterous women. In books and plays and films, from *The Scarlet Letter* to *Madame Bovary* and Tyler Perry's *Temptation*, we are taught again and again a lesson held dear by masculine society: that women of unwieldy emotion are neither trustworthy nor suited for coupling. In Margaret Atwood's *The Handmaid's Tale*, one of the theocracy's true believers might say that we are "unfit." But then, women like me—women who are Too Much—have never needed dystopian fiction to imagine how their sexuality, their flings and extramarital crushes and dirty talk, might be vilified and punished.

———

In the rearview mirror, my affair, a one-week cataclysm that cracked open the winter of 2010, seems ludicrous and resistant to comprehension: it's banal in its particulars, yet it was for me both shatteringly ecstatic and distressing. When I kissed Paul, it was the end of my first, frenzied semester as a doctoral student. I had only been married to my husband, Nick, since August. My panicked heart burned and sputtered.

I fell in love with Paul slowly, but easily. We met in a graduate seminar on nineteenth-century literature: I admired his
artful, quick-witted mind and his velvety warm blue eyes. After
collaborating on a class presentation, I was enthralled, but in a
way that seemed chaste, even sisterly. I had never found it difficult to maintain platonic male friendships while romantically
committed, so I assumed the band on my finger wouldn't bar
friendship now.

But once I acknowledge my attraction to a person, I am almost irrevocably distracted, my awareness totally reoriented by
piqued desire and curiosity. Such was the case when, one fall
evening, Paul and I grabbed a beer at a restaurant near campus. I had reassured myself that this outing was innocent—why
not make friends with my new classmates? But as the night
drew on and the beer eased my edges, Paul's own form, though
shadowed by the dim light, seemed to solidify before me, pe-
ripheries defined, precious matter within a nothing of space. I
could hold him, and I wanted to. Some obscure voice at the
back of my head admonished me to wave aside these thoughts,
to excuse myself to the bathroom and douse my face (a fool-
proof measure if ever there was one). But I was as curious about
my desire as my head was muddled by it. I hadn't had a crush
in years, and my affection for Nick had long lapsed into an
antiseptic lull.

Later that evening, Paul walked me to the metro station. As
we crossed a pedestrian bridge, we paused at the midpoint to
look at the night. Always keen to imbue any moment with cin-
ematic gravitas, I cast the two of us in my mind's off-brand
Nicholas Sparks flick.

After we were married, Paul would tell me that, over the

course of the evening, he had thought to himself, wryly, what a perfect date we were having. But in the moment, he betrayed not a trace of partiality or affection beyond the bounds of friendship. I left him at the train and returned home disappointed, though I muttered to myself punishing admonishments. It was ridiculous, not to mention hazardous, to dwell on this attraction. It was crucial—positively crucial—to get a goddamn grip. I tucked myself into bed and dreamily recollected the evening until I fell asleep. Paul's face drifting before my tired eyes, a gentle, sweet-hearted, imminent crash.

———

It always begins this way, doesn't it? Or so that is what the prevailing adultery narratives would have us think. Two people meet; one is attached, but they proceed without caution almost defensively, as if to say, "Why should I be careful when I would never *dream* of committing such a clichéd indiscretion?" (I pawed at the very same excuse.)

Then follow the swollen silences and lingering glances that you don't entirely want to go unnoticed. Perhaps there is a crisis of conscience a mere half a breath before succumbing to passion—but this isn't right!—and then, of course, the bittersweet, utterly rhapsodic consummation of desire. More often than not, these plotlines center around a woman who, despite some (never enough) effort, cannot stem the flow of sexual impulse, or one who is more unabashedly insatiable. And more often than not, the woman is punished—by man or by happenstance—for an indulgence that disrupts the harmony of a heterosexual pairing. Were women not so sexually greedy, were they not so lascivious or curious or mercurial, infidelity would not be the scourge upon matrimony that it has always been.

The Victorians, keen artists of stigma that they were, conceived of sexually excessive women in biblical terms. Women who committed adultery, divorced, made a living by sex work, or had a child out of wedlock—even if by rape—were branded as "fallen." The Edenic origin of the term is evident, as are the implications of a higher feminine ideal that the so-called fallen woman has betrayed. Victorian literature is well-populated by these women, sometimes as cautionary tales, or in the case of less ideologically rigid writers, to emphasize the impossible standards to which women were held.

For even if a woman did not exactly commit adultery, her reputation suffered as if she had. Author George Eliot, née Mary Ann Evans, lived at the periphery of polite society because her partner, philosopher and critic George Henry Lewes, was unable to divorce his estranged wife. While they were by no means the first lovers to engage in extramarital coupling, Lewes and Eliot were uniquely bold in declaring themselves husband and wife—Eliot even began referring to herself as Mary Ann Evans Lewes. Consequently, Victorian society regarded the couple, particularly Eliot, as sexually perverse polygamists. However illustrious her writing career, Eliot could not escape the puritanical rhetoric that interpreted her decisions as ones fueled by intemperate lust and disregard for the sacrament of marriage.

It's likely that Eliot's own "fallen" status inspired her, at least to some degree, to pursue narratives invested in similar themes. When I first read her 1860 novel *The Mill on the Floss* during my senior year of high school, I found a kindred spirit in Maggie Tulliver, Eliot's incandescent, frenetic heroine. From her childhood, Maggie is chastised for her rashness and intensity particularly by her brother Tom, the novel's foremost exemplar of patriarchal duty and intractability. And when she comes of age she encounters one of the signature predicaments of the sexy Victorian lass: mutual, forbidden attraction that her beloved chases, regardless of its ramifications for her.

Because *The Mill on the Floss* is a mid-Victorian novel, we only learn of Maggie's burgeoning erotic interest and, ultimately, her sexual indiscretion in evasive terms. During an extended stay with her cousin Lucy, she realizes, aghast, that she has developed feelings for Lucy's intended, Stephen Guest. Stephen not only reciprocates, but also pledges his devotion on multiple occasions, though Maggie, beating back her own desires, tells him that any romance is impossible. Finally, Stephen orchestrates a clandestine outing for the two of them, luring Maggie into a rowboat with him and then begging her to elope. She refuses, but as the boat careens farther down the river and into unfamiliar waters, the pair is forced to seek shelter on a larger vessel overnight. Alone on that darkened poop deck, anything may have happened between Maggie and Stephen—or perhaps nothing did. Regardless, Maggie's reputation can only be preserved, somewhat, by marrying her admirer; but, out of loyalty to her cousin, she refuses. Her name is thus irrevocably besmirched—what sort of licentious woman commits such romantic folly?—while the community gently chastens Stephen for being rather too flirtatious.

Mr. Stephen Guest had certainly not behaved well; but then, young men were liable to those sudden infatuated attachments... Maggie had returned without a trousseau, without a husband—in that degraded and outcast condition to which error is well known to lead... [her] conduct had been of the most aggravated kind. Could anything be more detestable?... Winning his affections? That was not the phrase for such a girl as Miss Tulliver: it would have been more correct to say that *she had been actuated by mere unwomanly boldness and unbridled passion.*[2] (emphasis mine)

As a child, Maggie embodies Too Much little girlhood par excellence: she is rash and petulant and prone to bouts of violent sobbing. She is no less passionate as a young woman, but her loyalties to kin and friends as well as her own ethical convictions run deep. Yet as the novel indicates, someone who exhibits "unwomanly boldness" cannot be trusted to demonstrate fidelity because, ultimately, she is the passive servant of her desire: like an automaton with a sex drive, she is "actuated" by "unbridled passion." To possess unwomanly traits thus emphasizes a female character's degeneracy. If women prioritize the safeguarding of their purity and honor the codes that structure home and the larger social web, someone like Maggie, someone wired to be sinful, is fundamentally incapable of choosing righteousness instead.

Tess Durbeyfield, titular character of Thomas Hardy's *Tess of the d'Urbervilles*—and perhaps the most famous of the Victorians' "fallen women"—is plagued by similar mythology in which a woman becomes the product of her ardent emotions and sexual history. If you know the story, perhaps you share my own disdain for her hypocritical husband, Angel Clare, who abandons her after learning that she was raped as a teenager, essentially kept against her will by said rapist, Alec d'Urberville, and in the aftermath bears his illegitimate child. (Naturally Angel has just admitted to a past weekend-long sexual romp, but, oh, how he has repented ever since!) To blame Tess for her trauma is the cruelest folly; even Maggie Tulliver is more directly responsible for her circumstances. But when Tess confides her history to Angel, he reminds us how women who are Too Much are denied power over their narratives, and, crucially, their identities. "Forgiveness does not apply to the case," he sneers. "You were one person; now you are another. How can forgiveness meet such a grotesque prestidigitation as that? ... [The] woman I have been loving is not you."[3]

Tess, whom Hardy sketches as a well-bosomed beauty, has always appeared to me as one of Dante Gabriel Rossetti's portraits of Elizabeth Siddal: all softly rounded curves, rose blush on cream skin, and a fulsome mane of hair. But the likeness is doubly fitting—Tess's short life is rife with suffering precisely because Angel enforces upon her his idealized narrative of feminine purity. He regards her not so much as a woman but as an art object, a portrait of a woman imbued by Angel's myopic conception of femininity. Tess's beauty is bewitching when he regards her as virgin soil, "a new-sprung child of nature," whose body is wholesome because, according to his fantasy, it has been thus far undisrupted. Refusing to parse event from person, Angel contorts Tess's rape and imprisonment into character traits, rendering her a mere signifier of lusty excess.

Angel eventually emerges from this bog of misogynistic idealism, but Hardy, true to form, reveals that his character's enlightenment comes too late. Together, Alec and Angel murder Tess: the first man through sexual violence and manic obsession, and the second by blaming her for being of the world, not—impossibly—transcendent.

———

I recall the uneasy sense that I too was bound for "fallenness," because I could never experience any meaningful emotion in a tempered way. It's nigh well impossible to hide from yourself when your feelings seem to press against you from the inside and, somehow, the outside as well. For this reason, among many others, the crush that blossomed out of my first evening with Paul should have spurred me to distance myself from him. But it makes sense to me that I didn't. Regardless of this burgeoning affection, I continued to rigorously deny that my relationship with Nick was askew. Marrying him—a respectable, sturdy, ambitious man—was, in retrospect, a way of disciplining myself, a way to suppress the timid but diligent whispers at the back of my brain. "Are you sure you're attracted enough to marry him?" it asked in a very small voice, one year into our relationship. "Didn't you used to love sex?"

At the time, we lived separately while he finished a graduate degree several hours outside of Washington, DC. But despite distance, Nick soon seemed to me insistently present. He, in fact, had become too much, and in a way that felt oppressive: he was too demanding, too aggravated by my professional aspirations. "I've never seen you this ambitious," he once said, his voice saturated with both disapproval and trepidation. When I had slogged through a sleepless week and, come Friday, gazed ravenously at my bed, I balked at his inevitable expectation of sex.

But Nick's behavior was surely influenced by my own disengagement. I regretted marrying him, though I would not admit it to myself, and if he had not yet deduced that, he certainly sensed my resistance, my yen for separateness. His summons, by way of phone and text and Gchat, became more and more frequent, all of them prickling reminders of marital obligation. I would squirm as my phone rang, exhaling with relief when voice mail finally swallowed the call. We'd fight later, but for the moment, I cradled my delusion of freedom.

This denial, of course, rendered me eager for greater familiarity with Paul. If I accepted the premise that my marriage was not problematic—or simply chose not to think about my marriage at all—then there existed no discernible reason to avoid someone whose company I enjoyed. Romantic longing ripped a gaping maw in that logic, but I was not operating according to logic anyway.

Throughout the fall, a collection of intimate rituals crystallized our relationship. While at school, Paul and I paid each other multiple office visits over the course of the day. He accompanied me on my morning walk to the campus coffee shop. Most suggestive, however, were the extensive late-night Gchat conversations where we eagerly confided in each other with the urgency and abundance of two people desperate to make the most of this kinetic bond before it became verboten. We were both aware that our friendship, as it stood, was marred by a certain transience, but we acknowledged this separately, unwilling to mourn the loss before it was inevitable. Instead, we told each other everything we could think to tell, unless it involved my marriage. Together we spun a delicate half-fantasy, neither of us traversing explicit lines of decency, yet willfully ignoring the existence of a husband who would move back to DC that summer and, understandably, would be skeptical of such intimate extramarital correspondence.

Every so often, I would take the measure of my computer screen, Gchat boxes for Nick and Paul winking side by side (and one sorely neglected). For brief moments here and there, it would occur to me that this fragile simultaneity would eventually crack. Then I would turn on Robyn and twirl around my bedroom, hell-bent on forgetting everything but the motion of my body.

As Thanksgiving break approached, my primary object was to stave off the assured misery of a long weekend with Nick— by now he would, rightfully, ask what the hell was going on— and devote the hours wedged between bouts of research and writing to spending time with Paul. We had not ventured to plan another one-on-one excursion since the night I first recognized my stirrings of attraction. Now we decided to see a movie, which, at my suggestion, evolved into the commonplace romantic pairing of movie and dinner.

Paul proposed that we see *127 Hours*, and such was my infatuation that I willingly agreed to see a film where a man frees himself from a boulder by sawing through his own arm. With equal enthusiasm, we subjected ourselves to the torture of sitting shoulder to shoulder in the charged obscurity of a movie theater. Always one to balk at violence, I shifted gingerly in my seat until the film's climax, at which point I plunged my face into Paul's shoulder. The impulse was born from fear and desire in equal measure, and as for Paul, well, he didn't remove his arm.

At the end of the night we parted on the train platform, Paul steeling himself for a red-eye back to Boulder, Colorado, for Thanksgiving break. As we hugged goodbye, nausea began to curdle in my gut. It was untenable, all of it: Paul's two weeks' absence; my husband's imminent arrival; the jagged realization that Paul signified far more than an idle crush. Meeting him had been a significant event, our intimacy a swell of warmth within a newly discovered emotional vacancy. Finally, I acquiesced to what I already knew: I had been wrong to marry Nick. After only a few months, Paul seemed more my match than my husband ever had.

Riding the train home, my body was weightless and queasy, as if buoyed by a quick suck of helium. "What the fuck do you have to be happy about?" I self-castigated. "You're holding a blowtorch and pointing it at two men you don't deserve."

It must have been late when I returned to my apartment, but, being in a rather self-absorbed frame of mind, I immediately called my friend Leigha. She already knew that I was unhappy; she also knew that I was spending an ill-advised amount of time with a schoolmate. The moment she picked up, I barely choked out "I'm in love with Paul" before stumbling to the toilet and vomiting convulsively.

But true friendship weathers a healthy heap of vomit, and Leigha waited calmly as I emptied my stomach of the day's meals and approximately half a lung. I returned to the phone, incapable of tracing out the plot points of the evening, whimpering desperate, befuddled fragments punctured by the refrain "I love Paul."

"No, you don't," Leigha soothed, and whether or not she—or I—believed it, that was precisely what I needed to hear, at least that night. It was not so much a statement of fact as an effort to steady me. After all, Leigha couldn't have known how I actually felt. She had never met Paul; she only knew my perspective of this pseudo-romantic quagmire. So when Leigha said, "No, you don't," what I heard was "Slow down." Her warm, easy conviction gradually placated me. I said good night, wiped the vomit from my lips, and collapsed into a grainy-dreamed sleep.

———

If the Victorians were singularly preoccupied with sexually de-viant women—according to their metrics, anyway—they by no means had sole purchase on the topic. Nineteenth-century literature across the continent meditated on the subject of unfaithful women and their havoc upon hearth and home. Gustave Flaubert is perhaps most famous for his 1856 debut, *Madame Bovary*, in which the protagonist engages in extra-marital affairs to beat back the banality of quotidian life. Leo Tolstoy's *Anna Karenina*, published in installments between 1873 and 1877, offers a relatively sympathetic depiction of the unfaithful wife, but that sympathy is largely predicated on her debilitating mental instability—paranoia, guilt, jealousy—in the wake of public shame.

Though we may mourn Anna's tragic end, within the logic of the novel that catastrophe seems inevitable after the social and familial chasms torn by her infidelity. If her affair with Vronsky culminates from unharnessed sexual passion, then the burden of that dangerous excess tips the scales in favor of tragedy. And were nineteenth-century Russian society kinder to "scandalous"

women, Anna still could not outrun the psychic trauma of abandoning her family and taking a lover whom, as a result of her
own reeling self-doubt, she could not trust. Anna, Vronsky,
Karenin—all three become entangled in the poisonous web that
begins to spin once marital vows are transgressed. And as Anna
demonstrates, the only exit strategy is death.

But far more damning—often hyperbolic—portrayals of female infidelity have endured into the present day. The femme
fatale trope slinked into American film noir, tempted her hapless gumshoe, and died, sketching a foundational twentieth-
century narrative for the hypersexual, unfaithful wife.

In 1944's *Double Indemnity*, Barbara Stanwyck portrays the
sinister, beguiling Phyllis Dietrichson who, rotten to the core,
effortlessly convinces an insurance salesman (Fred MacMurray)
to kill her husband so that she can collect his fortune. Walter,
the salesman, is nearly as corrupt as Phyllis: a cloying flirt from
their first meeting, he is only too eager to off an inconvenient
husband. Yet, it's Phyllis, not Walter, whom the film urges us
to regard as fundamentally irredeemable. She lies and cheats because she is sociopathic—incapable of selfless affection. Walter
proves himself a fool, and he suffers for his misdeeds, but his
willingness to trust Phyllis conveys the capacity for sympathy
and love—and all the more casts Phyllis in the cruel light of an
operator.

In 1981, Hollywood revisited the plot of *Double Indemnity*
with the sweaty, lascivious *Body Heat*. Again, a depraved,
voracious wife, Matty Walker (Kathleen Turner), inveigles
and seduces a dunderheaded underachiever, small-town lawyer
Ned Racine (William Hurt). Ned is utterly charmed by Matty,
and even more so by her reassurance of his sexual prowess; he

readily conspires to kill the man to whom Matty is tethered by matrimony. But like Phyllis, Matty schemes only for her own benefit. Regardless of its pleasures, each woman regards infidelity as a means to an end; it results from cool premeditation rather than romantic impulse. However, at the conclusion of *Body Heat* the moral skews to focus more squarely on the male culprit. During the span of their affair, Matty gifts Ned a fedora, both a throwback to the film's noir pedigree and a signal that he has unwittingly accepted the mantle of fall man. And take the fall he does, while Matty, flush with her murdered husband's wealth, escapes to sun-soaked beaches, contemplating the horizon behind dramatic, Audrey Hepburn-esque shades.

With whom should we sympathize here? No one, perhaps. The film implies that Ned has only himself to blame in the end. After all, did he not enter into a romantic entanglement with a married woman? A married woman, no less, whose palpable sexuality immediately marks her as pernicious, and who wields her desirability as the most potent tool in her kit. Matty's freedom might be interpreted as a misandrist fantasy, or even fraught with her own misgivings. "Ned, whatever you think— I really do love you," she tells her co-conspirator before framing him. But the film, committed to the trope of the femme fatale, cannot fully pursue this emotional complexity. Instead, *Body Heat* ultimately reads most clearly as cruel, if vague, irony, unfolding into the well-traveled narrative of the guilty woman flying free—others, innocent or not, often punished in their stead. It's a cautionary tale written toward heterosexual men. Don't be a chump, boys! Beware the poison of sexual excess. A woman who veers from the path of matrimonial fidelity, no matter her intentions, will only shatter you. Perhaps, like Vronsky, you'll emerge bereft and aching or, like Ned, you'll be tossed in jail, with only the emotional relics of your obsession to keep you company.

According to early 2000s Hollywood, affairs of the heart unravel into similarly hyperbolic catastrophe. Adrian Lyne's *Unfaithful* (2002), for example, might at first seem sympathetic to protagonist Connie (Diane Lane). At the film's opening, quotidian life, in its excessive familiarity, has become grotesque. Both Connie's eight-year-old son and her husband (Richard Gere) pee with the door open. Her son spits indistinguishable mush into her hand—her orders—before heading out the door for school. Sex has become a rare and hard-won activity. Why wouldn't Paul (Olivier Martinez), the French bookseller, appeal to her as a carefree erotic alternative?

Importantly, the film eschews the nuances of Connie's marriage; any displeasure that could be attributed to her husband, Edward, emerges as largely circumstantial, even inevitable. Connie, on the other hand, we are meant to interpret as well-meaning but ultimately too selfish to preserve the sanctity of domesticity.

Suspicious of his wife's recent distraction, Edward learns of her infidelity through the efforts of a private investigator, and the truth is his undoing. Jealousy and anger render Edward unrecognizable to himself, and during a vicious confrontation with Paul, he suddenly kills him with a blow to the head.

Reeling from these increasingly far-fetched circumstances—Edward attends his son's school play with Paul's body in his trunk—Connie and Edward find their way back to each other. Connie does decide to end the affair; Edward merely kills Paul before he can receive the message. And what is his explanation, once Connie learns of his violent deed? "I didn't want to kill him, I wanted to kill you," Edward sputters in desperate rage. In the logic of the film, Connie's alienation has conjured her husband's madness and, consequently, her infidelity is treated as a far greater crime than bludgeoning someone to death. Connie seems to resist this narrative, albeit feebly. "Everyone has accidents," she tells her son after he wets the bed. Her words are weighted with despair.

And yet infidelity is no accident. It is a choice, and rarely a healthy one. However, it need not follow that sexual deception yields romantic and emotional Armageddon. We need not cleave to a narrative that pathologizes women who have had affairs as hypersexual, prone to hysteric fits of lusts. When the institutional strictures of heterosexual matrimony, rather than the empathy due to our human fallibility, become the organizing principles by which relationships and women are judged, we limit ourselves to forecasting catastrophe and meting out punishment. We have not yet learned how to respect monogamy without worshipping it. And in our idolatry, we shift the burden of matrimonial upkeep onto women, charging one and all with custody of Penelope's legacy: to be patient and immaculately long-suffering, always waiting to serve our Odysseus. Gluttons for pat heteronormative romance, contemporary American society cannot recognize its own terrified devotion to what it understands as normal and natural, instead condemning women who deviate as the ones who cannot suppress our appetites for what we should not want in the first place.

Enter Tyler Perry and his 2013 film *Temptation*. A modern-day morality play, the protagonist's suffering is framed as punishment for her un-Christian deceit. When Judith (Jurnee Smollett-Bell), nourished and bred on southern Christian principles, hands herself over to the erotic passion dominating her lover, the cartoonishly villainous Harley (Robbie Jones), she quite literally risks death. And significantly, it is Judith's professional ambitions that lead her down this rabbit hole of dissolution. Determined to open her own marriage counseling business, she works late at her dating agency, preoccupation interpreted by her well-meaning but childish husband, Brice (Lance Gross), as neglect.

Harley, a business client, seizes at every opportunity to join Judith when she is alone at the office. Like *Unfaithful*'s Paul, he is an oversaturated trope of sexual danger, this time contorted to emphasize its fundamental evil. He is handsome, shifty, invested in pleasure before all else. And lest we not take Perry's overwrought moral—that engaging in this behavior means tangoing with Lucifer—Harley's red convertible sports flames on each side.

At the end of the film, once Brice has intervened, like a superhero, to save Judith from Harley's clutches, we learn that she has contracted HIV as a result of her affair. In the space of a few years, she grows feeble in health and with contrition: she now works as a marriage counselor—not at her own agency—and, divorced from Brice, only sees him when she visits his pharmacy to collect her prescriptions.

Brice, of course, has remarried a fresh Christian beauty; forgiveness does not mean condemning oneself to damaged goods. Judith, we understand, regards her circumstances with penitence. As Lindy West argues, Tyler Perry's women are never victims, but sinners.[4] For Judith to desire more than her lot—a puerile husband who forgets her birthday—indicates that wantonness has derailed her perspective and good Christian sense. If she had identified her lustful stirrings as sinful, rather than nurture them, then the most eligible bachelor would not have tempted her. And she would have immediately sent Harley packing, intuiting his hedonistic lifestyle as brutal contagion that would be doubly contemptible if she were to partake.

My sin started in earnest during the holidays that winter. The night that Nick arrived at my apartment for Thanksgiving, I told him we needed to talk, but the words at the back of my tongue—"I can't love you; I want a divorce"—were shoved to the side by more tempered speech. Feebly, I told him, "I know you're a really good guy."

"That's what people say when they're about to break up with someone," he quietly replied.

I don't know if Nick perceived what I was withholding, what pressed behind the vague, elliptical words I clumsily harnessed to convince both of us that everything would be okay. For my part, I attempted to swallow my own lie because I didn't see another choice. It never occurred to me that I could have made what would have seemed a rash and selfish decision and demanded an immediate separation. Perhaps in retrospect that would have been the better course of action. But we had only been married since August, and we still lived separately. Didn't I owe this man more time? Didn't I have an obligation to *try,* untenable and imprisoning as the idea seemed? If I found myself incapable, my own fears would be confirmed: I was both too impulsive and too unstable for healthy romance. I was one of the irredeemable people undone by a society that, somehow, scores of others could navigate. "You can't always do what you want," I chided myself, "because that's not being an adult." At the time I could not parse responsibility from misery.

My family gathered at my grandparents' house for Thanksgiving dinner, and as my mother and I sat together on the couch, tiny cousins rolling across our laps, she snatched a moment to ask, under her breath, if everything was "okay" now that Nick and I had spent some time together. Weeks ago I had confided to her about Paul during a long and aching phone conversation. She had met my desperation with sympathy, even remarking that it was difficult for her to fathom my wedding as an event that had really happened. Finally we were together, albeit surrounded, and I cannot remember what I answered her. I only know that I passed the evening trailing after my sisters and parents, attempting to shed the husband who was in turn always looking for me.

When I found my father in the basement, parked in front of Thanksgiving Day football, I situated myself on the couch directly behind his rocking chair. We were quiet—my father prefers quiet—but so much the better. I sat with him in silence, willing my heart's pace to settle to the creak of the rocking chair. Still, I felt alienated from his calm influence, set adrift in a marital calamity of my own invention. What if my parents—made aware of my unhappiness—seized me from Nick's grasp, whisked me home to Virginia Beach, and divested me of accountability for my mess? I'd be even more of a coward then, but at least I'd be safe. As far as I was concerned, I had forfeited my right to autonomy. It was tantalizing, this notion of my parents shooing Nick away on my behalf, leaving me unfettered and free to love Paul openly once the fires had burned themselves out.

My mind had relaxed into a fanciful free fall, and yet it was only a few moments after joining my father downstairs that Nick followed, again, in search of me. I looked at him and tried to love him. I could not. Nor could I conceal my irritation at his arrival. With a loaded sigh, I trudged back to the living room, taking my place among the family as a happy and gracious newlywed.

I cried when Nick left at the end of the break. He was relieved and seemed to pocket my tears as evidence of affection. In some ways, they were. Amidst the misplaced anger, physical disinterest, and the terrifying realization of our incompatibility, I'd located tendrils of melancholic fondness. We had spent five years together, after all, and I was grateful for everything that had been good between us. I wish I had had the courage to accept that our relationship had run its course years ago, to have left him honestly, and to have faced the solitude that can accompany living and navigating the world alone. In truth, I was crying in reminiscence, in mourning. I was also crying because somewhere in the depths of myself I had already decided to betray him.

By the time I returned to campus, my attention, previously straining in Nick's direction, swiveled back to Paul as if by magnetic pull. When he stopped by my office door to say hello, I nearly knocked over my desk chair in my haste to embrace him. I wore my love without trepidation. The shithouse was going down, and I was a terrible actress—why even make an attempt at concealment? I did not hold him long, but in that quick pause I arrived at an understanding. If Paul had committed himself to caution before, he was, just a little, letting me know what he had been protecting.

On the day the semester ended, we planned a night to watch movies and share music. I wanted Paul to see *Empire Records*, and we were both tickled by the prospect of sharing the stories tied to our favorite songs. (It's not lost on me that the characters of *Empire Records* would certainly have regarded our evening's agenda as fundamentally precoital.)

I woke the morning of our get-together vibrating with excitement. But I continued, as I had done for weeks, to admonish myself that our end-of-semester celebration was perfectly innocuous. Whatever Paul meant to me I would have to suppress—just enough, if not entirely—so as not to let the reins that had been gliding steadily out of my grasp fall away completely. And so I told myself that I wasn't shaving my legs for any special occasion, though I rarely touch a razor once the temperature drops beneath sixty degrees.

I spent all day masquerading as an easy, breezy gal who—no big deal—was headed over to a male pal's house for the most casual and chaste of get-togethers. The afternoon seemed contemptuously long, as if time, already aware of what would transpire, was implementing preemptive punitive measures. When Paul turned up at my office to escort me back to his house, I felt relief. Soon we were seated on the couch in his bedroom, narrating our lives through our iTunes libraries and wooing his cat, Hobo, out from behind the bed.

I don't recall why we eventually embraced; perhaps I had confided some intimate detail of my personal history. Perhaps we were looking for any sliver of opportunity. But when we pulled away, it was only for me to rest my head against his shoulder as he held me close.

Silence. But I could only stand it so long.

"Are we going to talk about the fact that I'm married?" I blurted out. Or so my memory tells me.

According to Paul, I spoke these words softly and calmly, albeit with distinct sadness. It's remarkable to me that this could be true. What I do know is that, as I broached this topic, the muscles in my chest throbbed, vibrating as if an invisible hand carelessly strummed across them. I did not especially want to discuss my marriage; in fact the mere act of pronunciation seemed beyond my physical capacity. And so, uttering this question—elliptical and uncommitting though it was—felt akin to choking out a tumor. It plunked out, sloppy and stumbling, but at last unavoidable.

"We can if you want to," Paul replied. But for his part, he said very little. I would not have blamed him for telling me to go, for coming to his senses that moment and realizing that I was foolish and selfish, the sort of woman who was careless with others' most tender emotions. Hadn't I been?

Not looking at him, but not letting go, I told him the truth.

"I have never felt for anyone what I feel for you."

Paul merely nodded in response.

Half convinced that I would be gently rebuffed—and aware that it would be for the best—I barely eked out, "Do you... reciprocate?"

My chest tightened with barbed joy when Paul replied, so softly, "Yes."

After that, I know we kissed with loving relief and with sorrow, and I know, too, that I sometimes gave into self-pitying sobs. Nick texted me later that night to ask if I was home; I lied. I promised myself I wouldn't stay the night, but by two a.m. I knew that I had intended to do so anyway. I slipped on one of Paul's old T-shirts, and gently, as if fearing the air around us would shatter, we made love in his bed.

For one night, my brain allowed me to play make-believe. I wasn't married—I wasn't myself—I was an obscure body and brain following impulse. The following morning, however, my brain had had the opportunity to take stock of recent events, and I crumpled.

I said goodbye to Paul and returned home with neither firm plans to return nor to stay away. I texted Leigha on the train, and she met me back at my apartment. We passed the day together, me scarcely aware of anything beyond my own frazzled free associations. Leigha, for her part, remained a steadfast wellspring of calm and refrained from scolding me because she was confident in my own self-condemnation. The truest friends, I have learned, expect the best from us without balking at each misstep.

But I'm sure I tried her patience, as I certainly tried my own. In the middle of that sticky, befuddling mire, only a few things seemed clear to me, and I recited them like the alphabet. First, that I was in love with Paul. Second, that I did not love Nick enough to remain married to him, and that I wanted to leave him. And finally, that however much I wanted to jettison my present life and begin anew with Paul, I felt certain that leaving then, after barely four months of marriage, was socially unacceptable to the point of futility. However, none of the above deterred me from seeing Paul every day for nearly a week.

The mundanity was at once dazzling and devastating. One night we ordered pizza; I waited downstairs to greet the delivery person. Paul intercepted me, laden with plates and utensils, and paused for a quick, rosy kiss before continuing up the stairs. I thought to myself, brazenly defiant, "I will never give this up." And for a handful of disoriented minutes, playing the runaway newlywed would seem plausible, even righteous.

But those moments quickly dimmed. As Paul and I worked side-by-side, thighs pressed together as if oxygen were the enemy, I would founder, pained by the fresh realization that this precious intimacy was purchased with deceit. The complexity of my predicament always reasserted itself. Paul never attempted to sway me, to coax me out of my marriage, but I also knew he wanted me to leave as much as I wanted to myself. Both of us, I think, understood that we toed the brink of alienation. So as the week stumbled on, and Paul prepared to return to Colorado that Saturday, we grasped at what we could offer each other: foolish, reckless love, the fear of hurting each other, and mutual pity for the fallout that we would each inevitably negotiate separately.

But all the while I was crumbling from the core. I saw clearly an inevitable trajectory of destruction, but I had been swinging my bat for too long to combat inertia. I won't credit myself with breaking anyone's heart besides my own. Yet I would close my eyes and see my likeness beating three of them, bloodied, sputtering, and suspended from dark air: Nick's heart. Paul's heart. Mine.

By Thursday, I forced myself to return home for at least one evening. My last term paper was due the following day, and I had barely written half of it. Moreover, Nick would be returning to DC in several days, and I needed to determine a next move before his arrival.

Or perhaps I should say: summon the courage to end my affair with Paul, a necessity I could not deny regardless of whether I chose to stay married. But the prospect of detaching myself from him made me miserable. Our immediate future was so bleak that, in his absence, it seemed that I had already lost him.

The solitude of my apartment meant being cloistered with my own increasingly panicked thoughts. I opened my laptop and pulled out *Villette*, reasoning that if I could just finish my term paper, I could more adeptly navigate my topsy-turvy circumstances. But anxiety coursed through my body without remission.

Nick, I knew, was studying for exams, but in more companionable times we had spent end-of-term trudges working together on video chat. I suggested we initiate one of these chats now, though I was not especially keen to talk. But the longer I fretted in that capsule basement apartment, the more my worries seemed to clutch and smother me. I felt like the most banal of stereotypes, but there's no solidarity in wandering a well-traveled narrative.

For perhaps a half hour, I choked up conversation with my husband, attempted to feign the demeanor of one merely unsettled by garden-variety academic stress. But as he turned his eyes away from me and back to his books, his face lapsed into glum worry. Did he already know? Was it fair for him to know? Shaking and sobbing, I told him anyway.

Nick grew quietly furious, muttering that he had already guessed my transgression—when, that week, I had assured him

I was home and alone, he counted it as one more lie charged to my account. And, of course, there was nothing to dispute: I had lied about everything until my feeble conscience broke open.

In an obscure corner of my brain, I wondered at my vigorous promises to be a better wife while every nerve screamed at me to get the fuck out. But it's emphatically clear to me now that I held my own judgment in deep suspicion (not without cause, perhaps) and instead panted after external guidance: family, novels, friends, song lyrics—it didn't matter, so long as the execution was confident.

And so it did not occur to me, as I admitted my deceitfulness to Nick, that I could have demanded a divorce and braced myself against the resulting familial tempest. My resolve was too limp; besides, I assumed what I wanted was impossible because it was both selfish and unconventional. Could a choice that seemed so solipsistic be fundamentally correct? Months later, I would read between choked sobs Dear Sugar's warm assurance: "wanting to leave is enough." But deep into that gnashing December night, I could only fathom the route of penitence. I contemplated the combined fury of my extended family and Nick's; it seemed to girdle me, shroud me so that there was no escaping it or my circumstances. Coward that I was, I feared Nick's anger too, and I was loath to supply any further information that would intensify it. Besides, protesting that I was in love with Paul was futile if I had already determined the inevitability of giving him up.

All week, I longed to follow my emotional compass, and in the abstract I had always touted the necessity of doing so. But I had been an irresponsible custodian of my emotions and impulses. I had explained away my diminishing affection for Nick, so careless of romantic love's absence that I had married him anyway. And then I had so freely indulged my desire for Paul that I had pursued an intimacy I knew was illicit. I was not the intuitive, emotionally perceptive woman I prided myself on being, but rather clumsy under the weight of my own contorted passions. How could I be confident that I would commit myself to another person when all evidence pointed to me as mercurial and impulsive? How could I claim to be informed by feeling when, in truth, I was haunted by emotions that terrified me or felled me in a deluge?

As my thoughts traveled down this darkening path, my present circumstances began to resemble a mire of roiling shit. I was begging forgiveness from someone I didn't want, someone whose forgiveness paled in comparison to the prospect of Paul's love. But I had to abandon Paul. We, but mostly I, had done everything wrong. I had wrecked my ship; now I was sinking with it.

Nick was sputtering mad. I was weeping. I glanced over at my unfinished seminar paper. At some point in the evening I had dashed off a frenzied email to my professor asking for an extension because "my husband was threatening to leave me." (He granted my request.) The world was absurd. And me? I was a fool.

I walked into my bathroom and pulled out a bottle of Tylenol, filled to the brim. I shoveled it into my mouth and forced every single one down. I heard Nick calling to me. I felt Paul in my bones. Would he be there when I died?

———

Were this a nineteenth-century novel or a Tyler Perry film, the story might end here. The camera would draw slowly back as I double over, heaving and spewing bile—paying the piper for my sins of lustful excess. The scene might then fade to black, emitting only the telltale moan of the ambulance, then the muffled bustle of the emergency room, and finally a heart monitor chirping listlessly before giving way to the flat line's monotone. A new scene would come into focus, bespeaking the ruin I had left behind. Perhaps we'd be faced with a long shot of Nick weeping in the hospital corridor, the indisputable victim of both marital treachery and my suicide. We would be urged, through our sympathy, to glance over his imperfections, not least because he had loved someone as flawed as me.

And then, of course, a mournful Paul would be presented to us, so that we might benevolently pity him in spite of his own transgressions. Maybe Nick would even shake his hand at my funeral, the perfect bastion of wounded gentility. Hate the sin, not the (male) sinner, right? My casket, like my narrative, would be shut: after all, cheating suicidal wrecks like me are events, not agents. We cannonball through innocent male bodies, dragging them to the brink of annihilation. But there is gruesome relief in the unfaithful woman's death. It is a reprieve; the space she vacates, however haunted, no longer heaves with the weight of her emotional largesse. Packed away in a coffin, she is subdued and contained, no longer speaking but spoken for.

My own story, as you may safely assume, does not end this way. I did not die: I immediately regretted the Tylenol and ran to my landlady, who drove me to the hospital. ("What happened, honey?" a nurse asked. "I cheated on my husband... I'm such a cliché," I slurred. My landlady, by now used to my pedantic literary monologues, sighed. "Oh, Rachel, of course you would give that answer now.")

But according to a glut of narratives across modern Western culture, my conscience awoke relatively on schedule, and my brush with death was inevitable. After a married woman consummates her infidelity, or perhaps immediately beforehand, we often expect some degree of emotional dissolution. In the 1996 film adaptation of *The English Patient*, a married Katherine confronts Almásy in his room, distraught by her longing for him, and by the deceit that now seems inevitable. She assails him with loud smacks until, finally overcome, she vigorously returns his kisses, and the two fall to the floor entangled. It's a fittingly violent beginning to a doomed affair. In an especially grim foretelling, Tolstoy invokes the specter of death as Anna Karenina and Vronsky grapple with the aftermath of their first sexual encounter. Vronsky, we are told, has the distinct sense that a corpse—not a living woman—kneels before him. For his part, he "[feels] what a murderer must feel when he looks at the body he has deprived of life."[5] The novel implies what Vronsky perceives: that Anna's illicit passion for him is fatal. Certainly it brings about her social "death." After the scandal of her affair, Anna is subjected to the vicious, shaming gossip of the Russian aristocracy. A so-called fallen woman, other respected personages, especially women, shun her company.

Vronsky's perception of Anna as a corpse draws on the trajectory of the unfaithful woman's catastrophe narrative, but in this case, the catastrophe seems untethered to any condemnation from the narrator. The text does not necessarily articulate a desire for the bad woman to pay for her sins. For if other characters recoil from Anna, Tolstoy's narrator does not. Likewise,

The English Patient does not condemn Katherine and Almásy for their love; indeed, it is romanticized and presented as fundamentally tragic. We are invited to mourn with them deeply in a way we are not even when *Unfaithful*'s Connie, after hearing about Paul's murder, penitently yet sorrowfully burns his pictures in her fireplace. But in both cases, nineteenth-century novel and late twentieth-century adapted film, the narrative universe cannot reconcile the breach of marital vows with a joyful, or even peaceful, outcome. Each work seems organized by an ambiguous higher power that demands, if not moral retribution, then adherence to the logic that a wife's infidelity catalyzes entropic misery.

Anna, for one, intuits a wretched end just as she comprehends the social isolation that her trespass ensures: "She felt herself so criminal and guilty that the only thing left for her was to humble herself and beg forgiveness; but as she had no one else in her life now except [Vronsky], it was also to him that she addressed her plea for forgiveness. Looking at him, she physically felt her humiliation and could say nothing more."[6] The practice of mercy, while so often inscribed in religious doctrine, will not, Anna knows, influence her peers even if their treatment of Vronsky remains unchanged. In fact, so lopsided is the parceling of social stigma that Anna, wracked with guilt, seeks deliverance from the person with whom she has committed this transgression.

But perhaps this is not so curious. Anna's survival depends upon Vronsky's continued affection; he must remain sturdy in his conviction that their love absolves them—that, critically, it absolves Anna, or else she will be utterly bereft. In the female infidelity narrative, we rarely make space for more than one villain,

and if, in the case of *Temptation*'s Harley, we do, the burden of
morality rests on the shoulders of their female conquest.

Cheating wives rarely see a happy ending. Many, perhaps,
would argue that they do not deserve one. Some, regardless
of their sympathy, might see domestic tranquility as impossible
when it has been so irrevocably destroyed in one domain.
"A woman who cheats often ends up alone," I recall being
told—with, of course, the implication that I would never
choose an unpartnered life. I expect some others might protest
that for me to take such a defiant tone in this chapter is both
insolent and unremorseful. If I am not confessing my sins, what
here is worth telling? And why should I, then, the perpetrator,
be the one to tell it? How could someone like me—someone
so at the mercy of her riotous emotions—be trusted? Of the
texts I have mentioned, none are narrated in the first person.

I would never diminish the toll infidelity can take, but I also
refuse to diminish myself for having been, as it were, unfaithful.
No woman's character begins and ends with a solitary oath, and
her self-possession cannot be so swiftly denied. Our fingers were
not crafted so that they could be cinched by wedding bands:
the union between body and the marriage industrial complex
is one ushered by capitalism, not destiny. Whatever symbolism
we embrace, or promises we utter, these are choices that must
conform to our desires, fragmented, fraught, and contradictory
though they may be. The long grind of history might declare
that a woman can do no worse than change her mind, at least
when that change signals a turn from heteronormative domesticity. I say that a woman's volatility is her prerogative, and that
her happiness is not for others to adjudicate.

In Augusta Webster's 1870 poem "A Castaway," we encounter

another fallen woman: a prostitute who has cobbled together a living by sleeping with all manner of men, a number of them married. Without question, the speaker is a marginalized figure, a specter at society's spokes, barred from conventional pleasures, including a relationship with her family. The poem aches with self-doubt, as our speaker struggles to assemble a coherent vision of herself—one apart from what society has designated. But suddenly, her cadence steadies like a piercing gaze. She declares in succinct defiance, "Aye let their virtuous malice dribble on— / mock snowstorms on the stage—I'm proof long since / I have looked coolly on my what and why / and I accept myself."

I read this poem for the first time while I was studying for my oral exams, a year or so after the events of that December night. One of my sisters had only just begun speaking to me again—circumstances I understood, though they broke my heart. I had lost a few friends in the English department, too, ever since the May afternoon when Paul had stuck his head into my door, after five months of silence, and asked if we could find a less clumsy way of coexisting in the same hallways.

To persevere in my relationship with Nick, I had initially resolved to cut Paul out of my life. The resolve did not last. That afternoon in May, I stood up from my desk, and I went to him. When we awoke the next morning, nestled into each other, my wedding ring no longer throbbed upon my finger.

Chapter Ten

LOUD

In college I worked as a writing tutor at my school's Writing Resources Center, and while the pay was meager, the work was pleasing to me, and the job came with a perk: each tutor was entrusted with a key to the center, which meant we could study there after hours. This privilege brought convenience, not to mention the touch of warm pride that accommodates an illusion of low-level elitism. Besides, the tutoring cohort was a small and relatively close-knit group; nights spent toiling in their company were preferable to trudging through homework alone.

But there was one tutor, Tara, who I knew wasn't particularly fond of me. I knew this because we were in the same sorority, and it had been communicated to me that she had vehemently protested my admittance. This, of course, was her right, and she had committed no meaningful crime against me. We are not for everyone; I certainly am not, though I have always struggled to accept this truth, and I certainly railed against it then. Mostly, I avoided her—I'm intimidated by those I am unable to charm—yet I also harbored a puppyish yearning for approval, particularly from people like Tara, who were disinclined to give it. So when I was in near proximity to her, I attempted to self-monitor, hoping that if I was sufficiently agreeable, her opinion of me would soften.

One evening, a small group of us were working in the center, but of course, the primary hazard of a study party is that it will develop into, well, a party. A gentle tone still prevailed across the room, but a few of us had nudged our work aside and begun chatting. I became distracted by the conversation and, as can be the case with me, my accelerating loquaciousness was accompanied by a significantly raised volume. I didn't realize this had happened—I very rarely do—until Tara snapped, in exasperation, "Rachel, you're SO LOUD!"

Tara was attempting to finish her honors thesis, no small task, and it must have been aggravating to have her focus broken by my exclamations. Still, I suspected that if she had liked me better, she wouldn't have responded so harshly, and as I folded into myself, chastened and shamed, I arrived at a glum conclusion: "She will never like me because she finds me obnoxious—and too loud."

Since girlhood I had squirmed with humiliation whenever I was told to lower my voice—by relatives, by teachers, by peers—and if I was not rigorously mindful, it was bound to happen. I am, and have always been, talkative and demonstrative; my every attempt at a poker face is doomed to failure by what seems to be a genetic disinclination. And until recent years, I was loud. I was loud until I finally, desperately, trained myself to mitigate some of my more bombastic tendencies, no longer willing to be addressed as if I were a perturbing child who, after chugging a case of Mountain Dew, had rocketed to hyperactivity. But even then, I was dogged by an ever-deepening sense that my voice and general disposition were disagreeably excessive—that others, particularly in professional circumstances, would always find the bigness of my expressions off-putting if I did not take care to modulate them.

———

It can be blisteringly painful to be an exuberant woman in a public setting, particularly a professional one. Oftentimes, we are positioned as if we're at odds with the environment. Exuberant women laugh loudly, whistle, and sing in the office. They are rarely blasé about their circumstances, nor are they concerned with appearing "chill" in the interest of keeping up appearances. If the exuberant woman finds reason to be excited, she will express it—that is, until she is maligned as immature, unprofessional, or even annoying. Somehow, expressions of joy and pleasure have become damning markers of stunted growth. If exuberance is not checked in youth, surely it will unsettle conventional expectations of womanhood. How could a thirty-year-old woman who has recognized the weight of her gendered responsibilities *not* sound jaded and sardonic and world-weary? But despite what American society insists, exuberance is not at odds with emotional and sexual maturity.

Exuberant women can demand respect without forsaking their buoyancy and playfulness.

Yet women in traditional office environments know all too well the necessity of muting their vibrancy. Already at risk of being treated like little girls playing pretend, an exuberant woman in a male-dominated workplace risks upward mobility and certainly the respect of upper management. We walk a fine line: after all, projecting confidence—an especial necessity for women in the professional world—requires women to gulp back any vestiges of meekness. We must demonstrate ourselves to be just as witty as our male colleagues, and after hours, we gain respect by holding our liquor at raucous happy hours. But for women, the line between confidence and exuberance is a fraught and muddied one indeed. One false step is damning, and we're never precisely sure where the traps are laid.

After I graduated college, I worked for one year as an administrative assistant at a private security company. It was a small, predominantly male office. The politics were overwhelmingly conservative, and much of the staff hailed from the military. I was twenty-two and blonde, my enthusiasm and naïveté palpable in equal measure. The purpose of the job for me was to fill a gap—I needed to make money while I applied to graduate school—but I was nonetheless determined, as usual, to impress. I wore suits during my first week. The heels of my shoes ascended to a sensible height.

But very quickly it became all too clear to me that I was something of a joke, not because I was incompetent (I wasn't) or because I was very young (although that was a contributing factor) but because it never occurred to me to mask my delight when the CEO brought her dog to the office or to refrain from hugging a friendly colleague. I was a joke because I was young and feminine and unaware that my wide-eyed and acutely earnest demeanor was incommensurate with the corporate vision of professionalism.

And to be sure, I was still a fledgling employee. When I worked in the company's human resources department and was responsible for fielding employee phone calls, I tripped over rhetoric and grappled wildly for relevant information. When one security guard called and told me that he wanted to quit, I exclaimed, before I could stop myself, "Oh, no! Don't quit!" My confidence in these endeavors lessened considerably after a coworker told me that our boss, while listening to me fumble through a call one day, said with a sigh, "I hate when Rachel answers the phone." To my recollection, she never attempted to mentor me in this regard. She had her own freight of responsibilities, but I believe she found me irritating and would have simply fired me if given the opportunity. But as it was, the turnover rate in that human resources department was flagrantly high; everyone was miserable and those who could afford to leave did precisely that. For my part, I dashed off to the bathroom to sob on more than one occasion because this boss spoke to me harshly. I felt silly and sophomoric for doing so, but navigating inhospitable circumstances demands a pressure valve of some sort.

After one year in this dismal corporate quagmire, I eagerly returned to school in order to pursue graduate studies in English literature. I fancied myself better suited for the "life of the mind," a phrase I relished in my early twenties and internalized with great solemnity and self-seriousness. Academia's liberal arts' quarter would be a harbor, I reassured myself, a sanctuary for a bookish girl who blundered in endeavors of emotional self-moderation. And in some ways, this was the case. I befriended likeminded classmates whose dispositions were similar to mine or who were amenable to my emotional largesse. When I began teaching college courses, which is its own sort of performance, I found that exuberance could be a boon, even if my students smiled indulgently and thought I was a bit of a goof.

But academia, in its own way, fetishizes a culture of flinty, productivity-absorbed coolness that often ground against my sensibilities. Being a focused and ambitious student did not suffice: what was preferable, it seemed, was to project the demeanor of someone who not only relished endless workdays, but who was blasé about it, too. Among a trusted inner sanctum I could reveal my insecurities and exhaustion—to the rest, I essayed an attitude of militant and self-punishing sangfroid (and was, I'm sure, lacking in my attempts).

I loved graduate school, and my tenure there was largely successful. I belong to that variety of person who assesses all of her achievements in terms of grades: as the saying goes, I'm still hoping to earn an A-plus in therapy, and I compulsively check my ride-share ratings. And so it smarted all the more when my too muchness resulted in the "wrong" sort of scholarly behavior: tears at an inopportune time, my failure to conceal distress during a serious meeting. During the opening statement of my doctoral oral exam, where I was tasked with delivering a presentation and answering questions from a committee of faculty members, I burst into tears—nothing had gone wrong, but the stress of the ordeal had quickened my pulse to a rabbit's pace and at last burst from my tear ducts. Everyone on my committee responded with perfect kindness, but I was mortified all the same. Lousy with chagrin, I would relive this scene, and so many others, ad infinitum. I had, after all, already internalized specific expectations of deportment, and even if an authority figure wasn't invested in them, I was. Gradually, as I checked my exuberance and gulped down my predisposition for soggy eyes, I put myself to the test, hoping that I would impress others with a veneer of stoicism. But I hardly triumphed; on this sort of examination I never could.

———

Docile quietude has long been wielded by conduct books as a specifically feminine virtue. In 1946, the magazine *Photoplay* published the article "That Romantic Look," an instructional piece for women who were aiding their soldier husbands in acclimating to civilian life after the Second World War. The paramount goal was to minister to one's head of household without injuring his proud masculinity:

> Listen to your laughter too. Let it come easily, especially when you're with boys who had little to laugh at for too long. Laugh at the silly things you used to do together. Laugh for the sweet sake of laughter. And if you hear your laugh sound hysterical, giddy, or loud, tone it down, *oh do tone it down!*
>
> Easy enough to say, "Speak gently. Laugh softly," I know. The tone of our voice and laughter generates within us. When we're worried or rushed, it's in our voice and laughter that hysteria will manifest itself... Serenity

is the very wellspring of a romantic look. In it you have the beginning of the smooth brow, the easy carriage, the low voice, the gentle smile. This Christmas with our men home, surely we should know serenity. So let us look happy and contented and starry-eyed.[1]

Historical context aside, these directives might have come from a Victorian lady's etiquette book. Mid-century America draws liberally upon the rhetoric of hysteria in admonishing its women to cultivate placid demeanors and soft, dulcet tones. And yet, with a more modern and progressive approach, this conversation—how to aid someone in the transition from a violent, traumatic context to the routines of daily life—would be a productive one. It would not be until the Vietnam War that we began even to discuss how to engage with those suffering from post-traumatic stress disorder: these early efforts to soothe those who had recently endured the unthinkable are well intentioned but, unsurprisingly, entrenched in gender-normative philosophies regarding femininity and distribution of emotional labor. Oh, do tone it down, ladies.

As for nineteenth-century etiquette books, their positions on women's voices and general dispositions are what you might suppose: if, as the old chestnut goes, children were to be seen and not heard, women's guidelines hardly differed. Feminine exuberance would have been received as unseemly at best when so much as opening one's mouth demanded special care and modulation. As in all other topics, Ella Adelia Fletcher's *The Woman Beautiful* takes a maniacally specific approach to addressing how a woman should speak without afflicting the genteel ears of those present. After instructing her readers in how to beautify their mouths and lips, Fletcher proceeds to tackle voice:

Naturally, the beautiful mouth and coral lips should be fittingly completed by a lovely voice; but, too often, this harmonious trinity is violated by a discordant, rasping, badly-placed voice. It is usually the result, not of any physical defect, but of careless habits: careless habits of breathing, of thinking, and of speaking. The commonest defect in a woman's voice is pitching it too high; and often this is accompanied by a nervous tension which holds the muscles of the throat taut and strained; and by short, hurried breathing which cuts the vibrations, destroys the overtones, and imparts an unpleasant rasping, dead, or shrill *timbre* to the voice.[2] (emphasis Fletcher)

Based on her account, it seems that Fletcher keeps close company with a hoard of verbal zombies, such is the purported ghastliness of women's faulty speaking habits. It's unclear how Fletcher has arrived at her conclusions regarding the ways that one might butcher her tone of voice—her description doesn't strike me as especially scientific—but her paramount motivation is not educating her readers on the mechanics of vocal cords and breath. Rather, the primary object is to render women more hesitant before they speak, less eager to pipe up in conversation, and more inclined to focus their efforts on adopting speech patterns that, while likely difficult to maintain, ensure that Victorian women uphold their foremost public role: emollient decoration. As Fletcher has made eminently clear, there is no aspect of one's person that cannot be chiseled and

squeezed and pressed upon until it obliges masculine sensibilities of female beauty and, above all, does not agitate a man's
amour propre. A woman should arrange herself so that she serves
as a complement to bolder, brasher masculinity:

> Train your ear to notice pleasant, agreeable voices, and lis-
> ten to your own critically. In the seclusion of your own
> room, try the pitch of your voice until you discover its
> most melodious one, that upon which you can develop
> the fullest and sweetest *timbre*, —the tone which you de-
> termine shall be known by your friends as your voice.[3]
> (emphasis Fletcher)

It's a wonder that anyone could proffer an argument for
essentialist gender types, when literature like this makes no
bones that femininity arises from an assemblage of learned behaviors and traits. Although Fletcher does not directly address
relations with men, the issue looms large in every page, with
the implicit argument that if one liturgically adheres to her
lessons, she will be the sort of woman who is pleasing to men
and will therefore attract their attention, as opposed to her
imagined "rasping, dead"-voiced competition.

While Fletcher was dispensing her advice across the pond,
Mrs. C. E. "Madge" Humphry, one of the first female journalists in Great Britain, was also publishing etiquette manuals for
men and women alike. In 1898, she released *A Word to Women*,
which followed her popular 1897 volume *Manners for Women*.
Her advice, rooted snugly in fin-de-siècle gender politics, acknowledges women's increased, but tenuous, presence in the
public sphere while adhering to the enduring philosophy of

the "Angel in the House"—in other words, the Victorian argument that a woman's rightful place was the domestic sphere,
which she should cultivate as a place of pacific harmony, a
palliative contrast to the rough-and-tumble of male-dominated
public life.

Humphry reiterates the necessity of maintaining tranquility
in the home, but moreover directs women to wield this influence in whatever social context they may inhabit. In her
chapter titled "Golden Silence" she posits that a woman should
limit her chatter without becoming tedious company:

> The lesson of quiet composure has to be learned soon or
> late, and it is generally soon in the higher classes of soci-
> ety. In fact the quality of reticence, and even stoicism, is so
> early implanted in the daughters of the cultivated classes
> that a rather trying monotony is sometimes the result.
> After a while the girls outgrow it, learning how to exer-
> cise the acquired habit of self-control without losing the
> charm of individuality. When maturity is reached, one of
> the most useful and delightful of social qualities is some-
> times attained—not always—that of silently passing over
> much that, if noticed, would make for discord. Truth to
> tell, there is often far too much talking going on.[4]

Humphry's lessons are evidently aimed at "the cultivated
classes" in English society, not surprising in such a trenchantly
hierarchical arrangement. And as she vigorously indicates, one
mark of good breeding is striking the balance between boring
one's company and not allowing the "charm of individuality" to
unravel into dreaded loquaciousness. A woman, she insinuates,

ought to be a peacemaker; that is to say, she should not address comments that are upsetting or inappropriate; after all, this would introduce "discord" into the atmosphere. Instead, one must suppress one's more ardent impulses to ensure smoother discourse. Being oneself was welcomed so long as that self was stringently groomed with the paramount goal of appealing to everybody and offending no one.

For, as Humphry elucidates in a later chapter, "Lightheartedness," it is not sufficient for a woman to monitor the quality and effect of her conversation; she must perform these feats with a smile. Unsurprisingly, the infuriating habit perpetuated by so many men—"Give me a smile, baby"—has firm roots in Victorian expectations of women to ameliorate every social environment, to transform their surroundings into pleasant, cheery contexts through the performance of good humor:

> Men are always telling women that it is the duty of the less-burdened sex to meet their lords and masters with cheerful faces; and if any doubt were felt as to the value of the acquirement—for cheerfulness often has to be acquired and cultivated like any other marketable accomplishment—shall we not find a mass of evidence in the advertisement columns of the daily papers? Do not all the lady-housekeepers and companions describe themselves as "cheerful"? Lone, lorn women could scarcely be successes in either capacity, and cheerfulness is a distinct qualification for either post.[5]

Humphry's chain of rhetorical questions is telling. For a late Victorian woman, what men desire—to be greeted as kings of

their castles with beaming, beatific faces—demands attention
and supplication (for sanity's sake, we'll pass over the suggestion that women are "the less-burdened sex"). "Well, 'tis our
duty to be cheerful," Humphry concludes, soon after these remarks. For that matter, she treats her commentary regarding
the necessity of "cheerfulness" in service positions as something of an afterthought; the greatest sign of "the value of
the acquirement" lies in male pleasure. But in mentioning
the necessity of a sunny disposition in "lady-housekeepers and
companions," two positions in which a woman joins a household as an inferior member, Humphry lays bare a larger truth:
that all women must be at the service of their so-called male
betters, and that they must quash their own, uglier sentiments
so that they may ensure they do not detract from the social
atmosphere. Humphry is not so naïve to overlook the "mar-
ketability" of this quality: by drawing a comparison between
good breeding and business transactions, she insinuates that
women are always, to some extent, selling themselves as welcome members of polite company. But in this case, that which
is "marketable" happens to be inextricable from iron-bound
duty.

And yet Humphry resists the perspective that a woman's purpose is exclusively to serve as a decorative vessel. Overlooking
the extent to which women's education has been obstructed
and regarded as unnecessary, she censures her readers in a
chapter aptly named "Deadly Dulness" *(sic)* for failing to el-
evate their minds beyond more trivial pursuits. "Ninety out
of every hundred women bury their minds alive," she declares. "They do not live, they merely exist."[6] But the fault,
she maintains, rests with women, for being inclined to indulge

in less intellectual activities, for occupying themselves with fashionable trends rather than, say, reading the newspaper:

The great world and its doings go on unheeded by us, in our absorption in matters infinitesimally small. We fish for minnows and neglect our coral reefs...And yet the news of the universe, the latest discoveries in science, the newest tales of searchings among the stars, to say nothing of the doings of our own fellow creatures in the life of every day, should be of interest. But we think more of the party over the way, and the wedding round the corner. Is it not true, oh sisters?[7]

On the one hand, it's not undesirable for a Victorian woman with some influence to encourage reading and self-education. But clearly she's referring to her "sisters" in equal or loftier socioeconomic classes: Humphry, like so many other Victorians, evinces little interest in empowering women of the working class. What's more, women were often condemned for acclimating to their prisons: while certainly intellectual curiosity varied—not every Victorian woman was a Brontë sister or George Eliot—it was a vastly uphill battle for women to procure the sort of education so readily available to men of a certain economic or social stature.

It was also not uncommon for intellectual women to accuse others among their ranks of silliness. In 1856, novelist George Eliot penned the scathing essay "Silly Novels By Lady Novelists," wherein she derides—with gusto—the sort of literature written by her female contemporaries, arguing that it is frivolous, detached from reality, and altogether an indication of what the novel should *not* be. Jane Austen delighted in the ridiculous social manners of men and women, although her critiques of women, in light of their often circumscribed opportunities, sometimes blistered with especial cruelty. And in this case, Mrs. Humphry castigates women of means for frittering away their days with dresses, parties, and—wouldn't you know—fiddling novels. Women, it seems, were enthusiastic about the wrong things precisely because they were coded as undeniably feminine. To edify oneself, according to Humphry, requires one to consider more sober goings-on. Not a deleterious endeavor on its own, but its purpose here is to teach women to behave so that they will be taken seriously by men, or shall we say, as serious as ever a man might have taken a woman in 1898 British high society.

Perhaps, buried within the coils of internalized sexism, is Humphry's genuine desire for women to navigate a world that regards them as subordinate and foolish. Three decades prior, American etiquette writer Florence Hartley undertook a different task, one that resembles Ella Adelia Fletcher's scrupulous methodology of behavioral micromanagement. In *The Ladies' Book of Etiquette and Manual of Politeness* (1860), Hartley reminds women readers through every possible avenue that their primary object in all things is "true politeness."[8] And in the chapter "Polite Deportment, and Good Habits," she delineates how politeness should manifest in a woman's every gesture, admonishing especially against exuberance and volume:

Many ladies, moving, too, in good society, will affect a forward, bold manner, very disagreeable to persons of sense. They will tell of their wondrous feats, when

engaged in pursuits only suited for men; they will con-
verse in a loud, boisterous tone; laugh loudly; sing comic
songs, or dashing bravuras in a style only fit for the
stage or a gentleman's after-dinner party...It may be encouraged, admired, in their presence, by gentlemen, and
imitated by younger ladies, but, be sure, it is looked
upon with contempt, and disapproval by every one of
good sense, and that to persons of real refinement it is
absolutely disgusting.[9]

Hartley's rhetorical maneuvers in this passage lean heavily
on emotional manipulation. You may believe that others enjoy
your company, that you are a social success, but everyone who
matters, everyone whose approval you *should* crave, finds you
"absolutely disgusting." For, as she insinuates, this "loud, boisterous" behavior only suits women of questionable virtue, the
so-called fallen women who often made their livings catering
to rich men in after-hours. What we now refer to as slut-
shaming Hartley deploys as a tactic of dissuasion: it's best to pipe
down or else everyone will think you loose and skanky.

But rather than merely dispense this warning against unwomanly conduct, Hartley offers guidelines that demand the
most punishing regimens of self-monitoring. It is not enough
to keep one's voice soft; every muscle must be trained to enact
genial docility:

Never gesticulate when conversing; it looks theatrical,
and is ill-bred; so are all contortions of the features, shrug-
ging of shoulders, raising of the eyebrows, or hands.
    When you open a conversation, do so with a slight

bow and smile, but be careful not to simper, and not to smile too often, if the conversation becomes serious.

Never point. It is excessively ill-bred.

Avoid exclamations; they are in excessively bad taste, and are apt to be vulgar words. A lady may express as much polite surprise or concern by a few simple, earnest words, or in her manner, as she can by exclaiming "Good gracious!" "Mercy!" or "Dear me!"

. . .

Avoid a muttering, mouthing, stuttering, droning, guttural, nasal, or lisping, pronunciation.[10]

The list continues in a similarly—and obsessively—fastidious manner. At base, Hartley, Humphry, and Fletcher share a common assumption: women should not gab so much that these exacting rules for discourse are difficult to follow. Being "cheerful" as Humphry directs is by no means a state to be confused with an easy, relaxed attitude; although, if one practices the appearance of it enough, perhaps verisimilitude will suffice. Nineteenth-century women generally understood the constrictions of their milieu: they would not be regarded as men's equals no matter their accomplishments or character. Women of privilege, those born to families with wealth and status, knew that, at best, they could distinguish themselves as examples of genteel femininity. But to achieve this distinction demanded an unyielding suppression of too muchness—of brash opinions and political fervor and heated emotions. After all, Victorian literary heroines like *Middlemarch*'s Dorothea Brooke were beloved for their gentle, not dispassionate, but certainly refined demeanors. Maggie Tulliver, from *The Mill on the Floss*, and the most famous of chatterboxes, Anne Shirley, learn to lower their voices and quench their confabulation as they grow older. Most of Victorian literature's notoriously headstrong heroines, like Elizabeth Gaskell's Margaret Hale or Charlotte Brontë's Shirley Keeldar, could hardly be described as bombastic, though Shirley Keeldar, who is proud and diffi-cult and sometimes deliciously rude, perhaps comes closest. To seize the tatters of respect and tolerance has always meant whit-tling ourselves into shapes that are legible and, above all, the easiest to swallow. And indeed: we've been swallowed whole, consumed for centuries in our most palatable, pleasing forms. To live authentically, and thereby refuse this protracted social annihilation—that's the aim.

———

As women have fought for, and gradually achieved, lives that extend beyond the domestic sphere, the terms by which we seek both empathy and respect have shifted; our emphases are broader, more diverse. To be sure, sexist ideologies still struc-ture the way much of Western society interprets and judges our behavior. Even in public, recreational spaces, boisterous, exu-berant, emotive women and femmes are regarded as liabilities—secondhand embarrassments, and depending on their company, perhaps even firsthand ones too. We have methodically erected cultural scaffoldings where women with big feelings are alien-ated from communal spaces. The tacit agreement that stoicism—or the appearance of it—and a general emotional re-serve are more easily navigable informs the brunt of our social rituals. It is unseemly to ask, implicitly, that others bear witness to our unravelings. To be loud and expressive in public is to invite accusations of immaturity and, worse, uncontrollability.

Gradually, however, the workplace has become the primary locus for these concerns. By now, forty-seven percent of America's civilian labor force are women, but the processes of adaptation and compromise continue to be a contentious trudge. Among debates regarding lactation rooms, warmer office temperatures, and other accommodations that would make working environments more hospitable to feminine persons, we confront larger ontological questions regarding how women should *be* in professional contexts. We tussle over what sorts of expressions or distress someone, particularly a woman or femme, can safely broadcast without being lampooned or risking her livelihood.

These questions have endured for decades, without any meaningful resolution. Perhaps for that reason, popular culture offers no shortage of depictions of women in the workplace, often focusing on what we must do to thrive in a corporate system built for white heterosexual cis-men. To be sure, this conversation is critical, and must continue, but we also need to put pressure on the prevailing theory that a woman's professional success demands a very specific performance of Stone Cold Bitch. The empress of *Vogue* magazine, Anna Wintour, already enjoys status as a print media legend, but not merely because she is a thunderously successful woman. We marvel at her because, by all accounts, she possesses a notoriously austere manner and utter intolerance for work that does not meet her rigid specifications. In short, we're impressed because she is mean. *The Devil Wears Prada*, both the book and its film adaptation, entice their audience precisely because a bitchy, brilliant female boss is a spectacle to behold.

But then, what of the Liz Lemon movement? When *30 Rock* first aired, Tina Fey's rumpled, uninhibited character seemed a love letter to creative nerds who had no interest in stiletto heels or frosted small talk. And yet Lemon's exuberance comes at the cost of her sexuality. Her boss, Jack Donaghy (Alec Baldwin) may be portrayed as an over-the-top sexist, but he nonetheless diminishes Lemon at every turn, often engaging with her as a sexless adult child. Tina Fey devises an even more extreme version of this character in her show *Unbreakable Kimmy Schmidt*, in which the titular character (played by Ellie Kemper) strives to acclimate to the modern world after being held hostage in a bunker by an apocalyptic cult leader (Jon Hamm). Although we are meant to understand Kimmy's naïveté and backwardness as a result of psychological and sexual trauma, it's her resilient smiles and exuberance that render her more childlike than anything else.

Meanwhile, conventional depictions of the covertly sensitive female badass prevail. On the long-running medical drama *Grey's Anatomy*, the heroic Dr. Miranda Bailey (Chandra Wilson) inspires viewers with audacity, deadpan hilarity, and talent, but particularly in the earlier seasons, it's always clear that what is softest inside of her must be concealed, even from some of those she calls her friends. Like so many black female characters, she is ever hoisting the burdens of others, whether professional or emotional. Perhaps our closest approximation to a character unwilling to suppress her sensitivity, no matter the context, is Leslie Knope (Amy Poehler) of *Parks and Recreation*. But, one of the show's running gags, Leslie's otherworldly productivity, seems almost a corrective, a means of assuring us that her exuberance and vivid emotional life never detract from her performance. Indeed, it's posited as one dimension of the relentless energy that enables her to carry her largely ineffectual employees.

On October 14, 2018, the *New York Times* addressed the matter of workplace expression directly with an interview entitled "Why You Shouldn't Feel Bad About Crying at Work." Conversing with *Ask a Manager* advice columnist Alison Green, Smarter Living newsletter editor Tim Herrera broached this knotted subject that, as Green candidly emphasized, cannot be so easily addressed. In fact, the headline is a touch misleading: crying at work, at least in the climate we have cultivated, is not something we can shrug off as incidental. "If you're regularly crying at work, or you break down in sobs at a staff meeting, or you're crying in response to mild feedback... yeah, it can hurt your reputation, for sure," Green remarks. "But getting a little teary in a one-on-one meeting where you're frustrated or stressed? An awful lot of people do that at some point during their careers, and while they tend to be mortified, it's usually fine."[11] This response seems reasonable enough; after all, Green is responding to the cultures of extant workplace environments. Moreover, making space for too muchness does not mean we can fully disregard the needs of others, but it does demand more flexibility than we are currently afforded. If I were permitted, say, one workplace crying episode every ten years, I would be in something of a pickle. Unsurprisingly, Herrera and Green draw on our terminology—too much—to sketch out the parameters of crying in conventional office settings. Green tackles the question directly:

> Let's talk about the times when it's too much! Full on, body wracking sobs are pretty much always out of place

at work (excluding something like news of a death). And if you're leading a team, you need to project confidence and authority, and *getting teary can undermine that.* Or if you routinely tear up in response to feedback about your work, your boss is likely to start worrying about your ability to take feedback (and may start giving you less of it out of discomfort with your reaction, and that's not good).

And you generally want your crying to be as private as possible; tearing up in a one-on-one meeting or alone in a bathroom stall is one thing, but crying while you're sitting around a conference table with a group of other people is likely to *harm your credibility and make people much more uncomfortable.* For better or worse, there's a higher bar in that situation for controlling your emotions.[12] (emphasis mine)

Green's observations regarding the too muchness of workplace distress are apt. It's quite true that in all manner of scenarios, tears detract from our credibility and cause our colleagues to squirm. The larger question is whether this should be the case and whether tearfulness is an index of someone's ability to manage a project or a delicate situation. As someone who struggles with especially leaky tear ducts, but who also taught college literature and writing for the better part of a decade, I would say that this is not necessarily the case. Too Much women know, far better than others often suppose, what we need to do in order to fulfill our obligations. If I were in danger of flatlining on an operating table I wouldn't be concerned that my surgeon was a crier unless her upset resulted in her fleeing from the OR rather than reviving me. My too muchness is without question a direct inheritance from my mother, and she was a trusted and beloved nurse.

But because we've nurtured a cultural fear of emotion, we've in turn perpetuated a pernicious lesson: that those of us who are more inclined to emote, and who would prefer not to suppress what we feel, reflexively shame ourselves for intense expressions of joy and distress. And when it comes to tears, Green explains, the anxiety is shaped by gender identity:

> It may just be because women are socialized to be more comfortable with tears, who knows. But I hear far more women talk about having teared up at work than men, and then there's also pressure on women not to seem too emotional in a professional context, so then they feel especially mortified. And the gender differences around this add an additional element of stress to it—for example, if you're a woman who cries in front of a male boss, is your male boss going to be more freaked out by it than a female boss would be? Maybe, and that's definitely something women worry about.[13]

It's not within this book's purview to discuss the vicious impact of toxic masculinity on male emotional expression, though, to be sure, their socialization has been deleteriously impacted. Still, American workplace culture was built by white heterosexual cisgender men, and throughout its development, they did not especially consider what people of other races and genders might require in order to matriculate effectively. Upon pushing past the gatekeepers, the rest of us were expected to assimilate without protest. And while Green's observation that "women are socialized to be more comfortable with tears" seems accurate, that comfort as she acknowledges does not extend to conventional office environments, where we have learned to fear the telltale sting at the corners of our eyes or the constriction of the throat. Certainly we should not accept the enduring circumstances that crying in front of a man is without question our problem and our fault.

A gamut of vulnerable female expression meets with skepticism and disapproval thanks to centuries of reinforcement: over time, the naturalized response to too muchness has become one of reprimand, discomfort, and doubt—in the woman's capacity to handle herself, or anything else. Meanwhile, white male tears are increasingly celebrated as the tabernacle of masculine emotional refinement. On the day after the 2016 presidential election, my husband Paul had to teach class, and he felt it would be disingenuous, not to mention impossible, to proceed as if we had not just experienced a terrifying historical juggernaut. As he spoke to his students, mostly left-leaning, but some conservative, he asked them to consider, whatever their politics, that many of their classmates, together with thousands of people living in America, were unspeakably frightened right now, and that we must support them and demonstrate empathy. In the process of addressing his students, he began tearing up—something he had not expected to do, and that caught him by surprise.

I was, and am, proud of him for saying what he did. What is curious to me, and to him, is the extent to which his students patted him on the back not merely for these remarks, but for becoming emotional while articulating them. One of his male students later told him that he appreciated Paul demonstrating a form of masculinity that did not preclude unfiltered expression. And yet, how different is the response to a white, hetero-sexual, cisgender man who cries before his students and the reactions to a woman who might do the same. Women are al-ready stereotyped as excessively feeling creatures; in our case, tears are often interpreted as a tipping point, a superabundant overflow from a hearty wellspring of emotion. Paul, like most men who present as conventionally masculine, is assumed as even keel unless he demonstrates otherwise. In his case, chok-ing up seemed to buttress the depth of his conviction, reassure the class of his sensitivity, and was even an index of his strength. This generosity afforded to male tears frustrates me, and, on a larger cultural register, it signifies problems of stigma and gen-der interpretation. But generally, male tears can be beneficial, in their way: in the case of Paul's students, they seemed to learn in real-time what nontoxic masculinity can look like. However, the cliché of the sympathetic crying man can be handily ex-ploited by those keen to manipulate. Brett Kavanaugh, the man appointed to the United States Supreme Court despite multiple accusations of sexual assault, knew precisely what he was doing when he began blubbering under oath.

Because they signify extremity, tears loom large in conver-sations about feminine emotional excess. Yet too muchness extends beyond crying to, among other traits, tone of voice and general exuberance, all qualities that women and femmes broadcast at the risk of censure. As I began my work on this chapter, I wanted to understand others' experiences in this re-spect and circulated questionnaires to more than 130 cis and trans women and nonbinary persons who identified as fem-inine or female-presenting, asking them to share testimonials about their experiences in office environments—to what extent they felt at liberty to emote, and whether they had ever been shamed for speaking loudly or simply for reacting to news or conversation with excitement. As the responses accumulated, and I sifted through them, I experienced a peculiar sense of mourning for something that has yet to come to pass: public spaces in which feminine emotion, and feminine too muchness, are not held suspiciously at arm's length, as if they are at best inconvenient and, at worst, dangerous.

For many who filled out my questionnaire, men's reactions to their voices and demeanors generated contentious environments. Kirsten, a thirty-year-old white woman, wrote to me that her "speaking style is something men tend to find 'bossy' or 'abrasive.' This has created a lot of problems for me . . . I once had someone say I was 'so abrasive it's professionally limiting,' and the genesis of that was apparently that I was too direct in expressing what I needed people who reported to me to do." She surmised, semihumorously, that she has been told to lower her voice "something in the order of 10,000 times." And as an "extremely" expressive and exuberant person, she has confronted a host of male persons who have sought to quiet her through tactics of humiliation. "I think people intend to make me feel bad when correcting my expression," she wrote. "I think it's mean-spirited and ill-intentioned. It used to embarrass me, but now I double down. Men in particular seem to want me to speak in a friendly tone, to accommodate them, and to express only positive emotions. They also don't like it when I'm too excited. I have found that tells me what I need to know about them."

Women of color confront the emotional strictures of an

office environment without the leniencies so often granted to those of us who are white or white-presenting. From the same survey, Liz, a thirty-two-year-old black queer woman, described how the larger sexist and racist social arrangement has shaped her self-presentation. "I self-monitor all the time," she wrote. "The balance between ego and self-advocacy is also a big one (impostor syndrome), especially as a black woman, so I engage in a lot of self-monitoring regarding my own perceived achievements as well." And yet, even her rigorous efforts to take account of her behavior could not prevent certain inequities:

> I recall being chastised about chatting with a fellow black coworker "too often" though we shared a work space and had very similar roles that often required collaboration. We seemed to be working under a microscope most of the time. Of course, we watched some of our white counterparts take long lunches and long breaks and [enjoy] the freedom to leave their desks more often and for longer periods of time... [They weren't] subject... to the same level of scrutiny. I even had a supervisor tell me I was on my cell phone too often! Not that I was "talking" on the phone, just that my phone was in my hand too much.

For, as Liz notes, it's not the tone of her voice that renders her "loud" in the eyes of supervisors; her presence, or the mere suggestion of a conversation—thus, the cell phone—has incited others to silence her. "The volume of my voice has rarely been an issue—the fact that I'm talking at all has more often been the target," she delineated. "'Be quiet' was not 'be quieter'; it was 'stop talking, period.'" Paula, a forty-eight-year-old black woman, explained that even responses she intended to project "neutrality" were interpreted as too intense. "[I've been] called combative for entering into what I thought was a conversational exchange, only to be told [that] by answering back I'm combative," she wrote. "Even if I'm addressing something in the most neutral voice, my confidence tends to make people uncomfortable."

This "confidence" or self-assurance, particularly from women of color, is, it seems, loud. That is to say, the mere act of being comfortable with oneself resounds in certain ears, precisely because it is unsettling to those who would prefer the Victorian woman's cheerful docility. Here is something we must understand about too muchness: it's an accusation that would be lobbed at us in most any case, whether we attributed it to ourselves or not. Most women, at some moment, will be marked as a Too Much woman. So much the better: we can all of us embrace the term, fold it into ourselves, and embody it as we see fit.

After all, we often realize that we're navigating a world distorted by gender- and race-based delusion. Lee, who is thirty-two, queer, and identifies as a nonbinary woman, recounted a particularly absurd office scrap. "Once, while engaged in a boisterous conversation with a male colleague (same tone and volume), I got taken aside and told to be quieter. He did not. I left the conversation and got chastised a second time for the noise, even though only men were still speaking."

These testimonials were not singular among the ones I collected; most of those who responded to my queries described intense, often painful efforts to suppress their emotions, to monitor their expressions, tone of voice, and volume. They testified the ways in which they reacted to the world unfolding in front of them lest they be told yet again to "calm down" or lower their voices or to be quiet. "If I had a nickel for every time I was told to lower my voice, I'd be a female Elon Musk," wrote V. Others' experiences reminded me of the familiar, infantilizing mortification that accompanies being "shushed," or the pricking sense that I was perceived as childlike for being excitable. Too many expressed a fear of laughing, particularly those who had been chastised for doing so in a way that was, for whatever wild or quibbling reason, received as unpleasant.

Extant conversations surrounding the gender and racial dynamics of office culture don't merely stifle possibilities for women's success, they preclude success according to individualized terms: a way of being without an emotional muzzle to stifle what would otherwise be sung. To forego strident self-moderation is a gamble for most women, and often an exercise in humiliation. When we live authentically, Too Much women risk the litany of assessments recounted to me, a liturgy of intended shame, although we strive to embrace it: loud, shrieky, shouty, shrill, intimidating, difficult, noisy, obnoxious, scary, strident, bitchy, bossy, pushy, not normal, intense, inappropriately lacking in deference, gobby, mouthy, unladylike, too friendly, too talkative, too emotional, too outspoken, too direct, too rash, too passionate, too much.

Chapter Eleven

OLD

When, on April 14, 1857, Queen Victoria gave birth to her ninth child, Beatrice, she was nearly thirty-eight—hardly what any reasonable person would call "old," especially today, but the arc of ageism is long, and lifespans in the nineteenth century were comparatively short (although Victoria proved an exception to this). After the delivery, her doctors admonished against having any more children, to which she reportedly replied, "Can I have no more fun in bed?"[1] Presumably she was not referring to the exertions of labor and delivery.

This anecdote flies in the face of the long-cherished assumptions about Victorian—and Victoria's—prudery: the good queen loved a hearty romp with her husband. And for all her vast privileges, Queen Victoria also lived according to the social clime. To bear nine children and to endure nine pregnancies before one turns thirty-eight is no small feat, and the queen abhorred much of what was involved, from breast-feeding to the nine-month gestational slog itself. But Victoria, for all she enjoyed having sex with Prince Albert, was also setting an example for her kingdom by modeling what was then considered a British woman's primary duty: motherhood. If the means to the end were pleasant for her, as they apparently were for the queen, then a woman was lucky, but the matter of her physical pleasure was so immaterial as to be nonexistent. That she bear sons who would grow up to defend Britannia and safeguard its vast empire—that was the paramount expectation. Victoria's question to the doctors—can I still have sex with my husband?—gestures to a culture at once preoccupied with women's ripe reproductive organs and, accordingly, disinclined to accommodate "aging" women—that is, those no longer capable of successful breeding. The royal physicians suggested that the queen guard against pregnancy because she was deemed too old to safely deliver another child. Victoria's immediate response is funny, but it's equally telling: women of her age were, for the most part, utterly desexualized. Even if the Victorians were discussing sex more than is typically assumed, those conversations were unlikely to reassure a woman in her late thirties that she was erotically empowered, that she ought to enjoy her coital proclivities. And they certainly weren't suggesting that women of Queen Victoria's age were desirable, because popular opinion, for all manner of reasons, dictated otherwise.

———

"Old" is a fraught and capacious term, and so by extension is the baggy pejorative "too old," an accusation lobbed with abandon at women of all ages with the paramount object of marking us according to a continuum of obsolescence and undesirability and, based on that metric, applying strictures of behavior. What sorts of acts and pleasures become "too much" for a middle-aged or elderly woman? In what ways are we permitted to age without being regarded as grotesque? Even in recent decades, as we see the rise of the "MILF"—women who embrace their sexuality long after their twenties and thirties and, most notably, after bearing children—it remains the case that aging women must combat de-eroticized invisibility. At best, what Western culture tolerates is the paradox of chaste sexuality: the older woman who has abandoned her sexpot days in exchange for genteel performance.

We have long struggled with the notion that a woman who has given birth and raised children can and should express her desires openly. One might say we cower under the shadow not of Queen Victoria herself, but instead what her appropriated image came to embody: the symbol of white maternity par excellence. "Modest, domestically inclined, and fertile: this was how Victoria's reign was depicted at mid-century. Her expanding family was a productive figure for England's expanding empire,"[2] explains literary critic Karen Chase. And so this narrative has endured, contributing to interpretations of adult women as sexless homemakers or grotesquely horny predators. When the term "MILF" entered our vocabulary with the 1999 film *American Pie*, it was saddled with ridicule. The acronym itself—shorthand for Mom I'd Like to Fuck—accommodates an anonymous subject while thoroughly objectifying "Mom"

as a pleasure vessel. The film draws on the term's rankest association: the MILF in question, played by Jennifer Coolidge, is
treated as both joke and novelty. It's unexpected that a woman
with an eighteen-year-old son would be sexually desirable;
moreover, that fact is treated as fundamentally humorous. In
the film, and on the IMDB database, she is reductively credited
as "Stifler's Mom," a blaring indication that her significance in
the film begins and ends with her curious maternal allure. In
2003 the pop rock band Fountains of Wayne enjoyed significant success with their radio-courting single "Stacy's Mom,"
which follows a similar premise: my girlfriend doesn't know
that I fantasize about her preternaturally hot, divorcée mother.
Even now, men in Hollywood toy with this trope. Take, for instance, the 2011 song and accompanying video "Motherlover"
by The Lonely Island, presumably a satirical spin on "Stacy's
Mom" and MILF jokes at large. To some extent, Andy Sam-
berg and Justin Timberlake render themselves ridiculous, but
the core joke is simple and the same: isn't it funny that I want
to fuck your mother who, in addition to having given birth to
you (hilarious!), is certainly too old for me?

As a matter of practice, Victorian fiction doesn't chronicle
the stories of middle-aged women; they are often sideline characters, figures of fun like Stifler's Mom or the haplessly eager
Mrs. George (played by Amy Poehler) of Tina Fey's 2004 comedy *Mean Girls*. What's more, the concept of aging was still
relatively inchoate until the Victorian period. "Senescence," or
old age, was a category that, while recognized, had not yet
ossified in either a cultural or socioeconomic way. Chase explains, "In fact, until the nineteenth century the attempt to
define 'old age' specifically by years was limited and variable.

Old age might be determined by looks, experience, feeling, or by the inability to bear arms or to work. Not surprisingly, it is the last—the capacity for work—which lent increasing value to the chronological definition of old age."[3]

Still, by the nineteenth century, those persons between the ages of forty and fifty, if not judged as positively decrepit, were seen as treading into their twilight years. Queen Victoria determined herself "old" by age forty-two—this was in 1861, the year she became a widow, and although she did not know it, only the midpoint of her life.[4] But then again, it might not have mattered. Widowhood concluded a distinct and weightily symbolic era: wherein a woman yoked her life to that of another and through that union produced a family. Even for a reigning monarch, this would have been framed as one's central endeavor, the years in which a woman could be productive in a biological way: for most, her preeminent contribution, according to cultural argument. Aging men might have shuffled home from their stores and their factories, backs bent and joints throbbing. Women became fundamentally extraneous to their purported moral duties, their bodies gradually alien to all that had once rendered them necessary.

If people of forty or fifty years were cycling out of the quotidian grind, they were simultaneously becoming less compelling figures to society at large. As literary critic Sarah Ross remarks, nineteenth-century novels, particularly those that chronicled women's lives, tended to exemplify the traits of the bildungsroman, that is to say, they were coming-of-age narratives that "catalogue the choices and missteps toward adulthood and a fully realized self."[5] For both young men and women, these steps lead them to marriage, and for women, they often lead to childbearing. The interior life of a middle-aged woman was, presumably, considered a less fascinating study for the majority of readers because she had already fulfilled her social debts. And if she hadn't, well, she had long been ousted to the margins of cultural life to keep company with spinsters and childless women and all the rest banished from the Victorian erotic circuit.

But this is not to say that Victorian novels lacked remarkable female characters who were middle-aged or older. In fact, stories teemed with them, but even in the most flattering cases, these women were generally sites of ludicrous excess. Betsey Trotwood of Charles Dickens's semiautobiographical novel *David Copperfield* (1850) emerges as perhaps one of the most beloved (she is without question one of my favorite characters): a flinty but vastly compassionate woman with little patience for men, she rescues David from an abusive household and the wretched labor of a blacking factory, seeing to his education and serving as a surrogate mother after his own dies. Dickens fashions her as something of an eccentric, a source of humor, particularly in light of her fanciful longing for a niece and bombastic fury at the start of the novel, when she finds out that David is not a girl. We learn, however, that Betsey's distrust of men comes from an abusive marriage she fled long ago, choosing instead to live with an intellectually disabled fellow, Mr. Dick, whom she treats with kindness and not a lick of condescension. We cannot always depend on Dickens—probably the most widely read author of his time, and certainly the most famous—to deliver a tenderhearted and thoughtful portrait of a woman. Yet with Betsey Trotwood, he more or less succeeds.

For Betsey Trotwood is something of an outlier in Dickens's

oeuvre. We need not look further than two of his other more famous novels for middle-aged or elderly women wallowing or even deteriorating in their own excesses. Most notoriously, the witchy Miss Havisham haunts *Great Expectations*, the too muchness of her fury and heartbreak rendering her a decaying jilted bride who obstructs the male protagonist's quest for love by manipulating a young girl to wreak romantic havoc on her behalf. In *Great Expectations* who abandoned Miss Havisham at the altar is far less significant than the spectacle she becomes: decrepit and bent with unfulfilled erotic longing, grotesque in her curdled happiness and fetid desires.

In *Bleak House* (1853) Dickens gives us the detached and disheveled Mrs. Jellyby, a marginal but scathingly rendered character who joins the ranks of his novels' lousy mothers. Preoccupied by her philanthropic endeavors in Africa, she wholly commits herself to letter writing campaigns while the Jellyby household, together with her gaggle of ragtag children, tumble into disarray. Mrs. Jellyby serves as one of Dickens's most choleric arguments against women who resist the demands of Victorian maternity and absorb themselves in more self-indulgent activities. Steeped in his own misogynist visions of motherhood, Dickens would have been unlikely to offer, with any degree of empathy, the interiority of a middle-aged woman who simply did not care about parenting. Betsey Trotwood is recuperable because, despite her suspicions regarding the male sex, she ministers to David with all the generosity and sage love of a surrogate mother. Mrs. Jellyby, unable to blame the follies of youth for her wrongheaded notions of charity, dwells in the text as an aging, ink-spotted monster: a woman who has, as far as Dickens is concerned, wasted her own life and all but destroyed her family.

This is not to say that Victorian literature diminished aging and old women altogether; oftentimes, mature female figures are crucial to a plot's mechanisms or, like Mrs. Pryor of Charlotte Brontë's *Shirley*, harbor a blistering secret, albeit one that is most crucial in the context of the young heroine's self-actualization. Chase reminds us that "the 'marginalizing of the elderly,' whether it is making the best of a bad lot or choosing one's destiny, is a complex fate and that it is compatible with central narrative interest... [W]hile the old are indeed relegated to the outside and while they can rarely choose to alter their position, they retain surprising powers of agency."[6] Without Betsey Trotwood, David Copperfield's future would have been far less auspicious. As readers of Emily Brontë's *Wuthering Heights*, we are largely at the mercy of narrator Nelly Dean, servant to three generations of Earnshaws and witness to some of the family's most lurid history. What her biases may color or shape, what her memory misremembers, and the extent to which she may dissemble we can only conjecture, but in the logic of the novel, the story is hers to tell. Lucy Snowe, of Charlotte Brontë's *Villette*, reflects on her youth as a much older woman, and she is perhaps one of the genre's cagiest narrators (Charlotte and Emily Brontë were fond, it seems, of leaving their readers to wonder whether they could trust what they were told). Hannah Thornton, of Elizabeth Gaskell's *North and South* (1855), is an imperious woman, but one whose focus is, to the point of myopia, on the fortune and future of her mill owner son. There are scores of older women in Victorian fiction who, as Chase argues, "retain surprising powers of agency" whether in terms of the story or its telling. Very often, they are important characters. But that does not mean that they are envisioned in full flesh, their histories considered beyond hearth and home, beyond the families they have cultivated dutifully or, as Dickens strives to make eminently clear regarding Mrs. Jellyby—not.

In the case of Elizabeth Gaskell's *Cranford* (1853), less a novel than a collection of sketches, the story focuses on the lives of elderly women but is narrated by a young woman, Mary Smith, who lives nearby and frequently matriculates among them. The concept of Cranford is, if not fantastical, unlikely: it's a small town that resembles a single-gender retirement community, with a vigorously entwined circle of elderly women who live together according to a precise, many might say absurd, social culture they have carefully developed, without giving much thought to the goings-on in the rest of Mother England. Gaskell's narrator begins by delineating these circumstances:

In the first place, Cranford is in possession of the Amazons; all the holders of houses, above a certain rent, are women. If a married couple come to settle in the town, somehow the gentleman disappears; he is either fairly frightened to death by being the only man in the Cranford evening parties, or he is accounted for by being with his regiment, his ship, or closely engaged in business all the week in the great neighbouring commercial town of Drumble...In short, whatever does become of the gentlemen, they are not at Cranford.[7]

The ladies of Cranford are unperturbed by men's tendency to exodus: in fact, they often find their company provoking, if not altogether agitating. They live according to simple, feminine rituals of gentility, which Mary Smith details with humor and a dash of condescension. Because Cranford inhabitants are poor, they regard displays of wealth as vulgar and weave a collective fable that enables them to recast privation as choice, even luxury—choosing to walk, for instance, in order to enjoy the weather and not because it would be too costly to pay for a carriage. "We none of us spoke of money," explains Mary, "because that subject savoured of commerce and trade, and though some might be poor, we were all aristocratic."[8] This sense of refinement informs even the smallest habits: Mary Smith's companions, the spinster sisters Deborah and Matilda Jenkyns, discover that eating an orange presents an especial quandary with regard to gentility. To fully enjoy an orange, one must suck the juice from it, but certainly no proper woman would ever *suck* among company. So, when Miss Jenkyns and Miss Matty choose to partake in this singularly tricky fruit, they separate to different corners of the house, where they might gorge themselves without fear of disrupting decorum. And when the Jenkynses procure a new drawing room carpet, the impulse for preservation obscures the object's primary purpose:

We were very busy, too, one whole morning before Miss Jenkyns gave her party, in following her directions, and in cutting out and stitching together pieces of newspaper, so as to form little paths to every chair, set for the expected visitors, lest their shoes might dirty or defile the purity of the carpet. Do you make paper paths for every guest to walk upon in London?[9]

Mary intermittently concludes these descriptions of her friends' more eccentric behaviors with this rhetorical refrain regarding London practices. She is charmed by her Cranford friends, and she indulges them in their nonsensical endeavors, paper pathways and all; she also implies, through her narration, that these behaviors are preposterous. In this way, she suggests to more cosmopolitan readers that they share an understanding when it comes to the little town's idiosyncratic conventions. One might also argue that the women of Cranford engage in these seemingly trivial exercises because they possess a certain economic understanding: nothing of value can be taken for granted.

For all the delight Mary takes in Cranford's more nonsensical traditions—and in some cases, who can really blame her?—she acknowledges too the robust connective tissue that renders these women, for the most part, allies and sites of mutual succor. When, in the middle of her party, Mrs. Forrester must ask her guests sitting on the sofa to move so that she can fetch her tea tray, no one makes mention of it: after all, to do so would draw attention to the modest size of her home, dimensions so skimpy she's forced to store serving platters under the sofa. Nor do Mrs. Forrester's friends raise an eyebrow when she pretends not to know what goodies will be brought from the kitchen (of course, because she cannot afford a cook, she has spent the day baking). And when death or economic calamity comes to pass, the women serve as fierce advocates for one another, particularly for Miss Matty who, Mary Smith concludes, is something of the town's moral compass. "We all love Miss Matty," she declares, "and I somehow think we are all of us better when she is near us."[10] Chase posits that "*Cranford* is a landmark text in the affirmation and celebration of old age, rejoicing in its labor of productivity,"[11] and certainly it is remarkable for its privileging not merely of women, but of elderly women, many of whom have never married, and most of whom prefer that men leave them to themselves, determining them to be, on the whole, troublesome bothers.

But while these character sketches do from time to time reveal secrets of the soul, they tend toward superficiality. Miss Matty emerges as the most gentle of the Cranford residents, having refused the man she loved for the sake of family, and choosing to live instead with her domineering older sister. The novel implies that she may be able to recuperate some of that romantic happiness after Miss Jenkyns dies and she is reunited with her former beau, Thomas Holbrook, but since they are all very much older, the ravages of time have their way: he dies before their courtship can resume. It is possible that Miss Matty would emerge from this bevy of loss and disappointment without bitterness—her character, as we know, is a beneficent one—but the novel assumes the reader's lack of interest in the shadings of her emotional recovery. Her romantic life holds, it is presumed, minimal fascination for the reader despite it being clear that she is quite ready, as a woman in her fifties, to reconsider her decades-old retreat from erotic life, and she is miffed at the suggestion that she would be too old for this. "'Martha, I'm not yet fifty-two!' said Miss Matty [to her housemaid], with grave emphasis; for probably the remembrance of her youth had come very vividly before her this day, and she was annoyed at finding that golden time so far away in the past."[12] Perhaps Mary intuits correctly, or perhaps she makes assumptions colored by her own youth—after all, her account of this exchange is editorial.

This moment of resistance from Miss Matty, however small, is notable and when, after Mr. Holbrook dies, she evinces her appreciation for romantic companionship, and perhaps even her regret, by finally allowing her housemaid to receive suitors. Ultimately, Miss Matty can only facilitate the erotic lives of younger generations, rather than her own: she instead returns to the woman-centered society upon which she has depended—and which brings her joy—but it is perhaps not all she might have desired, even if it is the ideal sanctuary for others in her community.

It's a fool's errand to attempt to "correct" Victorian fiction, to say what a society that precedes us by nearly two centuries ought to have done, or how their writers should have written. What we can do is consider the sorts of stories that were published and popular, and *Cranford* was quite popular. Far less amusing to readers would have been a novel set in England as most Britons knew it narrated from the perspective of a Miss Matty or a Miss Havisham or a Betsey Trotwood, with their pleasures and trials foregrounded in the narrative, rather than held aloft by an amused—or, in Miss Havisham's case, bewildered and somewhat disgusted—much younger narrator, or set aside in order to chronicle a child relative's coming-of-age. For them to unburden themselves on the page, without the imperative of entertaining or transforming into a punch line—that, I suspect, would hardly have been enough.

———

My conception of oldness has always been garbled and slippery. Most aspects of identity are to some extent relational—

something you can measure numerically is bound to be. When I was very little, "old" was a catchall signifier for anyone who seemed adultlike; in elementary school, girls who were thirteen were, in my estimation, enviably mature. I wasn't terribly concerned with what it meant to be "too old" unless the designation pertained to me and inflicted limitations: it seemed terrible, for instance, that I might one day be too old to play with dolls, and tragic that my mother would coddle me less. But youth meant that time yawned before me, languorous and infinite. There was too much time until, all of a sudden, there was not enough of it.

The years have only slackened my grasp on what it means to be old, or too old—often the "too" is implied—rendering it a near-incoherent vagary. My mother was sixty-two when she died, an age that is certainly not young according to Victorian standards for women, or ours. Yet—although she would disagree with me—she aged almost imperceptibly until the last months of her life, when the twinned ravages of ovarian cancer and various scorched-earth chemotherapy treatments settled into her silk-soft skin, turning her gaunt and jaundiced. But even then, she did not seem old, only sick and weary. Queen Victoria, who died when she was eighty-one, lived nearly twice as long as her husband, Albert, and buried two of her children. If fortune favors me, I will know decades denied to my mother. Although we expect to outlive our parents, this possibility strikes me as both bizarre and not a little cruel. After all, my mother did not outlive hers, nor did she meet her first granddaughter, my niece. These conventional, temporal benchmarks, so often barometers of advanced years, eluded her. She endures in my memory as young because her life was vibrant and gingery and brimful until it was severely clipped—because, when death came for her, she was too young, and it took her anyway.

Mom was several months shy of thirty when she gave birth to me; ushering in a new decade was, if nothing else, congruent with the unfamiliar terrain of parenthood. In my case, there was nothing so decisive; on the contrary, it was a keenly ambivalent birthday. I mostly felt young, but observed, with fresh vexation, how professional achievements lost luster in the public eye if they did not occur in one's twenties (every "Thirty Under Thirty" list insinuated this, anyway). In my case, turning thirty meant a second go: the year prior I had married for a second time and, after long, diligent work toward a doctorate in English literature, I was grappling with the queasy excitement of new, burgeoning career aspirations and the realization that while I was proud of the work that I had completed on my dissertation, I did not want to finish it (abandoning my doctorate was, ultimately, more painful than leaving my first marriage). As a newly engaged twenty-three-year-old beginning her graduate studies, thirty seemed decidedly mature, and certainly too old for profound change: after all, that was when I had decided I would finish school. Perhaps I'd even have a baby or two in the process. Every scrap of cultural evidence suggested to me that my twenties ought to be my most productive years, and that they would absolutely be my prettiest.

Imagine my surprise when, at twenty-five, I exploded my life and began ambling toward a writing career at twenty-eight. By thirty, I had almost completely reoriented, which should not have been cause for discomfiture, but was. Being a woman, I have learned, means that the world is always shrieking at you to hurry up, and harboring a viable uterus only exacerbates the duress. It's somatic and dizzying, my lingering anxiety over whether I am too old for this or for that. Turning thirty meant that I began to question what I "ought" to wear, even though I resisted capitulating and in fact began a short-lived campaign in which I wore sheer T-shirts that purposely exposed my bra. Perhaps this sartorial choice was perceived as "too much," particularly for a grown woman, but intellectually I knew such distinctions were sexist folly. To some extent, I was acting in protest: I have been hassled about my body more so now than in previous decades, and I seem always to face the question of whether its present size is acceptable or healthy.

The combination of entering my thirties and experiencing weight-shaming has produced a restive concoction of humiliation and insecurity that often, despite my best efforts, sizzles in my gut, turning my body into something chafing and disconcerting, a suit I want to shed or, better yet, dematerialize. I check my roots for gray hairs, the scoops of my eye sockets for wrinkles and newly sprung crannies. I grab at the flesh of my ass. I think of the Greek goddesses and gods who transformed into flora and fauna. I dream of turning into Echo, a disembodied breath, but acknowledge that I enjoy talking far too much for that particular metamorphosis.

Then I think of rapper Cardi B, who, on April 7, 2018, revealed her pregnancy while performing "Be Careful" on *Saturday Night Live* in a white crepe gown, her curves at once gentle and unapologetic. Attempting to draw likeness between myself and Cardi would of course be presumptuous. Cardi B is younger than I am, and a musical genius to boot. She also possesses a mesmeric sort of beauty, romantic and soft at the

edges. I am not a woman famous for my face, or for any reason
at all. But we are neither of us, strictly speaking, old, although
we are aging the inexorable way anyone does when they tumble onto this planet. Still, every time I see a woman honor her
body—whether pregnant, jacked, fat, or what we uselessly refer to as typical—particularly when it has manifested in a way
that provokes cries of vulgarity and too muchness, it seems of
a piece with this whack-a-mole question of "aging." It calls
to mind the impossibility of determining what "old" is when
every woman is seemingly and, according to the more misogynistic corners of our society, hilariously, too old for something
she should want to be.

That said, the prejudice against and rigid policing of women
who have entered into middle age, say, between the ages of
forty-five and sixty-five, is specifically diligent. And while it is
everywhere present, popular culture supplies us with our most
visible examples. Madonna is perhaps the most famous example of a woman rigorously censured for dressing and dancing
provocatively even as she has entered into her sixth decade. Famously and bombastically sexual in the 1980s, the most recent
criticisms levied against her take the form of retroactive shaming. How dare she assume people still want her, especially when
her brand of sexuality has always defied gentility?

Madonna, people might argue, has taken her schtick *too*
far. Her antics were permissible in youth; now her sexuality is
regarded as pathologically excessive, as if desire should evapo-
rate with every decade we age. "Much of the hand-wringing
around her age focuses on her lack of dignity," wrote Jancee
Dunn in 2015.[13] Dunn recounts some of this "undignified"
behavior, which involves kissing singer Drake onstage—raising

eyebrows, likely, because Drake is more than two decades her junior—and sporting an ensemble at the 2015 Grammys that featured her "fishnet-encased derrière."[14] Dunn examines her own mélange of discomfort and defensiveness—Madonna is, after all, waging a war against acute sexist ageism—but more often than not finds herself wondering whether Madonna is doing or *being* too much:

> Why does she have the seemingly compulsive need to shock and titillate, drawing from a playbook that is now three decades old? Yes, she is constantly reinventing herself, but is she evolving? "There comes a time in every Salome's life," Harvey Fierstein once wrote, "when she should no longer be dropping the last veil." Has the queen of reinvention reached that point?[15]

Perhaps Madonna does act according to a "compulsive" or imperious urge to resist social expectations; if she is, that would seem to be in keeping with the rest of her career. Why wouldn't the woman who scandalized audiences with a cone-shaped brassiere, who filmed the softcore music videos for "Justify My Love" and "Erotica," and who, amid flaming crosses, sexualized a black Jesus in the video for "Like a Prayer" bristle at the notion that reaching menopause demands a transition to sensible underwear? Madonna, after all, has always been aware of the misogynistic norms that she has condemned, and she has little patience for the notion that she should temper her dress and performance. Her Instagram account, like most belonging to celebrities, is riddled with selfies, her lips glistening with gloss and her long, kinked hair a beaming blonde. Her emoji usage is liberal, she enjoys a Snapchat filter now and then, and her captions generally include vocabulary like "slay," "vibes," and "bitches," which almost certainly elicits criticism that she is exerting too much effort to matriculate among today's youth.

On May 20, 2015, she posted a substantially filtered selfie accentuating the ridges of her cheekbones, firm thrust of her jawline, and plumpness of her upper lip. The caption reads, "Shut up jealous bitches! I hope you are as fun loving and adventurous as me when you're my age!!!!" The hashtag "#bitchimmadonna" follows a smattering of emojis, from a goofy ghost to a trio of chickens, as if to defy detractors by doubling down on social media rhetoric deemed too young for her. A litany of adoring comments follows the caption, bespeckled with accusations of paying for youth, giggled references to grandmotherhood, and cheap shots about physical deterioration. Four years later, on June 6, 2019, Madonna did not post a selfie, but instead the image accompanying the *New York Times Magazine*'s cover story, "Madonna at Sixty." A profile of the artist written by Vanessa Grigoriadis, it was published just prior to the release of her album, *Madonna X*. But Madonna was angered by the finished result, which she claimed was far more preoccupied with her age than with her work. Her remarks during the interview anticipate her later response—Grigoriadis attempts to engage Madonna in a conversation about aging, and the pop star refuses to dwell on the matter. "I think you think about growing old too much," she tells Grigoriadis, "I think you think about age too much. I think you should just stop thinking about it."[16] These are pointed remarks, but they are restrained, too: on Instagram, Madonna posts a caption unearthing the full thrust of her anger. "The journalist who wrote this article spent days and hours and months with me and was invited into a world which many people don't get to see, but chose to focus on trivial and superficial matters such as the ethnicity of my stand in or the fabric of my curtains and never ending comments about my age which would never have been mentioned had I been a MAN!" The profile does focus considerably on Madonna's age, and it seems intentional, if a tidbit preoccupied—one of the article's aims is to illuminate for readers Madonna's sense of her own legacy, and it leans heavily into the expansive trajectory of her fame. But Madonna, likely weary of conversations that fixate on famous women's maturity, was rankled by this approach. "I'm sorry I spent 5 minutes with [Grigoriadis]," she writes, adding the regrettable metaphor, "It makes me feel raped." (Madonna argues that as a rape survivor, "I'm allowed to use that analogy.") To be sure, Madonna's long career is rife with missteps, generally ones involving cultural and racial appropriation, but when Madonna draws outrage for baring her middle-aged ass on a red carpet she is, more than anything else, laying bare cultural assumptions of how so-called ladies of a certain age should appear. Even the *New York Times Magazine* profile, written by a well-meaning female fan of her work, belies, through its avid praise, agitation over how older women should present themselves (of course, Grigoriadis absorbs this snakebit social prejudice just as the rest of us do and is necessarily influenced by it). Often, discomfort over Madonna's enduring sexual provocations is dressed up in reproaches regarding decency and self-respect. We could debate the former matter at length, never uniting on a definition, and as for the latter, well, Madonna seems to be doing just fine.

When it foregoes performative hand-wringing in the name of modesty, Western media makes a game out of assessing aging beauties, to crow at their thickening waists and creased skin as if it were a sort of patriarchal victory. Watching former models Pamela Anderson, Jenny McCarthy, and the late Anna Nicole Smith age has also become a media bloodsport (granted, McCarthy has also come under fire, quite reasonably, for her crusade against vaccinations, but that is another issue altogether). By stark contrast, sleazy business mogul Hugh Hefner lived cozily in his model-stocked Playboy mansion until his death at age ninety-one. Hefner was a filthy man, and he faced his fair share of criticism over the years, but his appearance was never pilloried with the vitriol Anderson and her ilk surely faced at a third of his age. Like Madonna, these women were boldly sexual, though perhaps in ways that were more palatable to the male gaze: *Playboy* magazine catered to it, after all.

In the meantime, Jennifer Lopez's name has become synonymous with physical immortality: again and again—it has become a game of its own—the public expels collective gasps at her age, eyes darting from her documented birth year to closeups of her immaculate skin and her astounding physique. To be sure, the boons of genetic favor and wealth have facilitated Lopez's perennial youthfulness; it's also the result of profound and unyielding bodily toil. We demand that women of color be exceptional, and so when the media purports to celebrate Lopez for appearing two decades younger than she is, begging her to disclose skin and exercise regimens, it registers as less celebratory than the byproduct of a larger imperative. Middle-aged women of color maintain visibility by astonishing us with their perceived agelessness—"Asian Don't Raisin,"[17] reads the headline of one celebrity roundup, naming Lucy Liu and Michelle Yeoh and Constance Wu (who is in her thirties) as exemplars of graceful aging. Often, lists like these are compiled by members of the community, which is how it ought to be. Latinx journalists explore the question—prompted by Jennifer Lopez, as well as women like Salma Hayek and Sofia Vergara— of "Why Latina Skin Ages So Well."[18] But the larger, vastly white media exerts implacable influence over who, from marginalized communities, is allotted space in the arena of fame. It is not enough that women of color perform the rites of aging with aplomb, they should, ideally, render the process invisible. They should be nothing short of biological marvels.

If a famous woman does want to grow visibly older—somewhat—while still courting public approval, it's a delicate endeavor. The aging beauty must learn how to maintain her fame without becoming a figure of fun. White female celebrities have sought to triumph in this arena by refashioning themselves into "gurus." With her big-ticket lifestyle brand Goop, Gwyneth Paltrow markets herself as an elegant, accomplished, and worldly woman—witching her age into a sign of refined experience rather than a harbinger of obscurity. (We might even think of Goop, or any wellness brand, for that matter, as a modern-day conduct manual of sorts. Of course, for those of us with skimpier checking accounts, Goop is a convenient one to disregard.) Reese Witherspoon has followed suit with her clothing line, Draper James, drawing on the appeal of her Southern charm, and Kate Hudson has unleashed Fabletics, a line of fitness wear. Perhaps we might interpret the guru as the refined MILF: she positions herself above a term with such unseemly connotations, but the aim is not so different. Women entering middle age like Paltrow can still be regarded as desirable, but they must seem uninterested in the question, as if they have other, more age-appropriate concerns.

———

Feminine youth, as it is conventionally understood—blushing adolescence through one's early twenties—is a potent and tenacious fetish. I am happier now than I've ever been, and yet, when I am confronted with various incarnations of early adulthood, whether in a film, or in the image of a musician, or in a television show's rosily stilted manifestation of it, my reaction is a fickle one, a mélange of relief and covetousness. I'm grateful to have dispensed with years of agitated uncertainty and the eager willingness to rearrange myself according to others' predilections. Ultimately, I have benefited from the toil and tangle of living with myself. And yet, I'm susceptible to depictions of young adulthood that place exhilaration and beauty alongside the angst. I try, in spite of myself, to recollect juvenile missteps: perhaps euphoria, or even the unremarkable lull of contentment might have been possible had I behaved with more abandon and not dodged the risks. Maybe—probably—I was too ensconced in my own head.

According to a common lament, we can only discern the best parts of ourselves long after we've shed that skin. The most marvelous exploits glisten brightest once they've plunged into the cache of our personal histories. But moments cannot be so intoxicating and delicious if we are aware of them, if we appoint ourselves as characters in narratives of our own devising: either we retread these shimmering spaces by the grace of memory or they flee to a vast, unknowable archive littered with relics of time. Despite the reliable intensity of my feelings, I was pinned by an urgent impulse to editorialize every moment, not because I was especially profound, although I fancied myself so, but because I was terrified. If I had been more self-sure, I might have received murky obscurity as possibility. Instead, I tasked myself with rooting out meaning in every catalogued experience, as if dogged interpretation could harness my prodigious fear and pave a path to a life that suited me. These were the consequences of being young and Too Much: upon self-diagnosis, I looked at the world and saw peril at every turn, in romance and in creative aspirations and in my every small and colossal hope. If I was going to survive in this inhospitable place, I required discipline.

Now, at thirty-four—not aged, surely, but not especially young—I consider my Too Much youth with a flickering melancholy. In fearing myself, what did I miss? At my most vulnerable, I whip up recuperative fantasies: I imagine myself eighteen, unbound by the belief that I owe the world a more muted and stoic version of myself. I consider my future not with the timorous sense that I am unfit, but instead with exhilaration at my good fortune. I appreciate and honor both my body and my face rather than scowling at them with self-loathing. I come out as queer decades earlier. I have more sex. I spin this tale of an idealized and evolved girlhood because, in the thick of it, I'm fretting—about being too old and, still, Too Much.

Enduringly, I am tantalized by the talismanic power of a good story, the notion that everything is solvable and salvageable if I plot it out, even in retrospect. A good story led me to marry the wrong man, to deny my sexuality, to wound others and myself. To seek out a good story as both an organizing principle and an emotional bridle is, at best, a red herring, and at worst, a powder keg. Nowadays, I resist the impulse of contemplating more pleasing origin stories, with the recognition that they hardly soothe, but rather reinforce the great falsehood lobbed at us by a culture dazzled by youth: that with every passing year, a slice of something quintessential and cherished is, necessarily, lost.

————

On June 21, 1887, Queen Victoria celebrated her Golden Jubilee; she had reigned for fifty years on Great Britain's throne. She was glad, mostly. At sixty-eight years old, twenty-five years after the death of her beloved Prince Albert, she remained staunchly in mourning—on this occasion, as always, she donned a simple black dress—determined to glorify the husband she had lost and who, by then, many of her subjects had never known. The previous day, she had commemorated the occasion by documenting it in her diary. Her words are bald and forlorn: "The day has come and I am alone."[19] She had, by then, also outlived two children and five grandchildren, as well as John Brown, her dear and devoted companion.

And yet she found satisfaction in the day. Over fifty years, she had cultivated a sensational legacy as monarch of the world's most august empire. But despite Britain's grandiosity, Victoria dressed with a plainness that evoked middle-class English domesticity. She was avid in her efforts to oversee the kingdom, but positioned herself foremost as wife, mother, and then a bonnet-clad widow. This maternal iconography was pervasive. At the time of her Jubilee, the queen was hailed as the "Grandmother of Europe": numbered among her passel of descendants are the odious Wilhelm II, the German emperor who would declare war on England, and Princess Alix of Hesse, who would marry Czar Nicholas of Russia and, later, be killed in the Russian Revolution (she is perhaps best remembered as mother to Princess Anastasia). Among Britons, the queen was worshipped as a motherly goddess. "You go it, old girl! You done it well! You done it well!" applauded a crowd of working-class men as they met Victoria's carriage. She acknowledged them with a customary nod, but laughed too, and her eyes welled.[20]

If a woman must grow old, she might as well be the queen of an imperialist juggernaut. To be sure, status did not safeguard Victoria from woe and travails, but as she aged, she attained the luster of immortality (indeed, some thought she would be queen forever). From the British public's vantage point, the queen could never be Too Much; she was, after all, larger than life.

But Victoria, I suspect, did not share this opinion. While Albert lived, she was assiduous in her efforts not to puncture his ego, even when this meant diminishing herself. She knew her husband could not abide a power imbalance—in fact, he did not believe in women ruling kingdoms on their own—and so even attempted, unsuccessfully, to bestow him with the title King Consort (he was styled as Prince Consort).[21] Although women seeking the right to vote would later point to Victoria as an argument for universal suffrage—had she not ruled wisely?—the queen did not support it. When, during the Boer War, women sailed to South Africa to care for the beleaguered troops as well as prisoners suffering in British concentration camps, the elderly Victoria voiced her disapproval, remarking that these "hysterical" women would only be a bother. While she was known for being racially progressive, at least compared to many of her contemporaries, the queen never indicated concern for the indigenous women of India, China, Canada, Argentina, and the inhabitants of many other lands, millions of whom suffered brutalities in her name.[22]

When, on January 22, 1901, Queen Victoria's long life at last expired, the era that is her namesake came to a formal, if not ideological, close. Over eight decades, women in Great Britain had seen considerable social advancements. Victorian men might still demand an "angel in the house," the docile and chastely helpmeet, but women had begun to buck this expectation. Some chose not to marry, living alone, or together with other single women. A husband could no longer assume his wife's wealth; finally, she existed as an individual in the eyes of the law. The 1891 case *Regina vs. Jackson*, wherein a Mr. Jackson kidnapped his wife, enlisted guards to hold her prisoner at home, and took her to court for "restitution of conjugal rights," ruled, blessedly, in favor of the wife. Neither the ghoulish Mr. Jackson, nor any man, could claim legal proprietorship of his wife's body; this was unquestionably a landmark court decision.[23] These are marks of trenchant but circumscribed progress—the British colonies were not afforded the aforementioned liberties—and, because progress fundamentally suggests a process of evolution, it was also, without question, not enough. (For instance, it was 1991 before either England or Wales recognized "marital rape," and just two years before *Regina vs. Jackson* a judge ruled that a man afflicted with gonorrhea could rape his wife.)[24] But then it would be altogether oxymoronic, the concept of enough progress.

On her deathbed, it's unlikely that Victoria was dwelling on the legal and socioeconomic achievements of her female subjects. The monarch was no protofeminist, and she had always, even in widowhood, conceived of herself as Albert's wife with strident adhesion. However, as she prepared for their reunion beyond the grave, she did, it seems, muse upon herself. Inscribed in her funeral instructions was the following note to her children: "I die in peace with all fully aware of my many faults."

She was at peace. She was not enough—or she was too much: who is to say?

Chapter Twelve

SUBSTANCE: AN EPILOGUE

H ave I said too much?

Or perhaps not enough?

That's always the question, after all, and always a fact of our subsistence: we inhabit an illusory binary in whose stewing berth so many of us suspend on tenterhooks, marionettes pulling at our strings.

I wrote this book in order to articulate an argument that has long been clattering around my brain, sometimes unsteadily, but always persistent, like rain from the sky. I wanted to express it to you, but, of course, to myself as well—and in the latter case, it was something of a thought experiment. Was I simply making excuses for my too muchness? Perhaps I had gone to these lengths, ruminating over research, unspooling a thread between the Victorians—whom I love and who frustrate me—

and our quivering now, ultimately for the selfish purpose of ex-
onerating myself. A deliverance by book: I suppose, in any case,
it wouldn't be the first time.

In 2017, as I was beginning to draft my manuscript, I listened to New Zealand singer Lorde's sophomore album *Melodrama,* which recommended itself to me by the title alone and
which delivered the most cathartic emotional wallop. But I was
smote by one song in particular, "Liability." Though its lyrics
were resonant, more than anything else they filled me with
an ineffable sorrow: "They say, 'You're a little much for me
/ You're a liability.'" I felt it was my responsibility, to readers,
to my writing, and to myself, to approach too muchness from
confidence, and not a little righteous anger. I still believe that
mode was appropriate. And yet, Lorde reminded me of where
I had begun, and where I so often return—to melancholy and
resignation, to the gut-churning fear that I will never be capable of living in the world properly, and that I will always, at last,
wear out my friends, lovers, even family because I cannot help
but be utterly myself: a brimming body of conflicted, burning
feeling. Every day I wriggle a bit further from beneath this al-
batross, but it's an unwieldy and sticky burden.

I return, often, to that schoolgirl essay composed by a young
Charlotte Brontë, first-person narration wrapped in the cloak
of character, but indisputably autobiographical in sentiment:
"Without wanting to I allowed everything that passed through
my heart to be seen and sometimes there were storms passing
through it; in vain I tried to imitate the sweet gaiety, the serene
and equable spirits which I saw in the faces of my companions and which I found so worthy of admirations; all my efforts
were useless."[1] A Too Much heart, as Brontë conceives it, is a

thing indiscriminately porous, an organ permeable to joy and sorrow alike: a deluge from "storms passing"; other times, the emollient ripples of a sunbeam. Brontë, or as she would have it, her male speaker, resists this transparency, and despairs after the "serene and equable spirits," which are not so easy to muster and to project. Like Lorde, Brontë mourns the impossibility of concealing what demands to be witnessed.

I, too, have mourned this, but I no longer want to do so. I no longer want to pant after comely corsets, with all their trappings of performed equanimity and decorum—those cages that will only break my bones and stifle what is mine to declare. And all of it is mine to declare, every last tear and smile and shriek. And what is yours, that of course is your dominion, and your treasure, to brandish or to keep close as you will. Too muchness heaves with potential as a positive feminine force, but it is the choice to wield it that matters most of all.

Emotionally trussed for centuries, we deserve—we are owed—room to breathe. We've been taught that disaffection is au courant: better to be Ernest Hemingway's Cool Girl, Brett Ashley, rather than the beautiful but damned Catherine Earnshaw, killed by her own ravaged desire and abandoned to limbo on earth: a ghost keening over the moors and thwacking her beloved's windows. (Even I can admit that she's a bit of a drama queen.) And it's with good reason that we're encouraged to be stone cold bitches in the professional sphere. No one listens to a weeping woman.

No one listens until we decide to make ourselves heard. This prevailing narrative—one that champions stoicism at all costs—perpetuates the stigmas with which women are harpooned: we cannot be too sad, or too fat, or too in love, or too depressed.

We must whittle ourselves down, mind, body, and soul, our every inch contorted into decorum and cool.

But I cannot do this. I never could, and now, were I magically offered a serene disposition and the capacity for thin-lipped stolidity, I would hold fast to my own alluvion of feeling. It's a matter of principle and of empathy, too. More than ever, I'm devoted to celebrating too muchness rather than maligning it. To fostering a climate in which we do not simply acknowledge, but honor the various ways a person can dwell in their body and navigate the world. Isn't it glorious, and a blessing, that there are infinite ways to be?

So I will continue as I always have: as a woman who shows her hand with a flourish. I've joked, sometimes, that it would be cheating to claim honesty as one of my virtues because, when you lack a poker face, it's nigh well impossible to lie. What a relief to gradually—at last—perceive my too muchness not as a public menace, a cause for my shame and for others' repulsion, but instead as an agent of emotional integrity. A relief, indeed, although I cannot say that it is always easier. In Virginia Woolf's 1925 novel *Mrs. Dalloway*, the titular character, wading into the London morning, looks out at the street and thinks, "She always had the feeling that it was very, very dangerous to live even one day."[2] Unlike Clarissa Dalloway, who silently senses and beholds all the world's tremulousness, I cannot conceal what most stirs me; there is no smooth cohesion to my temper's skin, no opacity. I can only offer myself in raw unmediated doses, never "this...or that"[3]—Mrs. Dalloway contemplates how she no longer regards people in these simplified terms—but as all things at once: warm and kinetic, cluttered, exuberant.

This vulnerability, not chosen, but a twinned insistence of soul and physiology, does feel perilous. It can seem, at times, as if I'm handing myself over to the world and hoping, desperately, that it won't crush me between its fingers. And I have been crushed. I still prefer the risk. I prefer to feel it all, so as not to miss anything. We are all of us in danger, every day; it's the consequence of a pulse. We cannot remedy the cruelest parts of being human: heartbreak and loss and the torments we endure as we excavate severe self-truths. But we can, I believe, build little harbors for one another.

While the burden of history rests on our backs, no one is forcing our hands. We can sound our desires and demand witness to our too muchness. It would be a continental shift, and one that would demand empathy and reflection rather than the championing of reserve—or vulnerability—for its own sake. But we've sure as hell endured far worse.

"You're my favorite mess," a male friend once told me when we were in high school. At the time, I thought it was quaint and sweet. After all, I referred to myself this way—a mess— habitually; my friend, in fact, was probably responding to a comment of that sort. How kind people were to handle me with patience—because I was someone who demanded handling like some fretful, mercurial species of bird. I learned myself according to others' impressionistic remarks. When I was told that I was fragile, and crazy, I believed it. I assumed that these definitions could be depended upon for accuracy precisely because they were not my own and were therefore objective. There is no such thing as emotional objectivity—I knew this even then—and yet I succumbed to a fantasy fed to me through perceived consensus.

I am Too Much. I still type those words with trepidation, but soon I won't. I am Too Much because the sun gleams through the crevices and crannies speckled inside my heart, and sometimes I am overwhelmed by its broad warmth. Sometimes it still bewilders me, the too muchness of this life, even when I know, finally, that I would not choose another. Instead, I watch those beams across the middle distance, steady, yawning, and yellow. It feels like hope, and just enough of it.

ACKNOWLEDGMENTS

I am overcome with gratitude for so many people who have, over the years, offered themselves as shepherds, interlocutors, and mentors, in writing and in everything else. It feels impossible to fully communicate my thanks, but I'm going to try. First and foremost, I am indebted to my marvel of an editor, Maddie Caldwell, who inevitably understands what I am trying to say before I've said it, who asks the perfect questions, and who pushes me to excavate the heart of the thing—and, of course, who knows what is simply too cheesy to print. And to my agent—soul sister, really—Anna Sproul-Latimer, thank you for your conviction, which sustains me, for the warmth and steadiness of your support, and for being an incisive, clarifying reader of my work. I also so appreciate the support of Grand Central Publishing: in particular my wonderful publicist, Kamrun Nesa; my marketer, Alana Spendley; as well as Anjuli Johnson, my production editor; Becky Maines in copyediting; and Jacqui Young. And I'm thankful for the collaborative guidance of Anna's colleagues at Ross Yoon Literary Agency, in particular Dara Kaye, Howard Yoon, and Gail Ross.

Thank you to all the exuberant women and nonbinary persons who shared their experiences with me for the "Loud" chapter; I am so grateful to you for your time and your insights.

Since girlhood I have been positively spoiled with brilliant teachers, so many of whom encouraged me in my writing and, through their tutelage, made me so much better than I would otherwise be: Elizabeth Aldridge, Gareth Clement-Noyes, Patricia Kenan-Herrmann, Ken Miller, Jacqueline Davis, Beth Camper, Andrew Jackson, Sara Reich, and Clare Kerr (I am sorry for being an abysmal chemistry student). And to Carrie Hilborn Gantt: Years ago, at a Parents' Night, you told my parents that I would be a writer. I am still trying to earn your confidence in me.

I am also greatly indebted to my literature professors at the College of William and Mary, especially Suzanne Raitt, Melanie Dawson, Susan Donaldson, Carter Hailey, and Thomas Heacox. And to my mentors in graduate studies, Robert McRuer, Maria Frawley, Jason Rudy, Orrin Wang, and Sangeeta Ray—the capacious wisdom and insight you have imparted to me is beyond articulation.

Jonathan Auerbach, you have never failed to be at once a source of reason, comfort, and humor. Through you, I learned to teach and to think ever deeper.

Bill Cohen, my mind has been reshaped by your scholarship and pedagogy, and your mentorship is one of my life's greatest honors.

Deborah Morse, every possibility began with you—with the Victorian novels we read together, the afternoons of drinking tea and chatting about those Victorian novels, and through it all, your steady, affectionate love.

So many artists and writers and thinkers nourished me as I wrote this book, though they might not know it; among them are Maggie Nelson, Marilynne Robinson, Elena Ferrante, Cheryl Strayed, Tori Amos, Jenny Lewis, Robyn, Carly Rae Jepsen, Jane Campion, Paul F. Tompkins, and Lin-Manuel Miranda.

My profound thanks to the writers whose work illuminates and whose kindness has buttressed me, especially Heather Havrilesky, Robin Wasserman, Rebecca Traister, Celeste Ng, Roxane Gay, and Alexander Chee.

Thank you to Stuart and Leah Johnson, who drove me to the hospital and, as a result, saved my life. I am so fortunate that I lived under your roof.

To Hobo, who is a cat, but who, rightly, would expect to be included.

Sharon Alperovitz, you have my deepest gratitude.

To my community of friends, writers, and colleagues who astound and fortify me and who have been harbors across the years and miles: Devon Maloney, Caitlin Gibson, Becky Erbelding, Lindsay King-Miller, Chris Scott and Ona Balkus, Laura Lorenzo, Kathi Norden, Samyuktha Shenoy, Isabella Cooper, my shine theorists: Katie Stanutz and Liz DePriest, Kisa Lape, Jamison Kantor, Maura and Dan Collinge, Lisa Kirch and James Howes, Margot Anderson, Theresa Glatstein, Lucy Morse, Andy Black, Porter Olsen, Alex Afram, Briallen Hopper, Esmé Weijun Wang, Stassa Edwards, Helena Fitzgerald and Thomas Strickland, Vicki Lame, Mara Wilson, Evette Dionne, Alana Massey, Maris Kreizman, Josh Gondelman, Sarah Hagi, Beca

Grimm, Nikki Chung, Jia Tolentino, Kat Chow, Alice Bolin, R. O. Kwon, Nicole Cliffe, Laura June, Jason Diamond, Anne Helen Petersen, Julie Buntin, Jess Bergman, and Joe Berkowitz.

Leigha High McReynolds: It is the profoundest understatement to say that I'd be lost without you. Here's another understatement: You're one of the best things to ever happen to me, and your friendship is both a blessing and an honor.

Thanks to my beloved Fairy Godmother, Diane Brassil, who joined my family long ago and whose heart and contagious delight have been precious gifts. And, of course, thank you for rescuing my snowman.

Thank you to my dear family, whose love is by turns a buoy and a lantern: Maria Martin—truly a second mother to me—and Glenn Martin; Michael and Jeanne Cote; Ben and Anna Cote; Eric, Justine, and Malcom Cote; Michael, Jill, Megan, and John Florio; Andrew, Daniel, Carolin, Ben, and Harriet Vorona; Matthew, Jackie, Lauren, David, and Kate Vorona; Nancy and John Quackenboss; Nick Selle and Elena Katherine Selle.

To the Brownes: Eric, David, Julia, and my cousin-who-is-really-a-sister, Sarah Kaplan. I am more myself than I've ever been because of you. Thank you for bearing witness and for standing beside me.

To my grandparents, John and Olga Florio and Jack and Kappy Vorona: you taught me how to be a person in the world—to be kind and to listen and to consider.

Thank you to my sisters, Laura and Jinny, who are marvelous and talented and who teach me the many varieties of strength.

To Dad, my first reader and editor—and one of the finest at that. I understand what it means to unite principles and compassion because I have the great fortune to be your daughter. But please understand that I will never eat baked beans. To Mom, who asked to see the finished product: this was always for you.

And Paul, my fella and my darling. Nothing good comes from me that is not imbued by you. I love you.

NOTES

CHAPTER ONE: WONDERLAND: AN INTRODUCTION

1. Julius Althaus, *On Epilepsy, Hysteria, and Ataxy: Three Lectures* (London: John Churchill & Sons, 1866), 36.
2. Mary Kingsley (1862–1900) was an English explorer, ethnologist, and author who traveled and researched extensively in West Africa, publishing the popular *Travels in West Africa* in 1897, as well as *West African Studies* (1899) and other related works.
3. Jess Zimmerman, "Hunger Makes Me," *Hazlitt*, July 7, 2016, https://hazlitt.net/feature/hunger-makes-me.
4. Michelle Chen, "The Clothing Industry Is Set to Consume a Quarter of the Global Carbon Supply by 2050," *The Nation*, February 13, 2018, https://www.thenation.com/article/the-clothing-industry-is-set-to-consume-a-quarter-of-the-global-carbon-supply-by-2050/.
5. Andrew Scull, *Hysteria: The Disturbing History* (Oxford: Oxford University Press, 2009), 69, 93.
6. Cecilia Tasca, Mariangela Rapetti, Mauro Giovanni Carta, Bianca Fadda, "Women and Hysteria in the History of Mental Health," *Clinical Practice & Epidemiology in Mental Health* 8 (2012): 110–119.
7. Carroll Smith-Rosenberg, "The Hysterical Woman: Sex Roles and Role Conflict in 19th Century America," *Social Research* 39, no. 4 (Winter 1972): 652.
8. Scull, *Hysteria: The Disturbing History*, 23.
9. Frederick Hollick, *The Diseases of Woman, Their Causes and Cure Familiarly Explained; with Practical Hints for their Prevention and for the Preservation of Female Health* (New York: Burgess, Stringer, & Co., 1847), 205.
10. Hollick, 194.
11. Hollick, 199–200.

12. Hollick, 194–195.
13. Hollick, 200–201.

CHAPTER TWO: CHATTERBOX

1. Charlotte Brontë, *Jane Eyre* (London: Penguin Classics, 2006), 39.
2. M. O. Grenby, "Moral and Instructive Children's Literature," British Library, May 15, 2014, https://www.bl.uk/romantics-and-victorians/articles/moral-and-instructive-childrens-literature.
3. Claire Harman, *Charlotte Brontë: A Fiery Heart* (New York: Alfred A. Knopf, 2015), 43.
4. Harman, 43.
5. Charlotte Brontë, "Introduction," *Juvenilia 1829–1835*, ed. Juliet Barker (New York: Penguin Books, 1996), xv.
6. Harman, *Charlotte Brontë: A Fiery Heart*, 103.
7. Harman, 108–109.
8. Harman, 109.
9. Maria Edgeworth, "Simple Susan," *The Parent's Assistant; Or, Stories for Children* (London: George Routledge and Sons, Limited, 1891), http://www.gutenberg.org/files/3655/3655-h/3655-h.htm.
10. "The Girl's Own Paper," *The Victorian Web*, April 15, 2015, http://www.victorianweb.org/periodicals/girlsownpaper/index.html.
11. U. C. Knoepflmacher, *Ventures into Childland* (Chicago: The University of Chicago Press, 1998), 168.
12. Hugh Haughton, "Introduction," *Alice's Adventures in Wonderland* and *Through the Looking Glass* (New York: Penguin Books Ltd., 1998), xx.
13. Roger Lancelyn Green, ed., *The Diaries of Lewis Carroll* (Westport: Greenwood Press, 1971), 230–231.
14. Lynne Vallone and Claudia Nelson, "Introduction," *The Girl's Own: Cultural Histories of the Anglo-American Girl, 1830–1915*, ed. Lynne Vallone and Claudia Nelson (Athens: The University of Georgia Press, 2010), 3.
15. Gail Kern Paster, *The Body Embarrassed: Drama and the Disciplines of Shame in Early Modern England* (Ithaca: Cornell University Press, 1993), 25.
16. Lewis Carroll, *Alice's Adventures in Wonderland* and *Through the Looking Glass* (New York: Penguin Books Ltd., 1998), 20–21.
17. Chantel Tattoli, "Astrid Lindgren, the Gutsy Creator of Pippi Longstocking," *The Paris Review*, March 1, 2018, https://www.theparisreview.org/blog/2018/03/01/astrid-lindgren-gutsy-creator-pippi-longstocking/.
18. Tattoli, "Astrid Lindgren, the Gutsy Creator of Pippi Longstocking."
19. Tattoli, "Astrid Lindgren, the Gutsy Creator of Pippi Longstocking."

20. "An Interview with Beverly Cleary on *Ramona Quimby, Age 8*," *Ramona Quimby, Age 8* (New York: Harper Collins Publishers), 182.
21. Beverly Cleary, *Beezus and Ramona* (New York: Harper Collins Publishers, 2013), 1–2.
22. Beverly Cleary, *Ramona the Brave* (New York: Harper Collins Publishers, 2013), 140–141.
23. Cleary, 82–83.

CHAPTER THREE: NERVE

1. George Eliot, *Middlemarch* (New York: Penguin Books, 2003), 194.
2. L. M. Montgomery, *Emily of New Moon* (New York: Dell Laurel-Leaf, 1993), 80–81.
3. Montgomery, 81.
4. L. M. Montgomery, *Emily Climbs* (New York: Bantam Books, 1993), 32.
5. Montgomery, *Emily of New Moon*, 29.
6. Montgomery, 33.
7. Louisa May Alcott, *Little Women* (New York: Penguin Books, 1989), 162.
8. Frances Hodgson Burnett, *The Secret Garden* (New York: W. W. Norton & Company, 2006), 3.
9. Hodgson Burnett, 9.
10. L. M. Montgomery, *Anne of Green Gables* (New York: Bantam Books, 1998), 64.
11. Montgomery, 65.
12. Montgomery, *Emily Climbs*, 207.

CHAPTER FOUR: CLOSE

1. Sharon Marcus, *Between Women: Friendship, Desire, and Marriage in Victorian England* (Princeton: Princeton University Press, 2007), 1.
2. Marcus, 4.
3. Marcus, 175.
4. Wilkie Collins, *The Woman in White* (New York: Oxford University Press, 1998), 189
5. Christina Rossetti, "Goblin Market," Poetry Foundation, https://www.poetryfoundation.org/poems/44996/goblin-market.
6. Dinah Roe, *The Rossettis in Wonderland: A Victorian Family History* (Chicago: University of Chicago Press, 2013), 188.

7. Charlotte Brontë, *Jane Eyre* (New York: Penguin Classics, 2006), 97–98.
8. Marcus, *Between Women: Friendship, Desire, and Marriage in Victorian England*, 257.
9. After Juliet Hulme was released from prison, she took the name Anne Perry. Now, years later, she is a prolific crime novelist.
10. Charles Dickens, *Our Mutual Friend* (New York: Oxford World's Classics, 2008), 347.
11. Dickens, 233–234.
12. J. Sheridan Le Fanu, *Carmilla* (London: Hesperus Press Limited, 2013), 100.
13. Martha Vicinus, *Intimate Friends: Women Who Loved Women, 1778–1928* (Chicago: The University of Chicago Press, 2004), 26.
14. Laura Thompson, "Equality at the Gallows: The Hanged Women of England," *CrimeReads*, November 6, 2018, https://crimereads.com/equality-at-the-gallows-the-hanged-women-of-england/.

CHAPTER FIVE: PLUS

1. Anne Helen Petersen, *Too Fat, Too Slutty, Too Loud: The Rise and Reign of the Unruly Woman* (New York: Plume, 2017), 29.
2. Anya Krugovoy Silver, *Victorian Literature and the Anorexic Body* (Cambridge: Cambridge University Press, 2002), 72–73.
3. Helena Michie, *The Flesh Made Word* (Oxford: Oxford University Press, 1989), 19.
4. Michie, 26.
5. Michie, 13.
6. Charles Dickens, *Little Dorrit* (New York: Penguin Books, 2003), 96.
7. Silver, *Victorian Literature and the Anorexic Body*, 26.
8. Carolyn Day, *Consumptive Chic: A History of Beauty, Fashion, and Disease* (New York: Bloomsbury Academic, 2017), 91.
9. Michie, *The Flesh Made Word*, 21.
10. Michie, 21.
11. Silver, *Victorian Literature and the Anorexic Body*, 1.
12. Silver, 1.
13. Silver, 3.
14. Cesare Lombroso and Guglielmo Ferrero, *The Female Offender* (New York: D. Appleton and Company, 1898), 74.
15. Silver, *Victorian Literature and the Anorexic Body*, 34.
16. Ella Adelia Fletcher, *The Woman Beautiful* (New York: W. M. & Co. Publishers, 1899), 28.
17. Fletcher, 409.

18. Fletcher, 410.
19. Fletcher, 410.
20. Fletcher, 410–411.
21. Fletcher, 411.
22. Fletcher, 411.
23. William Makepeace Thackeray, *Vanity Fair* (New York: W. W. Norton & Company, 1994), 21.
24. Joseph Litvak, *Strange Gourmets: Sophistication, Theory, and the Novel* (Durham: Duke University Press, 1997), 72.
25. Julia Baird, *Victoria the Queen* (New York: Random House, 2016), 28.
26. Baird, 158.
27. George Eliot, *Middlemarch* (New York: Penguin Books, 2003), 7.
28. Eliot, 273.
29. Day, *Consumptive Chic: A History of Beauty, Fashion, and Disease*, 90.
30. George Eliot, *Adam Bede* (New York: Oxford University Press, 1998), 190.
31. Eliot, 159.
32. Michie, *The Flesh Made Word*, 58.
33. Eliot, *Adam Bede*, 84.
34. Michie, *The Flesh Made Word*, 26.
35. Charlotte Brontë, *Villette* (New York: Penguin Books, 2004), 260.
36. Michie, *The Flesh Made Word*, 22.
37. Sadie Stein, "For the Last Time: What Size Was Marilyn Monroe?" Jezebel, June 2, 2009, https://jezebel.com/5299793/for-the-last-time-what-size-was-marilyn-monroe.
38. Petersen, *Too Fat, Too Slutty, Too Loud: The Rise and Reign of the Unruly Woman*, 212–213.
39. Lanetra Bennett, "Local Teen Told Afro Is 'Extreme' and Can't Be Worn at School," WCTV.tv, May 19, 2017, https://www.wctv.tv/content/news/Local-teen-told-cant-wear-hairstyle-at-school-423232994.html.
40. Remy Smidt and Alec Bostwick, "These Teens Were Banned from Prom and Track Because of Their Hair, So They Challenged Their School," *Buzzfeed News*, May 22, 2017, https://www.buzzfeednews.com/article/remysmidt/these-teen-twins#.iqV6KYZAb.

CHAPTER SIX: CRAZY

1. "Art. VI.—Report of the Metropolitan Commissioners in Lunacy to the Lord Chancellor," *Westminster Review*, March–June 1845, via the British Library, https://www.bl.uk/romantics-and-victorians/articles/the-figure-of-bertha-mason.

2. Jane Austen, *Pride and Prejudice* (New York: Penguin Classics, 2003), 7.

3. Mary Elizabeth Braddon, *Lady Audley's Secret* (Oxford: Oxford World's Classics, 2012), 176.

4. Palko Karasz, "Charles Dickens Tried to Banish His Wife to an Asylum, Letters Show," *New York Times*, February 23, 2019, https ://www.nytimes.com/2019/02/23/world/europe/charles-dickens-wife -asylum.html.

5. Susanna Kaysen, *Girl, Interrupted* (New York: Vintage Books, 1993), 124.

6. Braddon, *Lady Audley's Secret*, 323.

7. Lyn Pykett, "Introduction," *Lady Audley's Secret* (Oxford: Oxford World's Classics, 2012), xxi.

8. Kaysen, *Girl, Interrupted*, 124.

9. Kaysen, 124.

10. Carol Atherton, "The Figure of Bertha Mason," British Library, May 15, 2014, https://www.bl.uk/romantics-and-victorians/articles/the -figure-of-bertha-mason.

11. Charlotte Brontë, *Jane Eyre* (New York: Penguin Classics, 2006), 353.

12. Brontë, 352.

13. Jean Rhys, *Wide Sargasso Sea* (New York: W. W. Norton & Company, 1999), 41.

14. Charlotte Perkins Gilman, "The Yellow Wallpaper," in *The Norton Anthology: Literature by Women*, 3rd edition, Sandra M. Gilbert and Susan Gubar, eds. (New York: W. W. Norton & Company, Inc., 2007), 1392.

15. Gilman, 1394.

16. Gilman, 1394.

17. Charlotte Perkins Gilman, "Why I Wrote The Yellow Wallpaper?" *The Norton Anthology: Literature by Women*, 3rd edition, Sandra M. Gilbert and Susan Gubar, eds. (New York: W. W. Norton & Company, Inc., 2007), 1403.

18. Virginia Woolf, *A Writer's Diary*, ed. Leonard Woolf (San Diego: Harcourt, Inc., 1954), 166.

19. Mitchell Sunderland, "Paparazzo Auctioning Off Umbrella from Infamous Britney Spears Attack," *Vice*, February 21, 2017, https://www.vice.com/en_us/article/9k9y45/paparazzo-auctioning -off-umbrella-from-infamous-britney-spears-attack.

20. Sunderland, "Paparazzo Auctioning Off Umbrella from Infamous Britney Spears Attack."

21. Alice Bolin, *Dead Girls* (New York: HarperCollins Publishers, 2018), 110.

22. Stephanie Marcus, "10 Years Later, Britney Spears' Head-Shaving Moment Is Still Unforgettable," *HuffPost*, February 27, 2017, https://www .huffpost.com/entry/britney-spears-shaved-her-head-ten-years-ago_n_ 58a5cff6e4b07602ad525d50.

23. Kathryn Lindsay, "Britney Spears Shares Positive Messages on the 10th

Anniversary of Shaving Her Head," *Refinery29*, February 17, 2017, https://www.refinery29.com/2017/02/141451/britney-spears-shave -head-ten-year-anniversary-instagram.

24. "Article 1. Detention of Mentally Disordered Persons for Evaluation and Treatment [5150-5155]," *California Legislative Information*, https:// leginfo.legislature.ca.gov/faces/codes_displaySection.xhtml?lawCode= WIC&sectionNum=5150.

25. Josephine Livingstone, "Freeing Britney Spears," *The New Republic*, May 16, 2019, https://newrepublic.com/article/153903/freeing-britney-spears.

26. Antoinette Bueno, "Britney Spears' Father Wants to Extend Conservatorship to Louisiana, Hawaii and Florida," *ET Online*, May 22, 2019, https:// www.etonline.com/britney-spears-father-wants-to-extend-conservatorship -to-louisiana-hawaii-and-florida-125725.

27. Ben Beaumont-Thomas, "Britney Spears Takes Out Restraining Order against Former Manager Sam Lutfi," *The Guardian*, May 9, 2019, https://www.theguardian.com/music/2019/may/09/britney-spears -restraining-order-former-manager-sam-lutfi.

28. Britney Spears, Instagram post, April 23, 2019, https://www.instagram .com/p/BwnqpG5g7qn/.

29. Jessica Hopper, "Fiona Apple's Bad, Bad Girl Moments," *Rolling Stone*, April 24, 2012, https://www.rollingstone.com/music/music-lists /fiona-apples-bad-bad-girl-moments-22292/.

30. "Fiona Apple Breaks Down After Being Heckled for Her Appearance," *Huffington Post*, October 4, 2013 https://www.huffingtonpost.com /2013/10/04/fiona-apple-heckled_n_4044449.html.

31. Elahe Izadi, "Kehlani's Suicide Attempt and the Double Standard of How Female Celebrities Get Criticized," *Washington Post*, March 30, 2016, https: //www.washingtonpost.com/news/arts-and-entertainment/wp/2016/03 /30/kehlanis-suicide-attempt-internet-bullies-and-chris-brown/.

32. Charles Keene, "The Clew," *The Victorian Web*, http://www .victorianweb.org/periodicals/punch/publichealth/2.html.

33. Andrzej Diniejko, "A Chronology of Social Change and Social Reform in Great Britain in the Nineteenth and Early Twentieth Centuries," *The Victorian Web*, http://www.victorianweb.org/history/socialism /chronology.html.

34. Elizabeth Gaskell, *Mary Barton* (Oxford: Oxford World Classics, 2006), 159.

35. Deborah Anna Logan, *Fallenness in Victorian Women's Writing: Marry, Stitch, Die, or Do Worse* (Columbia: University of Missouri Press, 1998), 130.

36. Andrea Ritchie, "The War on Drugs Is a War on Women of Color," Longreads, https://longreads.com/2017/08/03/the-war-on-drugs-is -a-war-on-women-of-color/.

37. Ritchie, "The War on Drugs Is a War on Women of Color."

38. K. Austin Collins, "Naomie Harris's Voice Is a Secret Weapon in 'Moon-light,'" The Ringer, February 15, 2017, https://www.theringer.com /2017/2/15/16037908/naomie-harriss-voice-is-a-secret-weapon-in -moonlight-794b881e9b37

39. Collins, "Naomie Harris's Voice Is a Secret Weapon in 'Moonlight.'"

40. Spencer Kornhaber, "When the Reality of Addiction Meets the Fantasies of Pop Stardom," The Atlantic, August 9, 2018, https://www .theatlantic.com/entertainment/archive/2018/08/demi-lovato-addiction -recovery/567047/.

CHAPTER SEVEN: CUT

1. Jennifer L. Geddes, "On Evil, Pain, and Beauty: A Conversation with Elaine Scarry," The Hedgehog Review, Summer 2000, https ://hedgehogreview.com/issues/evil/articles/on-evil-pain-and-beauty -a-conversation-with-elaine-scarry.

2. George M. Gould and Walter L. Pyle, Anomalies and Curiosities of Medicine (New York: Bell Publishing Company, 1896).

3. Sylvia Plath, "Cut," Ariel (New York: Harper Perennial, 1999), 13.

4. Robert E. McKeown, Steven P. Cuffe, and Richard M. Schulz, "US Suicide Rates by Age Group, 1970–2002: An Examination of Recent Trends," American Journal of Public Health 96(10), October 2006, 1744–1751, https://www.ncbi.nlm.nih.gov/pmc/articles/PMC1586156/.

5. Elizabeth Wurtzel, Prozac Nation: Young and Depressed in America (New York: Riverhead Books, 1995), 47.

6. Gillian Flynn, Sharp Objects (New York: Broadway Books, 2006), 63.

7. Leslie Jamison, The Empathy Exams (Minneapolis: Graywolf Press, 2014), 212.

8. Nicci Gerrard, "Why Are So Many Teenage Girls Cutting Themselves?" The Guardian, May 19, 2002, https://www.theguardian.com/society /2002/may/19/mentalhealth.observerfocus.

CHAPTER EIGHT: HORNY

1. Claire McEachern, "Why Do Cuckolds Have Horns?" Huntington Library Quarterly, December 2008, 607–631.

2. Michel Foucault, The History of Sexuality: Volume One, trans. Robert Hurley (New York: Vintage Books, 1990), 17–18.

3. "Michel Foucault," *Stanford Encyclopedia of Philosophy*, https://plato.stanford.edu/entries/foucault/.

4. Foucault, *The History of Sexuality: Volume One*, 11.

5. *The Pearl: A Journal of Voluptuous Reading* (New York: Grove Press Inc., 1968).

6. "A Visit to Miss Birch," *The Whippingham Papers* (Hertfordshire: Wordsworth Classics, 1995), 30–31.

7. "Reginald's Flogging," *The Whippingham Papers* (Hertfordshire: Wordsworth Classics, 1995), 64.

8. Glenn Everett, "A. C. Swinburne: Biography," *The Victorian Web*, http://victorianweb.org/authors/swinburne/acsbio1.html.

9. Algernon Charles Swinburne, "Anactoria," *Poems and Ballads & Atalanta in Calydon* (New York: Penguin Classics, 2000), lines 11–16.

10. Swinburne, lines 111–114.

11. Bram Stoker, *Dracula* (New York: W. W. Norton & Company, Inc., 1997), 60.

12. Stoker, 188.

13. Stoker, 187.

14. Stoker, 149.

15. Stoker, 193.

16. J. Sheridan Le Fanu, *Carmilla* (London: Hesperus Press Limited, 2013), 33.

17. Sheridan Le Fanu, 98.

18. Sheridan Le Fanu, 98.

19. Audre Lorde, *Zami: A New Spelling of My Name* (New York: Crossing Press, 1982), 78.

20. Karu F. Daniels, "Amber Rose Cancels Annual SlutWalk, Blames 'Abusive' and 'Toxic' Friends for Decision," *New York Daily News*, August 14, 2019, https://www.nydailynews.com/entertainment/ny-amber-rose-cancels-slutwalk-blames-toxic-friends-20190815-wfxgyrk3ijg2bdmiusa6ymp7si-story.html.

CHAPTER NINE: CHEAT

1. Cheryl Strayed, "Dear Sugar, The Rumpus Advice Column #77: The Truth That Lives There," *The Rumpus*, June 24, 2011, https://therumpus.net/2011/06/dear-sugar-the-rumpus-advice-column-77-the-truth-that-lives-there/.

2. George Eliot, *The Mill on the Floss* (Oxford: Oxford Word's Classics, 1998), 490–491.

3. Thomas Hardy, *Tess of the d'Urbervilles* (New York: Penguin Classics, 2003), 228–229.

4. Lindy West, "Tyler Perry Isn't Just an Artless Hack, He's a Scary Ideo-
    logue," *Jezebel*, April 3, 2013, https://jezebel.com/tyler-perry-isnt
    -just-an-artless-hack-hes-a-scary-ideo-5993523.
5. Leo Tolstoy, *Anna Karenina*, trans. Richard Pevear and Larissa Volokhon-
    sky (New York: Penguin Books, 2002), 149.
6. Tolstoy, 149.

CHAPTER TEN: LOUD

1. "That Romantic Look," *Photoplay*, December 1946.
2. Ella Adelia Fletcher, *The Woman Beautiful* (New York: W. M. & Co. Pub-
    lishers, 1899), 376.
3. Fletcher, 377.
4. C. E. Humphry, *A Word to Women* (London: James Bowden, 1898),
    Project Gutenberg, http://www.gutenberg.org/files/36330/36330-h
    /36330-h.htm#Page_51.
5. Humphry, *A Word to Women*.
6. Humphry, *A Word to Women*.
7. Humphry, *A Word to Women*.
8. Florence Hartley, *The Ladies' Book of Etiquette and Manual of Politeness*
    (Boston: G. W. Cottrell, 1860), Project Gutenberg, https://www
    .gutenberg.org/files/35123/35123-h/35123-h.htm#CHPTR_XVI
9. Hartley, *The Ladies' Book of Etiquette and Manual of Politeness*.
10. Hartley, *The Ladies' Book of Etiquette and Manual of Politeness*.
11. Tim Herrera, "Why You Shouldn't Feel Bad About Crying at Work,"
    New York Times, October 14, 2018, https://www.nytimes.com/2018
    /10/14/smarter-living/crying-at-work.html.
12. Herrera, "Why You Shouldn't Feel Bad About Crying at Work."
13. Herrera, "Why You Shouldn't Feel Bad About Crying at Work."

CHAPTER ELEVEN: OLD

1. Julia Baird, *Victoria the Queen* (New York: Random House, 2016), 281.
2. Karen Chase, *The Victorians and Old Age* (Oxford: Oxford University
    Press, 2009), 155.
3. Chase, 2.
4. Chase, 159.
5. Sarah Ross, "Middle-Aged Heroines: Locating Ageing Women in

Victorian Fiction," *Feminist and Women's Studies Association Blog*, http://fwsablog.org.uk/2015/09/08/middle-aged-heroines-locating -ageing-women-in-victorian-fiction/.

6. Chase, *The Victorians and Old Age*, 150.
7. Elizabeth Gaskell, *Cranford* (Oxford: Oxford University Press, 1998), 1.
8. Gaskell, 3.
9. Gaskell, 14.
10. Gaskell, 160.
11. Chase, *The Victorians and Old Age*, 138.
12. Gaskell, *Cranford*, 36.
13. Jancee Dunn, "Growing Older with Madonna," *New York Times*, June 24, 2015, https://www.nytimes.com/2015/06/25/fashion/growing -older-with-madonna-jancee-dunn.html.
14. Dunn, "Growing Older with Madonna."
15. Dunn, "Growing Older with Madonna."
16. Vanessa Grigoriadis, "Madonna at Sixty," *New York Times Magazine*, June 5, 2019, https://www.nytimes.com/2019/06/05/magazine/madonna -madame-x.html.
17. Brittany Wong, "27 Asian Celebs Who Prove That Asian Don't Raisin," *HuffPost*, August 20, 2018, https://www.huffpost.com/entry/celebs -prove-asian-dont-raisin_n_5b7afb91e4b0a5b1febdc546.
18. Patricia Reynoso, "An Expert Reveals Why Latina Skin Ages So Well," *Glamour*, January 18, 2016, https://www.glamour.com/story/why -latina-skin-doesnt-age-as-quickly.
19. Baird, *Victoria the Queen*, 436.
20. Baird, 434.
21. Baird, 159.
22. Baird, 467.
23. Baird, 466.
24. Baird, 466.

CHAPTER TWELVE: SUBSTANCE: AN EPILOGUE

1. Charlotte Brontë, "Introduction," *Juvenilia 1829–1835*, ed. Juliet Barker (New York: Penguin Books, 1996), xv.
2. Virginia Woolf, *Mrs. Dalloway* (San Diego: Harcourt, Inc.), 8.
3. Woolf, 8.